From the Republic of the Rio Grande

Number Thirty-five
Jack and Doris Smothers Series in Texas History, Life, and Culture

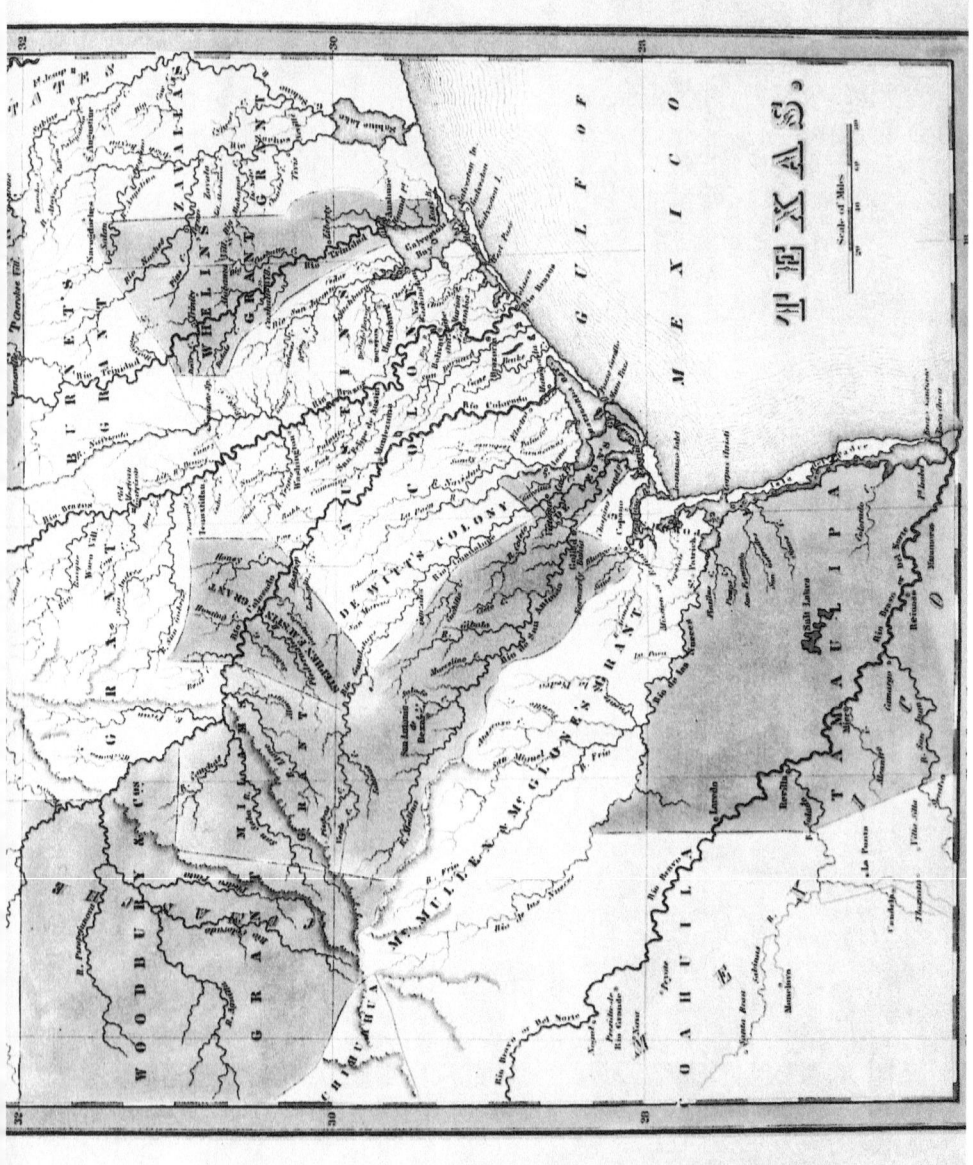

Texas, Coahuila, and Tamaulipas, circa 1833. Courtesy of the Austin History Center and Austin History Center Association, Austin, TX.

《 BEATRIZ DE LA GARZA 》

From the Republic of the Rio Grande

A PERSONAL HISTORY OF
THE PLACE AND THE PEOPLE

University of Texas Press   AUSTIN

Publication of this work was made possible in part by support from the J. E. Smothers, Sr., Memorial Foundation and the National Endowment for the Humanities.

All photos not otherwise attributed belong to the author.

Copyright © 2013 by Beatriz E. de la Garza
All rights reserved

First edition, 2013

Requests for permission to reproduce material from this work should be sent to:
  Permissions
  University of Texas Press
  P.O. Box 7819
  Austin, TX 78713-7819
  utpress.utexas.edu/index.php/rp-form

♾ The paper used in this book meets the minimum requirements of ANSI/NISO Z39.48-1992 (R1997) (Permanence of Paper).

LIBRARY OF CONGRESS CATALOGING-IN-PUBLICATION DATA
de la Garza, Beatriz Eugenia.
From the Republic of the Rio Grande : a personal history of the place and the people / by Beatriz de la Garza. — 1st ed.
    p.   cm. — (Jack and Doris Smothers series in Texas history, life, and culture ; no. 35)
Includes bibliographical references and index.
ISBN 978-0-292-76213-8
1. Mexico, North—History.   2. Mexico, North—History—Autonomy and independence movements.   3. Texas, South—History.   4. Mexican-American Border Region—History.   5. de la Garza, Beatriz Eugenia—Family.   6. de la Garza, Beatriz Eugenia.   7. Mexico, North—Biography.   8. Texas, South—Biography.   I. Title.
F1314.D44   2013
972'.1—dc23
                                                                    2012024688

doi:10.7560/714533

¿Y ha de morir contigo el mundo tuyo,
La vida vieja en orden tuyo y nuevo?
(And is your world to die with you,
The old way of life you made anew?)

Antonio Machado, *from* Galerías

Contents

Preface and Acknowledgments *ix*

CHAPTER ONE. The Republic of the Rio Grande *1*

CHAPTER TWO. The Kingdom of Zapata *23*

CHAPTER THREE. Grandfather's Revolution: The Horseman *48*

CHAPTER FOUR. Grandfather's Revolution: The Historian *74*

CHAPTER FIVE. The Prodigal *103*

CHAPTER SIX. "You and I Will Die of Love" *137*

CHAPTER SEVEN. "Not a Stone upon a Stone" *157*

CHAPTER EIGHT. The Streets of Laredo *177*

CHAPTER NINE. Voyages in English *190*

Works Cited *205*

Index *213*

Preface and Acknowledgments

This book had its origins in a small trunk—twenty-two inches long by eleven inches wide and high and made of tin reinforced with wood strips—filled to the top with papers either generated or preserved by my paternal grandfather, Lorenzo de la Garza. Among the first were dozens of typewritten copies of his personal and business correspondence on flimsy onionskin, dating from the first third of the twentieth century, as well as original replies to that correspondence—for example, a brief (printed) thank-you note from the recently elected Mexican president, Francisco Madero, dated November 1911. The second group, on more durable rag paper and either printed or in the flowing copperplate script of the nineteenth century, consisted of official documents, such as deeds to family lands signed by President Porfirio Díaz in the 1880s and correspondence on a variety of topics. Included in this correspondence were several letters relating to the deaths of two heroes of Mexican independence, Colonel Bernardo Gutiérrez de Lara and his brother, Father Antonio, whose dual biography (*Dos hermanos héroes*) my grandfather wrote in the early part of the twentieth century. At the bottom of the trunk lay the heaviest items, mostly sepia-tinted portraits on stiff cardboard, known as *cartes de visite*, of family members in stiff collars that gave their heads a haughty tilt and colorful postcards commemorating travels or special occasions.

My grandfather lived most of his life (and died) in Ciudad Guerrero, Tamaulipas, a small town founded in the middle of the eighteenth century as part of a chain of settlements known as Las Villas del Norte along the lower Rio Grande. Grandfather Lorenzo died in 1948, five years before Ciudad Guerrero was flooded by the construction of Falcon International Reservoir, and its inhabitants were relocated to a new town. How the small trunk made its way from Guerrero Viejo (Old Guerrero) to Guerrero Nuevo, when neither my grandfather (who was dead) nor his daughters, who had already moved to Laredo, Texas, were there to supervise its transport, remains a mystery, but the trunk ended up in the new town, together with miscellaneous items, in the storage room of my maternal grandparents' house. There I found it, some fifteen to twenty years after my grandparents' death. Nobody else was interested in old papers, so I carried it off to Austin, Texas, where it came to rest in *my* storage room, undisturbed, for some ten years. During that decade of repose, the paternal papers were joined by others from the maternal side that a young family member found stored in a ranch building. But the best was yet to come: my collection of family papers was finally complete when my sister gave me the letters exchanged between our parents during their courtship, letters that she had kept till then. These letters, from the late 1930s and early 1940s, detailed the joys and sorrows of the lovers, proving that, indeed, "the course of true love never did run smooth." In addition to revealing the hopes and aspirations of the writers, these letters introduced me to my parents, whom I had barely known, particularly my mother, who died when my sister and I were barely toddlers.

For years I figuratively sat on this wealth of family history without daring to delve into it. On the one hand, I was daunted by the practical considerations of sifting through the great number and variety of materials that would require, not only that I put them into some sort of order, but also that I make provisions for their conservation. For example, the oldest item in the trunk was a military appointment made by Mexican viceroy Francisco Venegas in 1812, and my parents' letters were, of course, priceless. On the other hand, I feared that poring through the contents of the small trunk and the boxes that had joined it later was dangerously akin to opening Pandora's box. My fears were that, upon my lifting the trunk's lid, myriad memories and feelings would fly out that would never be contained again. And indeed it turned out to be so, for as I read those old letters and documents, their authors came back to life through their words and resurrected their world with them. It was a world that had existed in a particular place—the northeastern Mexican states of Coahuila, Nuevo León, and Tamaulipas (which then extended into South Texas, up to the Nueces River), a region oriented toward but not divided by the Rio Grande/Bravo—and at a particular time, roughly bracketed between the middle of the eighteenth century and the middle of the twentieth. This was the world that had existed in the land that came to be known (rightly or wrongly) as the Republic of the Rio Grande.

Much like an archaeologist who reconstructs a lost civilization from the fragments of broken pottery found buried in the earth, I took these fragments of paper, long buried in the tin trunk, and worked to extract from each the stories that they contained. They were stories of personal milestones—weddings, births, and deaths—all happening within the framework of historic events, such as wars and revolutions, as well as times of recovery from the periodic strife. They were stories that deserved to be told; however, for these stories to rise above being merely a collection of anecdotes and form a coherent picture, they needed to be connected to the broader events of the time and the places in which they occurred. To accomplish this, I had to go beyond the materials that I had and consult not only the orthodox sources for the history of the region, but also privately published local histories and memoirs, which often provided details that the more general and academic works did not. In going from the particular narratives gleaned from the family papers and the personal recollections that I gathered to the broader accounts contained in history books, I have attempted to flesh out the world and the times only glimpsed in those individual documents and stories, while, at the same time, giving history a human face.

But although this work takes family history and genealogy as a point of departure for the events discussed, the ancestors and family members serve primarily as springboards or chroniclers for the narratives that follow. These narratives tell the story of a people who, while straddling two countries across a river, have managed to retain a common cultural identity, much as the Basques have done on both sides of the Pyrenees (as Mark Kurlansky relates in *The Basque History of the World*, an informative and entertaining book that I read only after finishing the final version of this manuscript). This work, though, remains a *personal* history, with a personal perspective in the telling of stories from which a reader without specialized knowledge can derive enjoyment, as well as information, following the old dictum of *enseñar deleitando* (teaching while delighting).

The work is made up of nine sections (in addition to the preface), with titles that usually intimate, rather than describe, the topic discussed in each. The arrangement of the sections is thematic, rather than strictly chronological, although the chapters are placed in a particular sequence that contributes to propelling the overall narrative. Nevertheless, readers who feel like reading the chapters out of sequence may do so without sacrificing too much coherence, and for this reason, certain facts may appear in various places, although, I trust, not to the point of tedious repetition. The family papers and other sources from which I quote are often in Spanish, and where the content is not clear from the context, I append an English translation. All translations are my own.

By limiting the time covered in this work to primarily the two hundred years from the middle of the eighteenth century to the middle of the twentieth, I realize that I have attempted to capture—as if in amber—a world already gone. The last fifty years of the twentieth century (and the first decade of the present) opened the old Republic of the Rio Grande to the rest of the world through expanded means of communication and commercial initiatives, such as NAFTA, and, in doing so, changed it permanently. I realize that this work is, therefore, also an elegy for a world and a time already lost. In the five years that have elapsed between the beginning and the conclusion of this work, I have also come to fear that I am writing the obituary of the place where I was born and grew up, as every day brings to light greater and more horrific tales of violence that threaten its existence. And yet I am reminded that in the past 250 years the Rio Grande frontier has endured, not infrequently, wars, military occupations, raiding parties by both the *indios bárbaros* and the *anglosajones*, local insurrections, and a ten-year revolution. The people of the so-called Republic of the Rio Grande endured and survived then and will probably do so again.

Along the way, in the time it took me to reach the end of this journey into the past (longer in duration and in extent than I had anticipated), I had—and still have—much cause for gratitude to many persons who helped me with their information, their memories, and their encouragement. Heartfelt thanks hereby go to all of them: Among close and extended family members, my sister, Alicia Margarita de la Garza; my niece, Evelina Teresa García; José Carlos de la Garza; and Mrs. Aurora García Cavazos. In Nueva Ciudad Guerrero, Tamaulipas, the late Mr. Jaime Gutiérrez, president of the association of Hijos y Amigos de Guerrero Viejo, and María del Carmen González, curator of the Municipal Archive. From Ciudad Victoria, Tamaulipas, state archivist Carlos Rugerio Cázares, a restoration architect who took time to answer my questions on the architecture of Guerrero Viejo. My thanks also to J. J. Gallegos and George Farías, for sharing their information about the leaders of the Republic of the Rio Grande (Antonio Zapata and Juan Francisco Farías, respectively); in Laredo, Texas, Joe Moreno, Special Collections librarian, Laredo Public Library, and Margarita Araiza, executive director of the Webb County Heritage Foundation; and in Austin, Adán Benavides and Margo Gutiérrez of the Benson Latin American Library and the staff of the Briscoe Center for American History, both at the University of Texas, as well as Galen Greaser, Spanish translator and archivist at the Texas General Land Office, who helped me discover unique aspects of my family history. In Austin, also, I thank my friend Dr. Joanna F. Fountain for technical and moral support and Mrs. Adela Flores Etcharren, my compatriot, for helping in my research of wedding customs in northern Mexico. Many thanks also to the academic readers, particularly to Dr. Stan Green, who guided me to the Texas State Archives, where my grandfather Lorenzo had had the foresight to deposit the priceless diary of Colonel Bernardo Gutiérrez de Lara. With their comments, both readers helped make this a better book. And last but not least, my thanks go to Theresa J. May, editor-in-chief of the University of Texas Press, for her patience and encouragement throughout the time that it took to complete this work and the confidence that she has shown in the final product. ¡Mil gracias!

From the Republic of the Rio Grande

《 ONE 》

The Republic of the Rio Grande

As a child, I dreaded the occasions when my aunts would pack me off to visit my maternal grandmother, for as soon as she saw me, her bright blue eyes, which reminded me of playing marbles, would fill with tears, and she would clasp me tightly to her bosom. Her reaction disturbed me profoundly because I did not understand it, but now I know that my presence reminded her of the loss of her daughter—my mother. I also know now that I reminded her of herself as a child and that she realized that our lives—hers and mine—ran in sad parallels, a case of history repeating itself, but in a mirror.

When my grandmother, who was born in Zapata County, in South Texas, was orphaned at an early age, she went to live with her paternal aunts across the Rio Grande, in Guerrero (the former Revilla). There she grew into womanhood, married, and had her children. When I, born in northern Mexico, in Ciudad Guerrero, Tamaulipas (now Guerrero Viejo, or Old Guerrero), was left an orphan by age six, I moved with my paternal aunts to Laredo, in South Texas, where I grew up. What was perhaps the most remarkable feature of our two parallel lives was that, in crossing the Rio Grande in opposite directions, neither my grandmother nor I felt that we had moved to a foreign country. And, indeed, we had not, for we had remained within the confines of the old Republic of the Rio Grande.

Yes, there was such a place for a brief, if not altogether shining, moment (the years 1839 to 1840, more or less), when the people of the lower Rio Grande settlements and their neighbors struggled to assert their autonomy against two countries—the Republic of Mexico and the newly declared Republic of Texas. The insurgent areas encompassed the northern Mexican states of Tamaulipas (the former province of Nuevo Santander, which had included Texas, south of the Nueces River), Nuevo León, and

Coahuila. The call for insurrection first sounded in Camargo, Tamaulipas, traveled up river to Guerrero, and was quickly taken up in Laredo, where the new government of the Frontera del Norte (Northern Frontier), later known as the Republic of the Rio Grande, established its capital and designated one of the principal houses on the main square, San Agustín Plaza, as the capitol.

It was natural that Laredo and the downriver settlements should link their destinies in this endeavor, as they had done in earlier days, since they owed their existence to a common impetus—the Spanish colonization of the banks of the lower Rio Grande by Don José de Escandón during the middle of the eighteenth century. For more than two hundred years after the Spaniards had first set foot on the shores of the mouth of the Rio Grande, the northern part of Nuevo Santander remained out of Spanish reach. The Spaniards had been more successful in colonizing the area around the source of the river (primarily in northern New Mexico) than where it emptied. Where the river met the sea and for some two hundred miles upstream there remained a land populated by "tigers, leopards, wolves . . . and snakes . . . the last-named being abundant" (Spanish Archives, Texas General Land Office [hereafter "GLO"], box 135, folder 10). The human inhabitants were no less hostile, among them the fierce Coahuiltecans, related to the cannibalistic Karankawas (Thompson, "Historical Survey," 19). Several times, beginning in the 1500s, the Spaniards had attempted to colonize this area, which they called *el seno mexicano* (in this instance, *seno* meaning a gulf or a cavity), and several times they had failed. Success did not come until the colonization project was entrusted to Don José de Escandón, the Count of Sierra Gorda, in 1746. Escandón had arrived in Yucatán from his native Spain as a fifteen-year-old and enlisted as a cavalry cadet. By 1740 he had been promoted to lieutenant general as a reward for having pacified the indigenous tribes of the Sierra Gorda, in the Sierra Madre Oriental of Mexico. It was from this campaign that he took the title of Count of Sierra Gorda when he was later ennobled by the Spanish sovereign (Herrera, *Breve*, 64).

According to Galen D. Greaser, in his excellent introduction to the *New Guide to Spanish and Mexican Land Grants in South Texas*, the successful colonization of Nuevo Santander was due not only to Escandón's "tireless industry and resourcefulness," but also to the "loyal captains he selected for the new settlements." Ultimately, though, these settlements took hold because of the people who put down roots in the towns founded under Escandón's direction: "Escandón's reliance on frontier families rather than on missionaries and soldiers to carry forward the colonization venture was justified." Greaser adds: "The results confirmed Escandón's belief that towns were better vehicles of colonization than missions or presidios" (148).

Escandón's plan called for multiple caravans, or *entradas*, of soldier-settlers to converge at the mouth of the Rio Grande from seven points on the frontier in early 1747, and, surprisingly, most did converge. Reconnoitering the south bank of the Rio Grande, Escandón noted also its tributaries—the Salado, the Alamo, and the San Juan rivers—for he hoped to establish settlements at their junctions with the Rio Grande, and he did. In all, Escandón founded some twenty settlements in what he called Nuevo Santander. Of these, some of his most successful were the four villages that he founded on the southern/western side of the Rio Grande—Camargo and Reynosa in 1749, Revilla in 1750, and Mier in 1752. The fifth village, Laredo, was the only one founded on the eastern/northern bank of the Rio Grande.

The five villages came to be known as Las Villas del Norte, and for their settlement Escandón attracted enterprising ranchers from the neighboring provinces of Nuevo León and Coahuila. These men, in turn, brought their own retainers and their families to populate the villages, as well as the flocks of sheep and herds of cattle and horses that were to form the economic basis of the new region. José María and Miguel de la Garza Falcón settled Camargo. Carlos Cantú founded Reynosa and, like his counterparts in the other settlements, took an oath to defend his village. Vicente Guerra, a prominent rancher from Coahuila, offered to settle twenty-six families at his own expense and did so in what became Revilla (named after the then viceroy of Mexico, the Count of Revillagigedo). José Florencio Chapa was in charge of the fifty-seven families that settled on the banks of the Alamo River, near the Rio Grande, in the place that came to be known as Mier. And Don Tomás Sánchez de la Barrera y Garza came from Coahuila and forded the Rio Grande at Paso de Jacinto with eleven families and founded the village of San Agustín de Laredo (Thompson, "Historical Survey," 24–31).

The bonds that held these five settlements together during the precarious years after their founding had their origins in a common conception and were strengthened by their shared experiences as frontier outposts where the settlers provided not only for their economic needs but also for their own defense. This requirement of self-sufficiency no doubt led to a strong, independent spirit among the inhabitants of the river settlements that also led them to embrace the struggle for Mexican independence from Spain that emerged in the first decade of the nineteenth century.

The cry for independence—*el grito de Dolores*—was first heard in the village of Dolores, in Guanajuato, on September 16, 1810. Father Miguel Hidalgo, the parish priest of Dolores, issued the proclamation that set in motion the War of Independence in New Spain (Mexico), but the impetus for the movement was not his alone. Hidalgo's sentiments were shared by a group of *criollos*, the Mexican-born children and grandchildren of Spaniards. The criollos had chafed for more than two hundred years, along with the *mestizos*, the Mexicans of mixed parentage (Indian and Spanish), under the domination of the Spaniards, the *peninsulares*, who controlled the highest civil, military, and ecclesiastical offices. Although criollos and mestizos together constituted roughly only one-third of the population of Mexico in the years around 1800, they—particularly the criollos—exercised a disproportionate influence in comparison with that of the indigenous majority, which was physically isolated and socially and economically marginalized. In addition, the criollos, often being wealthy, had the time and the leisure to think about political issues, something the others did not. Many criollos also became acquainted with the ideas of the Enlightenment and followed with great interest the French and American revolutions, which encouraged them to essay halfhearted and abortive attempts at rebellion. However, it was not until the mother country was thrown into turmoil by the Napoleonic invasion that the opportunity came for the criollos to stage a successful revolt, although the reason for their taking action was paradoxical.

Napoleon had invaded Spain in 1808 as part of his drive to achieve hegemony in Europe, imprisoning the Spanish king, Carlos IV, who abdicated in favor of his son, Fernando VII. Napoleon, however, disregarded Fernando VII and imposed his own brother, Joseph Bonaparte, as king of Spain (whom the Spaniards promptly dubbed Pepe Botellas, to underscore his fondness for drink), to the consternation and outrage of the inhabitants of the Spanish colonies. Many of the criollos were moved to call for severing the ties with the mother country, refusing to acknowledge the right of Joseph Bonaparte to rule them. These loyal but misguided subjects wanted to preserve the Spanish possessions in trust until Fernando VII could claim them someday. Other criollos, realizing that Spain had too many problems of its own to look after them, thought that it was time to chart their own course but were uncertain as to what to do. Still others, like Father Hidalgo and his co-conspirators, Gens. Mariano Jiménez and Ignacio Allende, decided that it was now or never and, gathering an impromptu army that some described as a mob, they called for independence and marched forward victoriously for a while.

The royalists regrouped after a few months, however, and pushed the rebels away from central Mexico and toward the north, where the insurgents found support. By early 1811 Allende and Jiménez found themselves in control of Coahuila, Nuevo León, and Nuevo Santander, winning the hearts and minds of many of the self-reliant *norteños* (northerners), among them the people of Revilla.

The proximity of the insurgents to the old Escandón settlements stirred the longings for freedom in two prominent natives of Revilla, the Gutiérrez de Lara brothers. They were Don Antonio, a priest, and Don Bernardo, a merchant. These two offered their services to Hidalgo and his generals, and their offers were accepted, each brother being given a specific task to carry out. Don Antonio was directed to use his influence as a priest to win over his parishioners to the cause of independence and to raise funds from among them. Don Antonio was happy to do so, and in addition, in a letter to General Allende, he volunteered to take up arms and to donate his possessions and his weapons for the cause. He related that he owned a carbine, a shotgun, a musket, a pistol, five pounds of gunpowder, and three hundred pesos that he had earned as headmaster of the local school for boys ("una carabina, una escopeta, una pistola, un gran fusil, cinco libras de pólvora, cuatro planchas de plomo"). He also had access to the collections from the daily Mass, a library worth two hundred pesos, and a house under construction (L. de la Garza, *Dos hermanos*, 13).

Don Bernardo, for his part, was commissioned a lieutenant colonel in the insurgent army and placed in command of the forces in the northern provinces, with orders to wage war in that area. He was also appointed envoy from the insurgent government to the United States and was directed to seek assistance from the neighboring nation, in particular loans of funds with which to buy weapons and ammunition. However, before Don Bernardo was able to depart on his mission, Hidalgo was betrayed, and he and his generals were defeated by the royalist forces, captured, and executed.

The Gutiérrez de Lara brothers now found themselves persecuted for their insurgent activities. Don Antonio went into hiding in the Sierra Madre, and Don Bernardo fled north, although he had to leave his mother, his wife, and his children behind in Revilla, where they suffered great privations because the royalists retaliated by confiscating the family properties. By December of 1811, after the many vicissitudes that accompanied an almost unimaginable overland journey from Revilla to the capital of the United States, Don Bernardo found himself conferring with the members of President James Madison's cabinet and with the president himself. Fortunately for us, Don Bernardo kept a diary of his journey to Washington in which he jotted down his observations and experiences during the trip. In it he noted his impressions, both of ordinary life, such as the people he met in the inns where he stayed, and of official Washington, such as his meeting with the president on December 16, 1811. Of the latter occasion Don Bernardo wrote succinctly that the meeting had been cordial but brief because the president did not speak Spanish: "[M]e recivio [sic] con mucha cortesía [pero] estube muy poco con el porque no entiende el ydioma español" (Texas State Archives).

Presumably there had been no interpreter to facilitate communication between the Mexican envoy and the American president; however, an interpreter must have been found for the meeting between Don Bernardo and the secretary of war, William Eustis, on December 12. At this meeting, Secretary Eustis had announced to his Mexican visitor that the United States, after having purchased the western lands from France, was now prepared to send an army all the way to the Rio Grande and, in the process, offer aid to the Mexican insurgents: "Me dijo que había facilidad de enviar un ejército hasta la orilla del Rio Grande, diciendo que hiban [sic] a tomar posesión de las tierras que el francés [Napoleón] les vendió y que estando allá el ejército serviría para auxiliar a los criollos." Don Bernardo saw the trap and sidestepped it, refusing the help that came with such compromising strings. "Y yo les dije que no," he noted in his diary" (Texas State Archives).

In spite of the sympathy that the Americans seemed to profess for the cause of the Mexican insurgents, the help that Don Bernardo received from them was more nominal and moral than material. Therefore, on the last day of 1811, he bid farewell to Washington and made ready to depart for New Orleans. From official Washington, Don Bernardo had received two hundred pesos for his expenses and letters of introduction to various persons, among them the governor of Louisiana (L. de la Garza, *Dos hermanos*, 30).

The Spanish ambassador, who, not surprisingly, viewed Don Bernardo's visit to Washington with a jaundiced eye, communicated his observations to the viceroy in Mexico, elaborating on the meager results of Don Bernardo's negotiations with the Americans. In his letter to Viceroy Venegas, the Spanish ambassador claimed that Secretary of State James Monroe had offered help to the Mexican insurgents to the tune of 27,000 troops, in addition to arms and ammunition, if Mexico agreed to adopt a constitution similar or identical to that of the United States in order to facilitate its annexation to the United States, once its independence from

Spain was assured. According to the ambassador, Don Bernardo had been outraged at the proposal and had broken off talks with Monroe (L. de la Garza, *Dos hermanos*, 37).

Once in New Orleans, Don Bernardo learned the discouraging news that the insurgency had been suppressed across the border in Texas. Clearly, then, he could not stop in San Antonio de Béjar on his way home, much less return to Revilla, which was also in royalist hands. All was not lost in Mexico, though, for he also learned that Hidalgo's place at the head of the independence movement had been taken by another priest, José María Morelos. There was nothing for Don Bernardo to do but bide his time in New Orleans, and while he waited, he conferred with the Louisiana governor and with numerous other Anglo-Americans and even French agents, all claiming to be eager to help the insurgents, in exchange for favorable treatment by Mexico when it achieved its independence.

Don Bernardo eventually left New Orleans and traveled by riverboat to Natchitoches, where he was close to the Neutral Ground separating Spanish territory from the United States, a place teeming with mercenaries and foreign agents, all eager to take part in revolutions and military expeditions that would bring them riches and power. War fever was rampant in this no-man's-land that summer of 1812 as hostilities escalated between the United States and Great Britain. It seemed like a good time to invade the Mexican province of Texas.

Don Bernardo, having made the acquaintance of a soldier of fortune named Augustus Magee, late of the U.S. Army, organized with him the Republican Army of the North out of the multitude of adventurers in the Neutral Ground and marched into Texas (Garrett 140–142). The Republican Army of the North, with Don Bernardo at its head, scored significant victories in Texas, taking first the settlement of Nacogdoches and later the Presidio La Bahía before marching to San Antonio de Béjar, which fell to the insurgents in April of 1813. However, this victory was marred by the conduct of the insurgents toward the royalist prisoners, including Texas governor Manuel María de Salcedo. The governor was executed by members of the Béjar militia, who may have been acting with Don Bernardo's tacit approval. The Bejareños had ample reasons to hate Salcedo for the cruel treatment he had meted out to them, according to Garrett (181), while Gutiérrez de Lara "had his own reasons for revenge," since Salcedo had been instrumental in the "capture and execution of Hidalgo, Allende, Jiménez, and other insurgent leaders" (Narrett 212–213).

The royalists were not yet vanquished, however, and made ready to counterattack. The Republican Army, under Don Bernardo's command, went out to meet the enemy on June 20 at a spot outside Béjar called El Alazán. Lorenzo de la Garza relates a particularly poignant incident that occurred before this battle: Don Bernardo's wife and children had traveled from Revilla to be reunited with him and met him at an oak grove outside Béjar, as he marched on his way to battle. After an undoubtedly emotional encounter, he had to leave them in the cover of the oaks while he departed to meet the enemy (*Dos hermanos* 56).

The insurgents were victorious on this occasion, but dissension was rife within the ranks of the Republican Army of the North due to the presence of a number of spies who had been planted among them by Spain and the United States. Among these were José Alvarez de Toledo, variously described as Cuban or Dominican, who turned out to be in the pay of Spain, and his allies, the American agents Henry Bullard and William Shaler. These two pressured the Junta de Gobierno that ruled Béjar to remove Don Bernardo as commander of the Republican Army (Schwartz 43). This action could not have come at a worse time, for the royalist troops were again on the march to engage the insurgents. On August 4, 1813, Alvarez de Toledo assumed the command of the Republican Army of the North, and Bernardo Gutiérrez de Lara was exiled to the United States (Garrett 220–221).

On August 18, 1813, the royalists, under General Joaquín Arredondo, defeated the rebels at a spot east of the Medina River known as El Encinar de Medina. At the end of the battle, the few hundred survivors were either captured and executed by Arredondo or managed to straggle to Louisiana. Among the latter was Alvarez de Toledo, who subsequently made his way to Spain, married well there, and was rewarded with a pension and eventually named by Fernando VII as ambassador to the court of Naples, where his wife had wealth and titles (L. de la Garza, *Dos hermanos*, 68–72).

Don Bernardo, with his family, returned to Natchitoches, and he remained there until 1824, earning his living as a blacksmith. He followed closely the sporadic uprisings of insurgents in Mexico until 1821, when Agustín de Iturbide, the commander of the royalist forces, made peace with the insurgents and sent the viceroy packing back to Spain. Ironically, this final act of insurrection came about for a reason similar to that of 1810—instability in the mother country—where Fernando VII had been forced by an armed uprising to swear allegiance to the liberal constitution drafted by the Spanish *cortes*, or parliament, in 1812.

Don Antonio Gutiérrez de Lara, the priest, had returned to Revilla in 1814, after receiving amnesty from the religious, civil, and military authorities. In 1821, following the conclusion of the War of Independence, he wrote to his brother in Louisiana, pleading with him to return home. Don Bernardo, however, was justifiably skeptical, for no sooner had Mexico thrown off the king of Spain than Agustín de Iturbide engineered a coup to have himself crowned emperor. The Mexican Empire lasted less than one year, when Agustín I abdicated under pressure from disappointed former supporters and staunch antimonarchists alike. He was allowed to go into exile, with the proviso that he not return to Mexico. A national congress then met and adopted a constitution in 1824 that established a federal and republican form of government. Now Don Bernardo was ready to come home.

His homecoming at first appeared to be most auspicious, for the newly formed legislature of the "Free State of Las Tamaulipas" (the former province of Nuevo Santander), of which his brother, Antonio, was a member, offered Don Bernardo the office of governor, which he accepted. However, even before Don Bernardo had been sworn in as governor, he was faced with a political and moral crisis: Agustín de Iturbide had landed on the Tamaulipas coast, in defiance of the federal law that had decreed his death should he return to Mexico. Don Bernardo was bound by his office to carry out the law, and therefore, in accordance with the congressional decree, he had Iturbide put to death in a "Christian and military manner," as he explained in his *Breve apología* that he published later in life to refute his detractors: "Comencé . . . a ejercer las funciones . . . del empleo, y . . . me estrené con el gravísimo y notable acontecimiento del ex-Emperador Iturbide, a quien hice morir cristiana y militarmente con puntual arreglo a la ley . . . y a la sentencia . . . del H. Congreso que lo condenó a sufrir esta pena" (L. de la Garza, *Dos hermanos*, 135). His political enemies used the Iturbide execution as a pretext to harass Don Bernardo to the point that he resigned from his office less than a year after assuming it. He was then commissioned a colonel in the cavalry of the state militia in 1825 and remained a soldier until his death in May 1841.

My grandfather Lorenzo de la Garza, although not a native of Guerrero, undertook in the early years of the twentieth century the task of writing the dual biography of Revilla's most illustrious sons in *Dos hermanos héroes*. Many years after my grandfather's death, I found, among his papers collected in an old trunk, three letters from José Ángel Gutiérrez de Lara, the eldest of Don Bernardo's children. The first, dated May 31, 1841, and addressed to his mother, Doña Josefa de Uribe, in Ciudad Guerrero, described the death and burial of Don Bernardo in Villa de Santiago, Nuevo León. In early 1841, Don Bernardo, already in bad health, had left Guerrero to visit Ángel, who resided in Linares, Nuevo León. During his stay there,

Don Bernardo's condition worsened, and he became determined to travel to Santiago, where his only daughter lived. Ángel described to his mother how he had arranged for his father to be carried on a stretcher from Linares to Santiago ("mandando hacer de antemano una Litera para conducirlo, pues de otro modo hera imposible"), where he died on May 13, 1841, and was buried in the local church.

It is interesting to note that, in the midst of grieving for his father's death, Ángel remembered the economic and legal consequences of a person's death. In his letter, he suggested to his mother that it would not be amiss for his brothers to round up the cattle—the drought permitting—and conduct an inventory of the herd ("No me parece fuera de propósito . . . que sería bueno, si la seca lo permitiese, que José Alejo y demás hermanos procediesen a juntar el ganado del rancho y formar un ymbentario completo") in preparation for the heirship proceedings that would, in due time, be held in Guerrero, Tamaulipas.

In the second letter, which Ángel addressed to his brother Januario in Ciudad Guerrero, he acknowledges having received the sad news of their mother's death in December of the same year, 1841. In this and in the previous letter, Ángel makes loving reference to his uncle, Antonio, whom the Gutiérrez de Lara children called Tata Padre and considered their second father, on whose wise guidance they all depended: "con la sabia dirección de nuestro segundo padre, que es Tata Padre." But Father Antonio Gutiérrez de Lara soon followed his brother and his sister-in-law. He died on November 14, 1843, in Ciudad Guerrero, and in the third letter, dated November 29, 1843, Ángel relates to Januario that, on the last time that he had parted from Don Antonio, their uncle had lamented that they might not meet again: "A Dios, hijo, puede ser que ya no nos vuélvamos a ver." And, indeed, they never did.

In the years following Don Bernardo's return home, he had lived through the violent severing of Texas from Mexico in 1836, an outcome that had been prefigured by the invasion of the Republican Army of the North, which had been made up, to a large extent, of Anglo-Americans. He also lived through the federalist uprisings from 1838 to 1840 that resulted in the installation of a new government for the people of the Frontera del Norte that came to be known as the Republic of the Rio Grande. The reason for the rebellion of 1838 was the same as that which had ostensibly driven Texas to rebel, the desire to reinstate the federal constitution of 1824. This charter had been abrogated in 1836 and had been replaced by a centralist plan, known as the Siete Leyes (Seven Laws), at the instigation of the political weather-vane president, Antonio López de Santa

Anna, infamous for losing Texas. The Texas colonists were not the only ones who had expressed their dissatisfaction with the change of constitutions, merely the most successful. For example, on his way to suppress the Texas rebellion, Santa Anna had paused to put down an uprising in Zacatecas. He was successful in Zacatecas but failed miserably in Texas.

The inhabitants of the old Escandón settlements, the Villas del Norte, were among those who felt aggrieved at the loss of autonomy that the repeal of the federal constitution represented. They had suffered chronically from the neglectful and overbearing attitude of the central government, which, while leaving them to defend themselves from the marauding Comanches, heaped insult on top of injury by demanding that the norteños support the government troops with horses and supplies when they passed through on their way to Texas (Wilcox 88–97). The norteños finally took action to remedy their situation and rebelled. In November of 1838 Antonio Canales, a lawyer from Camargo, Tamaulipas, issued a *pronunciamiento*, urging his countrymen to oppose the central government and to fight for the reinstatement of Federalism.

Antonio Canales was born in 1802 in Monterrey, Nuevo León, where he started school, but his family moved to Camargo when he was still a boy. His parents were José Antonio Canales Treviño and Josefa Rosillo. His mother was a niece of Fray Servando Teresa de Mier, the Dominican priest from Monterrey who had presented Mexico's claims before the Spanish cortes in 1812 but who was also one of the leading advocates of the centralist form of government. The Tamaulipas legislature granted Canales a license to practice law in 1829; however, he was no typical bookworm, since he also joined the local militia and took part in the frequent skirmishes against the marauding Comanches and Apaches (Zorrilla and González Salas 76–77). In addition, he practiced a most useful occupation: he was the official land surveyor of the state of Tamaulipas. As such, he surveyed many tracts in what later became Zapata County, Texas, among them the land grant awarded to his comrade-in-arms Col. Antonio Zapata, a tract known as Villa.

Canales's proclamation was soon echoed in the other Villas del Norte. In January of 1839, two months after Canales had issued his call to arms, the citizens of Laredo gathered at San Agustín Plaza and, with many demonstrations of joy and much ringing of church bells, passed a resolution stating that "this town will continue in the future to act under the Constitution of 1824" (Wilcox 99). Among the prominent Laredoans who supported the federalist cause were the alcalde, José María Ramón, and former alcalde, Bacilio Benavides (1836–1837), uncle of the then sixteen-year-old Santos

Benavides of American Civil War fame. Santos later recounted that he and his uncle "harassed the enemy [the Centralists] on their march, waylaid them in the defiles, and fired on them at night" (Thompson, *Laredo*, 97).

Canales's pronunciamiento was not the first incident of defiance against the centralist government. In March of 1838, Gen. José Urrea, who had fought with Santa Anna in Texas and had subsequently been appointed commandant general of Sonora, had rebelled against the government and declared in favor of the constitution of 1824. Urrea's rebellion was suppressed in October of the same year, but in that same month a fresh rebellion broke out in the port city of Tampico, Tamaulipas, which the fugitive Urrea was able to appropriate successfully (Nance 143–145). The rebellion in Tampico soon merged with Canales's pronunciamiento, which in turn prompted declarations in favor of the 1824 constitution in the state capital, Ciudad Victoria, and in lesser cities of the state, as well as in communities in Nuevo León and Coahuila.

In the last days of 1838 and the early part of 1839 it seemed as if the Federalists would topple the central government, taking important cities such as Monterrey and Saltillo and controlling foreign trade through the ports of Tampico and Matamoros. However, some of the Federalists' success was due to a major misfortune that afflicted Mexico at the time: the blockade of the Gulf of Mexico ports by the French navy and the threat of French occupation that arose out of the conflict that came to be known as La Guerra de los Pasteles (the Pastry War), which was the result of claims made by French merchants in Mexico for loss of property that had occurred during the many revolts of the 1820s. One of the claimants was a pastry cook whose pastries had been consumed without payment by a group of Mexican soldiers. The French king, Louis Philippe, demanded payment of $600,000 in reparation for the losses suffered by his countrymen in Mexico (surely not all for pastries!), and as payment was not forthcoming, he sent French ships to block the port of Veracruz and bombard the fortress of San Juan de Ulúa that guarded the harbor. When the French troops landed in Veracruz, Antonio López de Santa Anna came out of enforced retirement and led Mexican troops in a charge against the French and actually drove them back to their ships. The French then agreed to a settlement and sailed away (Meyer et al. 316–317).

One result of this episode in Veracruz was the temporary vindication of Santa Anna, especially as he was wounded in the affray and had to have his leg amputated; another was to free the centralist army to turn its attention to the federalist insurrection and to inflict serious losses on the rebels. The weakened Federalists, in turn, shifted their attention north and went to Texas to seek support, both from the government and from individuals. Francisco Vidaurri y Villaseñor, a former governor of the state of Coahuila y Texas and a leading Federalist, was in San Antonio in July of 1839, trying to convince Texans that they should make common cause with his party (Nance 186). On the military front, Cols. Antonio Canales and Antonio Zapata, the latter from Guerrero, moved their camp to Lipantitlán, on the Nueces River near San Patricio, to escape the reach of the centralist forces. (The area between the Nueces and the Rio Grande was claimed by the Republic of Texas but was not under its control, and Tamaulipas still exercised dominion over it.) From Lipantitlán, Canales issued a proclamation, exhorting Texans to join the federalist cause, and more than two hundred men responded, among them Cols. Reuben Ross and Samuel W. Jordan. On September 30, 1839, Canales and his men crossed the Rio Grande, after having met with Col. Antonio Zapata and two cavalry units near Carrizo (later renamed Zapata, in his honor). The Federalists then crossed the Salado River above its mouth and entered Guerrero early the next morning.

What followed resembled a page out of a novel by Alexandre Dumas. The centralist garrison in Guerrero was led by Don Bernardo Gutiérrez de Lara, the old warrior having been brought out of retirement and appointed its commander only a few days before, in spite of his poor health. It may seem surprising that Colonel Gutiérrez de Lara, having once rallied his fellow *revillanos* (residents of Revilla) to support the independence movement, now placed his services in the cause of the autocratic central government; however, according to Narrett, "[n]ational unity took precedence over all else" for Don Bernardo (227). He had learned to distrust foreign intervention in Mexican affairs after his experience with the Republican Army of the North, but now that early association came to his aid. After the garrison was overrun by the Federalists, Don Bernardo was captured as he tried to cross the Salado. One of the Texan soldiers recognized him and pointed him out, whereupon Don Bernardo demanded to be taken to the commanding officer, who turned out to be Col. Reuben Ross. Don Bernardo then asked him if he was related to Major Reuben Ross, who had fought with him in Texas in the Republican Army of the North. Colonel Ross replied that he was Major Ross's nephew, and Don Bernardo said that, in that case, he knew that he would be treated in a humane fashion (Nance 218–219). Antonio Canales, however, was not so inclined and fell upon the old hero, ripping off the gold epaulettes from his uniform, according to Lorenzo de la Garza's account. Then, not content with inflicting this humiliation on the hapless hero, Canales and his men also sacked his home. Don Bernardo was finally rescued by the appeals of his two sons, who were in the federalist army (*Dos hermanos* 201).

With a lesser man, the events relating to his capture by the Federalists would have engendered a desire for revenge, but three weeks after the incident, Colonel Gutiérrez de Lara addressed a conciliatory letter to Antonio Zapata, with whom he had had business relations in the past. In this letter, Don Bernardo counseled Zapata to lay down his arms for the good of his country, as well as for his own well-being. Reminding Zapata that his countrymen were grateful to him for his protection from Indian attacks, Gutiérrez de Lara assured him: "Todos ... deseamos ver a usted en su casa, con sus hijos, con sus amigos, con sus conciudadanos.... No puede olvidar este pueblo y parte de esta frontera los buenos servicios que le ha prestado, y por los cuales aún le conserva ... gratitud y aprecio" (We all wish to see you in your own home, with your children, with your friends, with your fellow citizens.... This town and this part of the frontier cannot forget your good services, for which they appreciate you and are grateful). The letter, which was written in Guerrero and dated October 22, 1839, was quoted extensively in *El Mañana*, of Reynosa, Tamaulipas, on April 24, 2008, in a series that the newspaper ran from April 24 to April 27 on Guerrero Viejo titled "Estas ruinas que ves" (These Ruins That You See).

After prevailing in Guerrero, Canales challenged the centralist army under Col. Francisco González Pavón at nearby Mier and engaged them in the battle of El Cántaro, defeating them decisively and taking González Pavón prisoner, as well as capturing their artillery pieces. Canales then decided to march on to Matamoros with approximately one thousand men; however, Matamoros was well defended, and the Centralists had superior manpower and firepower. Therefore, after a two-week siege of the city, Canales decided to try his luck elsewhere. Ross and fifty of his men then left the federalist army in disgust, and Canales set his sights on Monterrey. In Monterrey, Canales ran into Gen. Mariano Arista and a sizeable contingent of the centralist army and was defeated by them. Canales then returned to Texas in January of 1840 with a dwindling number of followers (Alessio Robles 2:215–217).

Antonio Canales, whatever his shortcomings and vagaries as a military leader, had a finely honed sense of political strategy. He sensed that the restoration of Federalism, by itself, no longer inspired men to follow him into battle. He needed a more proactive cause to rally people to fight. He therefore called a convention to bring forth an independent government for the Frontera del Norte.

Lorenzo de la Garza, in *La antigua Revilla*, relates that high-ranking persons in Guerrero and nearby towns decided, in the last days of 1839, to form a new government regime composed of Tamaulipas, Nuevo León, and Coahuila and held a convention in Guerrero for that purpose. They did this on January 18, 1840 (40–41). According to Juan José Gallegos in his master's thesis on Antonio Zapata, the representatives to the Guerrero convention then adjourned to Casa Blanca, on the Nueces River, possibly to remain outside the reach of the centralist troops (141).

At Casa Blanca the delegates organized a provisional government and called for a subsequent convention to include delegates from all the Mexican states. Jesús Cárdenas, a lawyer from Reynosa and a former political chief of Tamaulipas, was chosen president, and Francisco Vidaurri y Villaseñor, the former governor of Coahuila y Texas, was named vice president. José Antonio Canales was appointed commander in chief of the army, and Juan Francisco Farías, who had served on the Laredo municipal council, was named secretary. A legislative council of five members was also chosen. This council consisted of the president, the vice president, and a representative from each of the three participating states: Tamaulipas, Nuevo León, and Coahuila. Juan Nepomuceno Molano, former alcalde of Matamoros (and a kinsman of Canales's wife, whose name was Refugio Molano), represented Tamaulipas, while Manuel María de Llano, former governor of Nuevo León, represented his state, and Francisco Vidaurri represented Coahuila. José María Carbajal was named secretary of the general council (Nance 252–253).

Laredo was chosen as the capital of the new government. During January and February of 1840, however, the seat of government remained in Guerrero because that town possessed a printing press, which allowed the Federalists to establish their official newspaper, the *Correo del Río Bravo del Norte*. On Sunday, February 16, 1840, the *Correo*, in its first (and only) issue, published the convention results mentioned above and announced that the motto of the new government was *Dios, libertad y convención*— God, Liberty and Convention (L. de la Garza, *La antigua*, 40–41).

When the delegates finished their work at Casa Blanca, they returned to Guerrero, where the president and the vice president of the new government were sworn into office. After the inauguration, a ball was held at Col. Antonio Zapata's house, which overlooked the plaza, to celebrate the event, "and all were welcome who chose to attend"; but many of the soldiers did not do so, because their clothes were practically in rags. To alleviate their destitute state, each soldier then received two dollars in partial payment for past services (Nance 254).

One of the first things that the new government of the Frontera del

Norte undertook was a diplomatic overture toward the Texas government, much as the leaders of the War of Independence had done regarding the United States when they sent Col. Bernardo Gutiérrez de Lara to Washington. Although Canales had written to President Mirabeau B. Lamar of Texas soon after his pronunciamiento of 1838 and had sent federalist general Juan Pablo Anaya to solicit material help and volunteers in San Antonio, Austin, and Houston, the first official approach was made by Jesús Cárdenas, president of the government of the Frontera del Norte, in February of 1840. Cárdenas wrote to José Antonio Navarro, one of the founders of the Republic of Texas, offering him an appointment as agent in Texas for the new government. Navarro declined the appointment (Vigness 312–317). Neither Navarro nor President Lamar was willing to be seen as aiding the Federalists in Mexico, since Texas was still trying to receive formal recognition of its independence from the Mexican government, and the Mexican government, whether the Texans liked it or not, was the centralist government.

On the other hand, the first approach that Canales made after the installation of the new government was to General Arista, the centralist commander, asking for an armistice. This action may have been the product of pragmatism, rather than cowardice or treachery. After all, why continue to fight if your enemy is willing to call it quits? Arista, however, wanted nothing to do with an armistice and mobilized his troops to go in pursuit of Canales.

Canales remained in Guerrero until February 18, 1840, when he decamped ahead of Arista's army. Arista reached Guerrero on March 6, 1840, and found a deserted town. The townspeople, afraid of bloody reprisals, had fled into the brush. The opposite of their fears happened. Arista issued a general amnesty to all the inhabitants who would acknowledge the centralist government and encouraged all to return to their homes. Arista then resumed his pursuit of Canales, who continued his own flight up the river to Coahuila, where he established his camp at the Presidio del Río Grande (L. de la Garza, *La antigua*, 41). According to Gallegos, Canales and Zapata had a disagreement at this point, and Zapata took his squadron to the nearby settlement of Santa Rita de Morelos while Canales moved to San Fernando—present-day Zaragoza, Coahuila (149).

When Canales abandoned Guerrero, President Cárdenas left the town as well, and, escorted by one hundred Mexican rancheros and a few Texans, he moved the seat of government to Laredo. Today the house that is known as the Capitol of the Republic of the Rio Grande is a museum in

Laredo. Like the other houses of the leading citizens of the day, it faced the main square, San Agustín Plaza, and was located on what is now Zaragoza Street. When the house was placed at the disposal of President Cárdenas in 1840, it was relatively new, having been built about 1834 for Bartolomé García, a fourth-generation descendant of the founder of Laredo, Don Tomás Sánchez. Architects describe it as a "one-story, stuccoed, sandstone vernacular structure" in the shape of an L and consisting of four rooms built around a courtyard (*A Shared Experience* 144).

From Laredo, Cárdenas sent Capt. John T. Price to Texas to recruit volunteers for the weakened federalist army, promising those enlisting a pay of twenty-five dollars per month for privates, plus the booty that might be taken from the Centralists. President Lamar of Texas, fearing that Price's offer might induce desertions from the Texas army, issued a proclamation declaring that future deserters would receive the death penalty but past ones would be pardoned if they returned to their posts (Nance 259). After occupying Guerrero, General Arista headed for Laredo, and President Jesús Cárdenas deemed it prudent to abandon the town and seek refuge in the brush country of the Nueces Strip, the disputed land between the Nueces River and the Rio Grande, setting up camp at Laguna Espantosa on the Nueces, later moving east, still on the Nueces, to Casa Blanca.

Meanwhile, in his pursuit of Canales in Coahuila, General Arista came upon the detachment led by Col. Antonio Zapata. In his official report, Arista describes how the force that he commanded, the División Auxiliar del Norte, caught Zapata and his thirty men by surprise at Santa Rita de Morelos and took the leader and twenty-three men as prisoners, killing the remainder. After some delay, Canales attacked the Centralists in an effort to rescue Zapata, but he was completely repelled. According to Arista's report, some 200 Federalists were killed and 176 were taken as prisoners. In addition, the Federalists lost their artillery pieces, ammunition, and flags. In the same report, Arista mentions that Zapata would be tried by a military court, which would determine his fate. We know that Col. Antonio Zapata was killed by a firing squad, after refusing to recant his political beliefs and loyalties (L. de la Garza, *La antigua*, 41–43).

After his defeat at Santa Rita de Morelos, Canales took refuge at Laguna Espantosa, but he soon left his headquarters there to seek support in Texas. He first went to San Antonio to confer with Juan N. Seguín, who was a senator at the time. Seguín sent him to Austin to meet with President Lamar. Lamar was cordial but offered only moral support, much as President Madison had done with Col. Bernardo Gutiérrez de Lara some twenty-eight years earlier. However, Lamar must have turned a blind eye to the recruiting efforts in Texas, because Canales was successful in raising troops and supplies.

While Canales was negotiating in Austin, President Jesús Cárdenas had established himself around Victoria, Texas, where he was warmly received. The local population, particularly the merchants, was eager to trade, not only with the soldiers, but also with the inhabitants of the Villas del Norte. Joseph M. Nance recounts in *After San Jacinto* that eighteen persons who described themselves as merchants of Victoria and who carried on extensive trade through Lavaca Bay had petitioned President Lamar in the spring of 1840 to consider "the propriety of affording protection to the Mexican Trade" from the depredations of armed Anglo-American bandits who "rob and otherwise molest the traders" (290). The population of Victoria took so well to Cárdenas and his government that a dinner was held in his honor on April 10 "under the shade of the venerable post oaks on Diamond Hill" (Nance 294).

By June, Antonio Canales had established his headquarters in San Patricio on the Nueces and had gathered additional forces. These included Juan Seguín, who, having resigned his Texas senate seat, had raised one hundred men, together with his fellow Bejareños Antonio Pérez and Leandro Arreola, who brought in another hundred. By July, the reconstituted federalist army was on the march again. Canales sent Colonel Jordan with fifty Anglo-Texans and Col. Luis López with one hundred Mexican rancheros to retake Laredo and to collect the six to eight thousand pounds of lead that the Federalists had hidden in Laredo, according to a letter from José María Carbajal to President Lamar (cited by Nance 326).

The march through the brush country at the height of the summer heat must have taken a toll on the troops. One thing in their favor was that they rode at night, to escape both the heat and centralist patrols. By July 25 they were in the outskirts of Laredo. It was not yet dawn, and they left their horses in a corral and silently entered the town on foot, hiding in the bushes lining the riverbank, within a hundred yards or less of San Agustín Plaza. Just before daylight, an old woman, on her way to draw water from the river, discovered the hidden men and sounded the alarm. The Federalists then rushed out of the bushes and charged the troops garrisoned in the square. Taken by complete surprise, the troops opted for fleeing (Wilcox 100). There is no mention of any harm having come to the old woman who revealed the intruders' presence. As a matter of fact, although Lamar's adjutant general, Hugh McLeod, commented that the "Federalists plundered Laredo when they took it—friends and foes" (as cited by Nance

327), contemporaneous reports, including the understandably self-serving one from Colonel López, make reference to amicable relations between the townspeople and the occupying forces (Thompson, *Laredo*, 102).

The Federalists remained for a few days in Laredo before rejoining Canales at his camp at Lipantitlán on the Nueces. After the success of the Laredo expedition, Canales made plans to return to the Rio Grande. He ordered one of his Texas lieutenants, Col. Samuel Jordan, to go ahead of the main body of the troops to clear the stretch between Guerrero and Camargo of Centralists. While en route to his objective, Jordan met Col. Juan Molano, the representative from Tamaulipas on the governing council, who delivered a change of orders. Their combined forces of Anglo-Texans and rancheros were to proceed south of the Rio Grande, toward Ciudad Victoria, the capital of Tamaulipas (Wilkinson 170–171).

Along the way to Ciudad Victoria, Molano would declare "federal constitutional order restored" in the towns where they stopped, such as Linares, Nuevo León, and then would appropriate tobacco taxes, stamp taxes, and even tithes to support their expedition. Jordan and Molano's troops took Ciudad Victoria by surprise on September 29, 1840, put in place a federalist government, collected the available taxes, and withdrew on October 6 (Vázquez 29). This sudden withdrawal underscored the different purposes pursued by each of the two groups—the Anglos and the Mexican Federalists—in their joint adventure. The first had engaged to fight in the pursuit of "the spoils of war," as Colonel Molano described it in a letter to the editor of *El Ancla*, a newspaper from Matamoros (cited by Nance 336–337). The Federalists, according to Molano in the same letter, could not afford to alienate their countrymen by engaging in pillage, since such depredations could become "an insuperable barrier to the progress of the revolution." This letter from Molano to *El Ancla* came almost six months after the occupation of Ciudad Victoria, and it was clearly in the nature of an apologia, in view of the intervening events. An opposing version of the occupation came from Anson G. Neal, who later recounted that the local people had received the troops with open arms; the merchants in particular "threw open their stores to the credit of our men." Nance has the grace to add: "They could scarcely afford to do otherwise" (339).

After Ciudad Victoria, Molano and Jordan marched toward Saltillo, the capital of Coahuila. On the way there, depending on which point of view the reader prefers, either Molano had an epiphany that revealed to him that bringing armed foreigners into his homeland was wrong and that his cause was hopeless (Vázquez 29), or he was bribed by intermediaries from General Arista into surrendering (Nance 352). In either case, Jordan's men were left to their fate after an armed encounter near Saltillo caused Molano and his men to lay down their arms. Some of the norteños were caught in the middle, refusing to follow either Jordan or Molano. Such was the case of Col. José María González of Laredo, who, with his men, left the affray outside Saltillo and headed for home (Nance 354–355). Later González met up with Jordan's band at Candela, Coahuila, and accompanied them to Laredo. At Laredo they encountered Juan Seguín, who had information relating to the agreement that Antonio Canales had made with the Centralists for ending the war. This agreement gave the Federalists, both Mexican and Anglo-Texan, the option of joining the centralist army at the military ranks previously conferred by Canales and of collecting the back pay owed to them. Seguín and Jordan wanted to hunt down Canales, apprehend him, and hang him as a traitor; however, they soon learned that their quarry had already disbanded his army and was in the process of negotiating with centralist general Isidro Reyes in Mier (Nance 362). It was time for all parties to call it quits and go home.

In capitulating to General Arista's forces, Colonel Molano had negotiated surprisingly favorable treatment for himself and Canales and the troops who likewise surrendered. In addition to a general amnesty for the former members of the federalist army, the Mexican government also guaranteed their property and their safety. The government also assumed the debts contracted by what was termed the "provisional government" (Vázquez 30). This generosity—which seemed remarkable, and even a sign of weakness, to foreigners—was part of the usual rules of engagement, an attitude necessary for survival in a land plagued by frequent strife, since the winners today might be the losers tomorrow (Olivera and Crété 170).

The conclusion of what is usually termed the Federalist Wars at the end of 1840 came at a crucial time, for by 1845, when the United States moved to annex Texas and thereby precipitated war with Mexico, Mexico did not need to be at war with itself. In those circumstances, it needed all the military talent it could muster, and Antonio Canales, a seasoned frontier fighter, acquitted himself well in the forlorn attempt to repel the invasion from the north. Canales reached the rank of brigadier and took part in the battles of Palo Alto and Resaca de Guerrero (Resaca de la Palma), losses that resulted in the fall of Matamoros and the Villas del Norte to the invaders. He was also with Gen. Pedro de Ampudia in the brutal defense of Monterrey and with Santa Anna in the grueling battle of Buena Vista near Saltillo.

After the Treaty of Guadalupe Hidalgo was signed, General Canales continued his military career, putting down an 1852 uprising near Camargo known as La Rebelión de la Loba, where he defeated his old comrade-in-arms from the days of the Federalist Wars, José María Carbajal, and served briefly as governor of Tamaulipas. His two sons, Antonio and Servando Canales Molano, were also governors of their native state and exerted great influence in the area, especially Servando, who distinguished himself in the War of the French Intervention, particularly in the battle of Santa Gertrudis, which was fought successfully near Camargo in June 1866 (Zorrilla and González Salas 74–77).

Contemporary historians writing on this subject have raised the question of whether there was ever such a thing as the Republic of the Rio Grande. Josefina Z. Vázquez, in *La supuesta República del Río Grande*, asserts that "the so-called Republic" was a creation of the propaganda arm of Gen. Zachary Taylor's invading army, which published a bilingual weekly called *La República del Río Grande* in Matamoros in 1846 in an attempt to rekindle separatist feelings along the river settlements (5). However, George Fisher, a Serbian adventurer passing himself as a businessman and a journalist, had already used the term "Republic of the Rio Grande" to refer to the Frontera del Norte in 1840. In a letter to the editor of the *Morning Star* of Houston (March 3, 1840), Fisher had advocated for improved commercial relations between Texas and the incipient neighboring republic: "Therefore, the success of the independence and the final establishment of the Republic of the Rio Grande, is much to be desired by every friend of Texas" (Nance 197). As a good propagandist, Fisher knew how to coin a catchy name, even for a republic that had not yet come into being. Vázquez claims that the term was never used by the Federalists, and she may well be correct, because Spanish speakers referred to the river—then and now—as the Río Bravo. The name of the official publication of the putative republic was *Correo del Río Bravo del Norte*. It was published in Guerrero, and in its first and only issue it carried a presidential address to the citizens of the area that began: "JESUS CARDENAS, Presidente de la frontera del norte de la república mejicana a sus habitantes." It is clear that at the time of this publication—February 16, 1840—a name had not yet been coined beyond the descriptive term used by Cárdenas, "the northern frontier of the Mexican republic." Two weeks later, George Fisher apparently remedied this omission with his reference to the "Republic of the Rio Grande."

Juan José Gallegos also questions the existence of the Republic of the Rio Grande, pointing out the lack of documentary evidence, such as a declaration of independence, to prove its existence. Gallegos adds that Lorenzo de la Garza, in *La antigua Revilla en la leyenda de los tiempos*, refers only to a "new governmental regime" (*un nuevo régimen gubernamental*) composed of Tamaulipas, Nuevo León, and Coahuila (Gallegos 178). However, de la Garza also mentions the motto of the new government: Dios, Libertad y Convención, implying that some kind of constitutional convention had been held or was in the planning stages (*La antigua* 41).

And we must not forget that there was a flag with the three bands and the three stars, representing the three states—a flag that the warriors of the Republic of the Rio Grande (by whatever name) insisted on flying in the disputed territory between the Nueces and the Rio Grande (Alessio Robles 2:219). Ultimately, whether the Republic of the Rio Grande was a political reality or the fabrication of foreign propagandists is not the most important issue. What is important is to recognize that the people of the area encompassed by the three stars—and this included the disputed Nueces Strip—thought of themselves as belonging together. In 1848, after the signing of the Treaty of Guadalupe Hidalgo, when the residents of Laredo learned that henceforth they were to be part of the United States, they petitioned to be allowed to remain part of Mexico. Three of their most prominent members, former mayors José María Ramón and Bacilio Benavides and Col. José María González, all supporters of the Republic of the Rio Grande, wrote a letter to Mirabeau B. Lamar, the former president of the Republic of Texas and now the United States general in charge of the occupation army, asking to be allowed to continue their union with Mexico (Wilkinson 222). Perhaps the Laredoans felt that a known devil was better than an unknown angel. Most likely, it was their desire to remain united to the other Villas del Norte, their sister settlements, and not to be divided by the Rio Grande. The request was not granted.

Yet, in 1906, more than fifty years after the political severing of Laredo from the other Villas del Norte and from Mexico, the idea of a common union was still evident in the people of the area. Among old family papers, I came across a yellowed newspaper dated November 30, 1906. Someone had saved it long ago because it contained a notice regarding the probate proceedings related to the death of my maternal great-grandfather. It was a tabloid of only four pages, published in Ciudad Guerrero, and it was called *La Unión Fronteriza* (The Border Union).

《 TWO 》

The Kingdom of Zapata

In the early 1950s, when Hollywood producers made a movie about the Mexican revolutionary hero Emiliano Zapata, with Marlon Brando in the title role (*Viva Zapata!* 1952), they chose South Texas, particularly Zapata County, as the location for shooting the film. Why they did so, when Zapata had lived and waged war mostly in south-central Mexico, in the vicinity of his native state of Morelos, is a mystery. The contrast could not have been greater than between the semiarid brush country of the lower Rio Grande Plains and the lush sugarcane-growing region of Emiliano Zapata's birth. Perhaps the filmmakers wanted to depict authentic Mexican architecture, such as could be found in San Ygnacio in northern Zapata County, or in Roma in neighboring Starr County, even if the geography was not authentic. Most likely, the movie people—even the writer John Steinbeck, who penned the script—believed that Zapata County had been named after Emiliano Zapata and thought it fitting to film his life there. They surely had never heard of Col. Antonio Zapata, who had lived, fought, and died almost a century before the better-known revolutionary and at the northern extreme of Mexican territory, where Emiliano Zapata had never set foot.

Zapata County, Texas, was organized in 1858 and was named in honor of Col. Antonio Zapata at the behest of the first county judge, an Englishman named Henry Redmond, who was obviously an admirer of the colonel. Redmond was a resident of Carrizo, the county seat that was later renamed Zapata too. However, before the county seat acquired its present name in 1898, the site, in addition to having been called Carrizo (after the Carrizo Indians who inhabited the area in the eighteenth century), was also known as Habitación, which means "dwelling" in Spanish, or Habitación de Redmond, for wherever Henry Redmond dwelled was the county seat.

According to Virgil Lott and Mercurio Martínez in their history of Zapata County, Redmond was a merchant who came to the area in the 1830s and married a woman from Guerrero, Tamaulipas. He carried on trade between present-day Zapata County and settlements in the neighboring Mexican state of Nuevo León, such as Cerralvo and Agualeguas, as well as the Villas del Norte along the Rio Grande (42–44). As a merchant, Redmond would have been acquainted with Antonio Zapata, who, according to Lorenzo de la Garza, devoted himself in the 1820s and 1830s to commercial activities, mainly the buying and selling of livestock in the area around Revilla/Guerrero (*La antigua* 38).

Cattle traders, like horse traders, may be admired for their shrewd dealings but not necessarily for their honesty. Yet, almost twenty years after his defeat and violent death, one of Antonio Zapata's fellow merchants—and perhaps competitor—petitioned the State of Texas to honor Colonel Zapata by naming the county after him as a tribute to his character. Lorenzo de la Garza states that, in business, Zapata's credit was unlimited, because of his reputation as an honorable man (*La antigua* 38–39). As an example of Zapata's honesty, it is often related that in the mid- to late 1830s, coinciding with the rebellion in Texas, or because of it, Antonio Zapata suffered catastrophic business losses. Most likely, his cattle were requisitioned without payment by the centralist forces under Santa Anna on their way to and from the battlefields of Texas. Zapata, having operated under "unlimited credit," found it necessary to liquidate all his property to pay off his debts, which, according to some versions, amounted to seventy thousand pesos, a veritable fortune at the time. In order to meet the debts, he had to sell even his wife's jewelry (Huston 67). However, one creditor, Don Bernardo Gutiérrez de Lara, did not call in Zapata's debt, thereby showing his faith in the man who later became his military antagonist when they found themselves on opposite sides of the Federalist Wars, the movement that spawned the Republic of the Rio Grande (Gallegos 9).

It is remarkable that a man like Antonio Zapata—who, unlike a prophet, achieved great honor and respect in his own land—came from very humble origins. Juan José Gallegos, in his exhaustive study of Antonio Zapata, cites the parish records of Nuestra Señora del Refugio in Revilla, which contain the baptismal entry made on the twenty-ninth of January in 1797 by the priest who baptized "José Antonio Serapio," a days-old *mulato*, the legitimate son of Ignacio Zapata and María Antonia Rocha (19–20). That a child born not only of poor parents but also as a member of a *casta*, as the people of mixed race were known, could rise during his lifetime to both wealth and military honor is an example of the egalitarian spirit that could be found in the Villas del Norte and evidence of social mobility in what was supposed to be a stratified society.

Mulattoes were the products of combined European and African parentage. Moreover, Antonio seems to have been born of two mulatto parents or, at least, of parents who were a mixture of indigenous and African. Gallegos traces the Zapata lineage through the Revilla census of 1780, which listed the household of Ignacio Zapata and his wife, Alberta Esparsa. Among the dependents, or *arrimados*, was a single woman named María Ignacia Calderón, aged thirty-nine, and a young boy of seven named Ignacio Calderón. Gallegos adds that both were identified as *pardos* (42). *Pardo*, which one Spanish-English dictionary translates as "gray, drab, brown; a mixture of black and white, containing some yellow or red," was the term originally used by the Spaniards to designate a person of African and Indian parentage (Lafaye 30). However, according to the same author, eventually *pardo* simply came to refer to a member of the *castas*, much as "colored" came to be used in English-speaking countries. Perhaps the *bachiller* Don José Cayetano González, the parish priest in Revilla, was merely trying to be precise when he described José Antonio Serapio as a *mulato*, rather than using the general term *pardo*. Equally precise was the 1791 ecclesiastical census of Revilla, which again enumerated Don Ignacio Zapata and his wife as the householders and named among the servants Ignacia Calderón, aged forty-nine, a *mulata libre* (free mulatto), and a young man, Ignacio *Zapata* (emphasis added), aged twenty, described as mulatto, who had been raised in the house (Gallegos 42).

The dry information contained in the census documents suddenly gives rise to speculations, which, although perhaps melodramatic, are nonetheless pertinent. First we notice that Ignacio Zapata's servant, Ignacia Calderón, had given birth some twenty years earlier to a son, Ignacio Calderón, indicating an illegitimate child. It is quite possible that simple coincidence accounts for the same given names of master and child, just as with master and servant (in its masculine/feminine forms). However, between 1780 and 1791, Ignacio Calderón becomes Ignacio Zapata. There is, of course, the possibility that Don Ignacio and his wife may have adopted the young Ignacio as an act of kindness, but it is also possible that young Ignacio may have been Don Ignacio's *hijo natural* (illegitimate child) whom he legitimated eventually, to coincide, perhaps, with his mother's manumission. One may have required the other. It may have been legally necessary for Ignacia to receive her freedom and become a mulata libre before Don Ignacio could adopt her child. Slavery and the system of castas were not abolished in Mexico until Hidalgo's successor as leader of the War of Independence, José María Morelos, convoked the Congress of Chilpancingo in 1813, during which slavery was outlawed (at least in theory). As of 1791, though, it was still necessary to set down the racial—and, therefore, legal—status of persons on all important documents, and these included church records, a practice that, although abhorrent, is of great value to researchers.

If there was a question about young Ignacio's parentage, this was not the case with José Antonio Serapio, who was declared at his baptism to be the legitimate son of Ignacio Zapata and María Antonia Rocha. Antonia was the daughter of Francisco Rocha, also a mulatto, who worked on a ranch belonging to Captain Miguel de Cuéllar on the eastern bank of the Rio Grande. Francisco Rocha was killed by Lipan Apaches in the summer of 1790 (Gallegos 48–49). Francisco's widow, Magdalena Martínez, who died in 1799, was also listed as a mulata in the burial records of the church in Revilla (Fish, *Borderland*, 22).

Gallegos points out that, at the time of Zapata's birth, mulatto families constituted 30 percent of the families in Revilla, the second-largest group, next to the Spaniards (42). The percentage of mulattoes seems surprisingly high, but only at first blush, if we remember that relatively few Indians were attached to the Villas del Norte; consequently, there were also few mestizos. That the history of the Villas makes little or no mention of the African element probably reveals a high degree of integration between the two groups. This was not the case with the Indians.

The relationship between the inhabitants of the Villas del Norte and the indigenous peoples of the surrounding area was one of persistent conflict, and it was this state of intermittent warfare that shaped the character and the destiny of Antonio Zapata. Even more than for his business probity, Antonio Zapata came to be valued by his countrymen for his bravery and skill as a warrior in the frequent encounters with the *yndios bárbaros*, the term used to describe the Indians who had not been pacified by either religion or force of arms and who were a constant threat to the survival of the Villas.

In his years of exile in Louisiana before 1824, Don Bernardo Gutiérrez de Lara had devoted whatever spare time he had to devising schemes for achieving peaceful relations with the Indians. One plan revolved around making various gifts amounting to some twenty thousand pesos to the Indians in exchange for the return of the captives they held—basically a ransom plan. However, his brother, the priest Don Antonio, remained skeptical and advised Don Bernardo to abandon or postpone such ideas and come home instead: "[S]oy de sentir que abandonando o dejando para después las ideas de convertir a los indios del norte, pienses únicamente en transportarte con tu familia a ésta tu Patria." Don Antonio saw nothing but pie in the sky in the ransom scheme and pointed out that obtaining the twenty thousand pesos was his main—but not the only—objection to the plan. Neither the central nor the local governments had the money to buy the Indians' cooperation, and even if the sum had been available, there was no certainty that the Indians would abide by the truce for long. Don Antonio repeated his plea for his brother to come home and forget about the Indians: "Déjate de indios y piensa solamente en venir con tu familia" (L. de la Garza, *Dos hermanos*, 89–95).

Don Bernardo's hope for buying the Indians' friendship was not only proof of the desperate state of insecurity in which the settlers existed along the northern frontier but also an acknowledgment that the proximity of Anglo-Americans played a large part in the increase and ferocity of the raids. As long as the Indians raided the Spanish settlements only to meet their needs, the losses suffered by the *pobladores* (settlers) might have been tolerable; however, as the Anglo-Americans pushed west, particularly after the United States acquired Louisiana in 1803, they often provided a market for the booty taken by the Indians (Weber 95). At least one incident that transpired near Guerrero bears out the claim that the Indians raiding the Villas had had previous contact with Anglo-Americans. Lorenzo de la Garza recounts a bloody Indian attack on the Rancho Los Moros in 1844 during which one of the raiders killed by the ranch defenders was found to have on him a silver medallion weighing four ounces and bearing the image of President Martin Van Buren, while another wore a tin medallion with the effigy of President John Tyler. De la Garza adds that the dead Indians were neither Comanches nor Lipans and that they had many carbines (*La antigua* 57–58).

Sometimes the "booty" sold by the Indians consisted of human beings, the captives that Gutiérrez de Lara was attempting to ransom. Lott and Martínez relate the story of twenty-year-old Manuel Ramírez Martínez of Revilla, who was abducted from his ranch by the Comanches in 1819. His captors first took Manuel to a village near the Brazos River and kept him there as their slave until they transported him and three other captives to Cherokee country, where they sold him to a man named Macurine. Macurine then took Manuel to Natchitoches, Louisiana, and there sold him to a man named Denis, who paid Macurine for Manuel with three old black slaves. Denis treated Manuel in a kindly fashion and allowed him to work on the plantation until Manuel had paid for his purchase price, after which Denis let him go free to return home with a trading party. Manuel had been gone two years, and his parents had already given him up for dead. Manuel later wrote some verses that recorded his ordeal, which are quoted by Lott and Martínez (92–96): "Fue el caso que andando activo / El año diez y nueve / Por una partida leve / De Comanches fui cautivo" (While busy working / In the year nineteen / A small party of Comanches / Took me as their captive).

Jean Louis Berlandier, a French-Swiss naturalist who traversed the northern Mexican provinces accompanying Gen. Manuel Mier y Terán in 1827, noted that Comanches and Lipans had waged "a lengthy war against the inhabitants of the inland provinces of the east [of Mexico], and particularly against the villages along the Río Bravo del Norte," and he described the treatment of those inhabitants whom they captured: "Men were usually massacred on the spot, while women and small children were carried off into slavery. . . . Captives who have somehow escaped the fury of their masters are often led into the villages and sold" (*Indians* 75–76). Manuel Ramírez had apparently suffered the latter fate.

Weber also points out that the Anglo-American traders paid the Indians with firearms and ammunition, as well as whiskey, for the cattle and horses that the Indians took from the Spanish and Mexican frontier settlements, thus compounding the harm done (95). The Spanish and the Mexicans at times also engaged in this self-destructive barter with the Comanches. Berlandier observed this practice in San Antonio de Béjar and remarked on its harmful effects in his diary: "In time of peace, the Comanche come to Bexar to sell buffalo hides and deerskins, meat and bear grease to the inhabitants, who, particularly the soldiers, give them ammunition in exchange, as well as weapons which are shortly turned against them" (*Indians* 31). It was a point of debate at the time whether the Indians were more lethal with guns or with bows and arrows, but the point became moot as the guns and the powder improved in quality.

Still, one of Antonio Zapata's most famous battles with the Indians involved the use of arrows, not guns, on the part of the Indians, and hand and foot combat on his part. In *La antigua Revilla*, de la Garza recounts an anecdote that is repeated whenever the life of Zapata is told. The story relates that as Zapata and some thirty men from Revilla returned from a skirmish along the Nueces River, they encountered a band of Comanches. Zapata and his men had taken a defensive position along an arroyo, with Zapata in the front line, when he noticed that the Comanche chief was approaching him. Zapata then moved forward to meet his enemy. When Zapata had almost reached him, the Comanche shot an arrow that lodged in Zapata's leg, pinning him to the saddle. The Comanche then turned his horse and fled. Zapata pulled the arrow from his leg and, spurring his horse, overtook the Comanche, grabbed him by the hair of his head, and threw him to the ground. Then, dropping from his own horse, Zapata proceeded to stomp the Comanche to death with the metal heel of his boot. On this occasion, Zapata had been armed with a pair of pistols and a saber, but he used none of his weapons (39–40). According to Lott and Martínez, Zapata's favorite weapon was a blackjack, a short iron rod encased in leather with which he "beat out their [the Indians'] brains" (50).

The fierceness of Zapata's fighting methods bordered on—or even strayed into—barbarism. However, we must remember that his conduct was probably no worse than the treatment that the settlers received at the hands of the Indians. This was true whether the settlers were taken captives or were casualties of the bloody attacks perpetrated in places such as the Rancho Los Moros, where in 1844 more than forty settlers were killed in battle or burned to death when the main house was set on fire (L. de la Garza, *La antigua*, 55–59). De la Garza also reproduces in the same book the recollections of Don Candelario Rendón, who in 1890 recounted an Indian attack that he had witnessed as a child at the Rancho Las Tortillas. In old age, Don Candelario still recalled the dread and panic produced by what the locals called *un día de indios*, "an Indian day." Don Candelario remembered that the dogs had begun howling in response to the beat of the approaching drums and the piercing wails of the war whistle ("el estridente gemido del 'patito'"). The child Candelario then saw his eighteen-year-old sister running from the direction of the creek, clutching at her breast as blood streamed down from it, staining her white blouse and skirt. As she reached her young brother, he saw an arrow protruding from her chest, just as she dropped to the ground, dead, before him (61).

The warrior is always valued by people living under the threat of constant attacks, and Antonio Zapata was an outstanding warrior and defender of his people. Thus, it is not surprising that he was able to transcend his humble origins and to achieve material success and respect among his countrymen in Las Villas del Norte. Therefore, when the Villas found themselves oppressed more than usual by the central government, it was natural that Zapata should take the leadership in their defense. This was not a position that he sought out at the beginning, however. Zapata's main concern at the time was still the Indian threat to the Villas and their surroundings. Gallegos tells us that the day after Antonio Canales and his sympathizers declared their rebellion against the central government, in November 1838, Zapata was in Mier, discussing the Indian situation with Colonel González Pavón, the centralist commander (102).

Still, Zapata was not without sympathy for the Federalists' cause and shared their grievances against the central government. In particular, he resented the lack of support from the government in repelling the Indian attacks and — the final straw — a tax law enacted on June 9, 1838, that further burdened the Villas and aggravated their misery (Gallegos 93). Thus, when the rebels approached Zapata, they were able to persuade him to join their ranks, and he was commissioned a colonel in the federalist army, in charge of a cavalry unit assigned to carry out hit-and-run operations against government troops, which he did with frequent, lightning-quick strikes (Gallegos 106).

Although Antonio Canales was the military and political leader of the Federalists, it was always acknowledged that Zapata was the best fighter they had. But a daring and impetuous warrior like Zapata was not always the most disciplined soldier. His fierce attacks on the Centralists often spilled over to the citizenry and generated hard feelings against the Federalists among the inhabitants of the affected areas. Gallegos states that "Zapata and his men's behavior . . . neutralized the good will he had accumulated in the region as a result of his reputation as an Indian fighter" (113).

The early successes of the Federalists in the first part of 1839 dried up by the second half of the year, and Antonio Canales was forced to look to Texas for reinforcements. Unfortunately for Canales, the troops that he brought from Texas consisted mainly of the same types of adventurers and cattle rustlers that, together with the Indians, had preyed on the ranches near the banks of the Rio Grande. Many of the rancheros who supported Zapata and made up his cavalry were opposed to the inclusion of this element in the federalist group. Col. Bernardo Gutiérrez de Lara, not only a hero of the War of Independence but also Zapata's generous creditor, addressed a letter to Zapata, urging him to disassociate himself from the Texas adventurers and return to his home (*El Mañana*, Reynosa, Tamaulipas, April 24, 2008). Zapata, however, disregarded this advice and continued waging war.

The infusion of new troops from Texas helped the Federalists achieve a series of successes in encounters such as that in Guerrero, where Don Bernardo Gutiérrez de Lara was captured and allegedly mistreated by Antonio Canales, as was recounted in chapter 1. However, the more important prizes of Matamoros and Monterrey eluded the Federalists, and in Monterrey they suffered a serious defeat at the hands of their ultimate nemesis, Gen. Mariano Arista, and were forced to retreat toward the Rio Grande. That retreat exacerbated the miserable condition of the federalist forces, and Zapata tried to alleviate their situation by demanding loans of money and supplies from the inhabitants of Villa Aldama, Nuevo León, an action that provoked them to animosity against the Federalists (Gallegos 136).

Once back in Guerrero, Zapata tried to reach an armistice with General Arista, and Canales did likewise from his camp in Mier. It was a false olive branch from Canales, though, a dilatory tactic to buy time, since he also directed Jesús Cárdenas to call a meeting in Guerrero of the alcaldes of Camargo, Reynosa, China, Los Aldamas, and Marín—the latter three settlements in Nuevo León—to organize a provisional government (Vázquez 19). All this took place in early January of 1840, but in spite of the primitive means of communication (letters sent by ship or couriers on horseback), the propagandist George Fisher reported on the convention— held in Guerrero on January 18—in the *Houston Morning Star*'s March 3 issue (Vázquez 19–20). In his report, Fisher also made reference to the subsequent meeting held in Casablanca on the Nueces River, but Vázquez, in her study of the "So-Called Republic of the Rio Grande" (*La supuesta República del Río Grande*), is inclined to agree with Joseph M. Nance, who identifies the latter convention site as the Oreveña Ranch, near the present-day city of Zapata (Vázquez 20).

It does make more sense that the Federalists should have continued the Guerrero meeting across the Rio Grande, rather than traveling up to the Nueces to organize the provisional government. This scenario is also more credible if we remember that the delegates, after concluding their business, returned to Guerrero to be sworn into office and to celebrate their inauguration with a ball at Colonel Zapata's house. This was undoubtedly a fine house, as befitted a man who had been the alcalde of Guerrero in 1835. It was at this ball that the soldiers were reported to have sworn allegiance to and kissed the flag with the three stars that came to be known as the flag of the Republic of the Rio Grande (Wilkinson 166).

According to a map of Guerrero Viejo drawn by Lori B. McVey in 1993, Zapata's house faced the main plaza and was catercornered to the Church of Nuestra Señora del Refugio. There was no better proof of the elevated status that Zapata had attained in the community than the location of his house. Most prominent citizens in the Villas sited their houses facing the main plaza, in accordance with town planning guidelines used by the Spaniards: "On the street fronting the plaza, sufficient ground was assigned for a church, a jail, and a municipal building; the remainder of the lots were assigned for the residences of the captain and other important citizens" (Scott 66). In Zapata's case, the house on the plaza was a further testimony that he had joined the ruling class, for that structure, according to the McVey map, had originally belonged to—and probably had been built by—Don Cristóbal Benavides, one of the original settlers of Revilla.

That inaugural ball on January 29, 1840, at Zapata's house must have been the last celebration of a happy occasion within those four walls, for soon after that Zapata and the Federalists left Guerrero, escaping ahead of Arista's forces, and the house may have been left empty in his absence. Antonio Zapata had married Asunción Salinas, described by de la Garza as an orphan of his same social sphere, in May of 1821 (*La antigua* 38). The couple had five children—four daughters and a son—but the boy died within days of his baptism in 1824 (Fish, *Borderland*, 2). In March of 1836 Asunción died too, of dropsy, according to parish records (Fish, *Borderland*, 23). Therefore, in February of 1840 Col. Antonio Zapata was the sole parent of four young daughters, the oldest of whom, María Petra, was a few days shy of turning eighteen.

The question then arises of what happened to the four girls when their father went to war. Perhaps the girls stayed alone in the house under the care of María Petra, a not unheard-of situation in those times and places where young people had to grow up fast. It was also possible that the motherless girls went to stay with grandparents or other relatives, for they were not likely to have had a housekeeper or woman servant to look after them. In Guerrero, as in the other frontier settlements, the inhabitants mostly managed their households without servants. Only the richest employed help, and such workers were not usually indoor servants but, rather, ranch hands. The census taken during the inspection by José Tienda de Cuervo in 1757 of the Villas del Norte showed that Revilla, seven years after its founding, had a total of 357 inhabitants, broken out into fifty-eight families and eighteen servants, including a mulatto and a slave. That meant that more than half of the families of Revilla had no servants at all, although the captain, Don Juan Báez Benavides, had two, Don Cristóbal Gutiérrez four, and Don Juan Soberón three. More than eighty years later, the Zapata family, like many others, probably made do with no domestic help, beyond what the daughters and dependent friends and relatives (arrimados) could provide.

In any case, once Col. Antonio Zapata left his home and his daughters in Guerrero on February 18, 1840, he never returned to them alive. In fleeing ahead of Arista's forces, Canales and Zapata traveled up the river until they reached the vicinity of the Presidio del Río Grande, in the state of Coahuila. There they received word that a party of Comanches was nearby. Canales detached two squadrons of his cavalry to go in pursuit but did not include Zapata among them. Gallegos recounts that Zapata was displeased at being left out of this mission. The old warhorse wanted to go into action against his traditional foes, the Indians. "Zapata always wanted to fight," recalled Santos Benavides, who, as a youth, aided the Federalists (quoted in Gallegos 148).

Gallegos also quotes from a letter dated March 26, 1840, from Antonio Canales to Jesús Cárdenas, the president of the Provisional Government, in which Canales tries to justify the disastrous results of the encounters with the Centralists on the two previous days. According to Canales, Zapata, who was "contrary and headstrong," disobeyed orders to stay with Canales's forces and took off for the settlement of Santa Rita de Morelos to obtain provisions for his squadron (Gallegos 153). Santa Rita de Morelos was not a hotbed of Federalism; on the contrary, it had previously sided with the Centralists. If Zapata believed that the villagers there would willingly provision his soldiers in exchange for protection from the Comanches, as Gallegos surmises, he was fatally wrong. The villagers instead sent out word to the approaching centralist forces commanded by Gen. Isidro Reyes that Zapata was in their town, demanding money, maize, and horses (Gallegos 153).

General Reyes immediately detached a Captain Galán and sent him with some eighty local presidial soldiers to Morelos to trap Zapata. In the meantime, the treacherous villagers of Morelos had persuaded Zapata to delay his departure on that fateful day of March 24, 1840, offering food and drink to the tired men and their weary mounts. As Zapata and his men allowed the villagers to lead the horses to the corrals, Galán's troops galloped into town. Zapata and his men, realizing their predicament, barricaded themselves inside a house facing the plaza and returned fire, hoping that Canales and his forces, who were only a league and a half away, would come to their aid. Instead, cavalry and sharpshooters from General Reyes's forces arrived to reinforce Galán. Zapata, out of ammunition and realizing the hopelessness of his situation, surrendered with twenty-three of his men. Three of his men had been killed and four seriously wounded (Gallegos 154–155).

Apparently, Canales did not become aware of Zapata's capture until late in the day. When he did, he descended on Morelos with his troops and attacked General Reyes at nightfall, but without success, according to General Arista's report. The battle continued the following morning of March 25, but it soon concluded after General Arista's arrival with reinforcements. Canales and his troops then abandoned the field of battle. Arista reported that his soldiers had pursued the rebels after capturing their artillery pieces, ammunition, and flags. He also reported that some 200 Federalists had perished and 176 had been taken as prisoners, among them Col. Antonio Zapata, who would be court-martialed within two days (L. de la Garza, *La antigua*, 41–42).

The verdict of the court-martial was that Antonio Zapata was guilty of treason, and his sentence was death by a firing squad. The sentence was carried out at ten in the morning on March 29, 1840, at Santa Rita de Morelos. The facts about Zapata's death are indisputable; however, the inevitability of the event and how it came about are open to inquiry. Gallegos, basing his account on General Arista's report to the Ministry of War in Mexico City, relates that before Arista made the final attack on Canales on March 25, the imprisoned Zapata requested an interview with the centralist general. Arista reported that Zapata had assured him that Canales would surrender if he (Zapata) asked him to do so. Arista agreed to Zapata's proposal and sent a federalist prisoner to relay Zapata's message, along with his own ultimatum, giving Canales thirty minutes to lay down his arms or be destroyed. Arista claimed to have waited forty-five minutes to hear a reply from Canales, but none came (Gallegos 156).

The day after the battle, March 26, General Arista announced his victory in a letter to the minister of war, a copy of which he circulated also to newspapers in Mexico and Texas. He then convened the court-martial of Col. Antonio Zapata and presented the case against him, as well as whatever mitigating circumstances were in his favor. Gallegos includes reports of witnesses who stated that during the jury deliberations General Arista had offered to pardon Zapata if he would lay down his arms and renounce the Federalist cause (161). De la Garza relates that Zapata "disdainfully refused" to become a turncoat (*La antigua* 43). Gallegos adds that Zapata urged Arista to shoot him because he "would never lay down his arms as long as he was at liberty" (161–162).

Perhaps Antonio Zapata was a reincarnation of the hero of the medieval ballad quoted by Don Quijote: "Mis arreos son las armas / Mi descanso es el pelear" (Weapons are my attire / Fighting is my repose). Perhaps Santos Benavides had been right when he told Mirabeau B. Lamar that Antonio Zapata always wanted to fight, as Gallegos recounts (148). Perhaps Zapata would rather have fought and died than lived as a defeated man. But if that was so, why did he approach Arista before the battle with Canales, offering to persuade Canales to surrender? Of course, we have only Arista's word that the conversation ever took place.

It was fortunate for Zapata's memory that the story of the second incident, the "disdainful refusal," prevailed, and we are left with the image of

Zapata as the defiant warrior, rather than that of the defeated prisoner. The legend of Antonio Zapata, the man of unflinching valor and integrity, had already taken shape during his lifetime, but it became part of the regional consciousness after his death, as an unintended consequence of the ultimate humiliation heaped on him—the desecration of his body ordered by Arista. Just as Father Hidalgo, after his execution in 1811, had been decapitated, so was Antonio Zapata. And then, to exacerbate the already grisly act, Arista had Zapata's head "pickled" in alcohol in a wine cask, to be preserved for the trip back to his hometown. De la Garza relates that a convoy headed by Gen. Pedro de Ampudia brought the head of Antonio Zapata to Guerrero and exhibited the macabre trophy on a spike planted on the main plaza, facing Zapata's home (*La antigua* 43). This gruesome sight confronted his daughters—if they were in residence there—for three days before the parish priest was allowed to bury the head on April 12. The parish priest of Guerrero, Don José Antonio de la Peña Berástegui, entered this act in the burial records of the parish, giving the cause of death as *ajusticiado* (executed). He also added that Antonio Zapata, a widower, had not left a will (Fish, *Borderland*, 24).

Antonio Zapata had left, instead of a will, a legend and land—land to which his descendants and the descendants of his neighbors clung with grim determination throughout that century and the next as the new sovereign, the State of Texas, tried to wrest it away from them. Zapata's physical and spiritual heirs could not afford to lose the land that had nurtured them and their ancestors. In the place that came to be known (only half in jest) as the Kingdom of Zapata, the land provided not only sustenance and even wealth but, more importantly, a sense of belonging, roots in a community without which a person had no home. A historian of Tejano ranching in South Texas, Armando C. Alonzo, has summed up the long history of Tejano landholding, saying that it "fostered a deep economic and psychohistorical attachment to the land, still cherished today" (275). In *New Guide to Spanish and Mexican Land Grants*, Galen Greaser adds: "The fight to extract a living from an unpredictable and dangerous environment produced, at times, an almost visceral connection to the land" (109). To support his assertion, Greaser quotes from an 1828 petition for land by a resident of one of the Villas del Norte: "'That love of the land where one is born precludes aspiring to other prospects ... even when these frontier Villas are totally lacking in agriculture and other arts, being solely devoted to the raising of large and small stock, in spite of droughts and the hostilities of the barbarous Indians'" (109).

This psychohistorical attachment to the land was the legacy of the promise that Don José de Escandón had held out to the settlers who followed him to the banks of the Río Bravo del Norte—the promise that they would have their own land. The first thing that these original settlers, the *pobladores primitivos*, did upon reaching the places that came to be known as Las Villas del Norte, was to select the plots of land they were to cultivate or were to pasture their cattle. Yet it was not until 1767 that a Royal Commission was set up by the Spanish Crown to give the pobladores formal possession of the lands that supported them. In the meantime, between 1749 and 1767, new settlers had arrived to the Villas del Norte, also clamoring for land, and it became necessary to rank the rights to be conferred. The commission determined, not surprisingly, that the original settlers, the primitivos, would have the first choice of the lands within the jurisdiction of their respective Villas, lands that most of the settlers were already occupying. These settlers were granted long, rectangular tracts with river frontage that were known as *porciones*.

A series of requirements had to be fulfilled, however, before the individual settlers could have ownership of their land. The first step was to select the surveyors who were to survey the tracts. Half of the surveyors were selected by the Royal Commission representing the Crown, and the other half by the settlers to act on their behalf, although the surveyors were usually residents of the area who were familiar with the land. In Revilla, for example, the *agrimensor*, or surveyor, chosen to represent the settlers was Don Vicente García, my maternal great-grandfather, four times removed. Before the surveyors began their measurements, though, it was stipulated that six leagues in each direction would constitute the jurisdiction of a particular Villa, and henceforth each porción would be identified as belonging to a particular Villa (Scott 63–64). The jurisdiction of each Villa extended to both banks of the Río Bravo/Grande, as well as to the lands of its tributaries that flowed by the Villas, such as the Salado at Revilla, the Alamo at Mier, and the San Juan at Camargo.

After a porción had been surveyed and adjudicated to a settler, there still remained one final act to be performed to confer ownership, the Act of Possession (Acta de Posesión). This was a ceremony in which the chief justice (*justicia mayor*) or the captain of the Villa took the grantee by the hand and led him around the land that was to be his. My ancestor, Don Vicente García, was given possession of Revilla Porción 47 on the banks of the Río Salado in an act that, like the others, was recorded at the time and subsequently copied and deposited in the Spanish Archives of the Texas General Land Office. The English translation of this act, as it pertains to

Porción 47, reads: "[O]n the margin of the river Salado . . . on a tract belonging to Don Vicente Garcia . . . in the name of his Majesty I went with him around the corresponding circle, he picked up stones and threw them to the four winds, plucked herbs, took water and irrigated the earth and performed other demonstrations in proof of delivery and was well satisfied, obligating himself to erect permanent landmarks and to persevere in the cultivation and settlement" (GLO, Revilla Act of Possession, 213). The ceremony described was an ancient one, harkening back to feudal Europe. Long after feudalism had disappeared in western Europe, its spirit survived in the northern reaches of New Spain, not only in the rites of conferring possession of land, but also in the close identification of the people with their land.

However, Antonio Zapata's ancestors had not been among the pobladores primitivos. He had had to acquire his land under different rules, as did others who came after the primitivos. These later grants, or *mercedes*, were much larger than the porciones since they usually did not have any river frontage and were made at the request of individual applicants (GLO, Guide, 2). In 1808, for example, Don Andrés Bautista Pereda and his son, José Manuel Pereda, from "la Villa de Revilla," petitioned the Royal Vice Patronato de Tierras y Aguas, the entity charged with administering land and water rights in New Spain, for the grant of two large tracts of grazing land that were vacant (*tierras realengas de agostadero*) on the eastern side of the Rio Grande, in the jurisdiction of Revilla, just east of the porciones awarded earlier to Capt. Miguel de Cuéllar and to Clemente Gutiérrez. In due time, Don Andrés received a grant known as Charco de la India, containing 17,713 acres, and his son, José Manuel, the adjoining Cerrito Blanco grant, with 17,712 acres, in what later became Zapata County, Texas. The files containing the *testimonios*, or documentation supporting these grants, are among the most complete in the Spanish Archives of the Texas General Land Office (San Patricio Files 1–564 and 1–570, respectively, box 135, folder 10).

These files contain, among other documents, the entire testimonio that evidenced the grants of land from the Spanish monarchs Carlos IV and Fernando VII to the Pereda men. The testimonio recited that the petitions from Don Andrés and Don José Manuel had been received by the Intendancy of San Luis Potosí on September 22, 1808, and that the surveys and field notes of the tracts had been completed in 1809. The testimonio also referenced an earlier appraiser's report of 1807 as to the nature and value of the land in question. The report concluded that the land was inhabitable but problematic, according to the translation of an early archivist at the Texas General Land Office. Regarding the flora of the area, the appraiser reported that "[t]he plants are chaparral, huisache, mesquite and retama, and such vegetation is so plentiful that it makes the land inhabitable and beneficial." However, the fauna was not uniformly hospitable: "The animals are tigers, leopards, wolves, coyotes, rabbits, hares, deer, antelope, and snakes, and these last-named are abundant." The appraiser concluded, "There is no timber which can be used to any advantage; there is only pasturage for stock, and I do not consider the tract suitable for any kind of settlement whatsoever. . . . Skilled appraisers value the leagues at ten pesos each as water is absolutely lacking" (GLO, box 135, folder 10).

The testimonios detailing the history of the Pereda grants were deposited in the Texas General Land Office by A. Winslow of Laredo, Texas, without any explanation as to his role in the transaction; however, since A. (Andrew) Winslow appears listed as an attorney in the Laredo, Texas, City Directory for the year 1900, he may well have been acting on behalf of a client. If that was the case, he performed a valuable service both to his client and to history, for the Pereda files are of enviable thoroughness, in addition to containing an unusual notation made by the Spanish archivist, who remarked: "[The testimonio was] written on fifteen pages, front and reverse, of heavy linen paper bearing the seals of Charles IV and Ferdinand VII. When it was deposited in the Land Office in 1902, it had been folded to pocket size in three horizontal sections, and three blood stains, diminishing proportionately on the successive pages, had penetrated forty-five thickness of paper" (GLO, box 135, folder 10). The presence of these bloodstains has led to this land title being known in the General Land Office as "the Blood Title."

Since Don Andrés Pereda was my maternal great-great-great-grandfather, it is tempting for me to speculate that, along the years, some ancestor of mine had defended this land and that it was his blood that had soaked the document, but there is no support for this supposition. The remaining documents in the Pereda file merely reflect a series of transactions whereby the heirs of Don Andrés and Don José Manuel transferred their interests in the lands in Zapata County to various purchasers, among whom was Don Alejandro Treviño, another maternal ancestor of mine who acquired an interest in Cerrito Blanco in 1843.

The Pereda land grants were made contemporaneously with the outbreak of the War of Independence in Mexico. Understandably, then, the awarding by the Spanish Crown of mercedes came to a halt in the Villas del Norte after the commencement of hostilities in 1810. After Mexico's independence from Spain was consummated in 1821, the grants were resumed by the new sovereign, the Republic of Mexico, and its subdivision, the State of Tamaulipas, whose boundaries extended up to the Nueces River. As a consequence of this third wave of grants, by 1822 José Manuel Pereda had acquired new neighbors: Antonio Zapata and his step-uncle (his stepmother's brother), Pedro Bustamante, had settled on tracts that came to be known as Villa de Antonio Zapata and Las Comitas, respectively, the latter adjoining Charco de la India and Cerrito Blanco, and Villa abutting Las Comitas. Zapata and Bustamante were close friends, in addition to the family connection, according to a Zapata historian (Fish, *Borderland*, 2).

The Zapata and Bustamante tracts, however, were not surveyed until 1835 by the official surveyor of Tamaulipas, Antonio Canales, the future leader of the Republic of the Rio Grande. The impetus for awarding these late land grants was the promulgation of an edict known as Decreto 24 on October 19, 1833, by the State of Tamaulipas. Article I of the decree stated: "To the inhabitants of Camargo, Mier, Guerrero and Laredo, who may have no lands of their own, and who may possess stock to occupy them, there shall be given at once not exceeding five leagues each, and in compensation they shall pay the state $10 for each league." Article II explained that the reason for this magnanimous act was to compensate the inhabitants of those Villas for the hardships that they had undergone in their struggle with the Indians: "Those only are comprehended in the foregoing article who lived in said villages during the last Indian war now passed and who did not emigrate previous to the year 1821" (Sayles and Sayles 1:137).

Antonio Zapata had obviously lived in Guerrero during "the last Indian war now passed," having been one of the foremost Indian fighters in the area. Under the decree of October 19, 1833, he would be able to obtain legal ownership of the tract of land to the east of the Rio Grande that he had been occupying since the early 1820s, and he took the required steps to do so, as did Pedro Bustamante. Another resident of Revilla who also qualified for a land grant under Decreto 24 was my paternal ancestor Jesús Benavides, who "denounced," or petitioned for, and surveyed a 9,809-acre tract known as El Pedernal in present-day Zapata County.

These titles emanating from the State of Tamaulipas subsequently proved problematic for many of their owners after the Treaty of Guadalupe Hidalgo of 1848 stripped Mexico—and therefore the State of Tamaulipas—of the lands north and east of the Rio Grande. The Zapata, Bustamante, and Benavides tracts—among others—although having been surveyed in 1835, did not receive their titles from the state until January of 1848, only a few weeks before the signing of the treaty that officially concluded the war with Mexico. The Treaty of Guadalupe Hidalgo stipulated the recognition of land grants made by the previous sovereigns in the territory ceded by Mexico to the United States, to the extent that these titles were "legitimate under the Mexican law in California and New Mexico up to the 13th of May 1846, and in Texas up to the 2d March 1836" (del Castillo 181–182). The question that came to haunt the successors of Zapata and his fellow countrymen was whether the titles to their lands had been legitimate as of the cutoff date. More than fifty years would elapse before the question was settled.

In the aftermath of the Treaty of Guadalupe Hidalgo, the State of Texas, which, under the terms of its annexation to the United States, had retained ownership of its public lands, wanted to know if any or all of the lands south of the Nueces River were held under legitimate title. Therefore, it began an inquiry in 1850 into the legality of "titles and claims emanating from Spain and Mexico . . . in the territory recently ceded by Mexico" (Greaser and de la Teja 450). The instrument for this inquiry was a legislative commission known as the Bourland-Miller Commission, created for the purpose of quieting "the uncertainty and confusion about the validity of these grants" (GLO, Guide, 2–3). In order to fulfill their task, the two men who made up the commission—William H. Bourland and James B. Miller—traveled to the newly created counties of Webb, Starr, and Cameron in South Texas. They intended to examine the titles of all those claiming lands in those counties and convoked them to present proof of their claims; however, not every landowner presented evidence of title to Bourland and Miller, nor was every claim subsequently confirmed by the legislature. In all, 343 claims were presented, of which 78 were rejected (Greaser and de la Teja 460).

Perhaps it was just as well that the Zapata, Bustamante, and Benavides heirs—among many others—did not respond to Bourland and Miller's call, for on the commissioners' return trip to Austin aboard the steamboat *Anson*, all the title papers collected in Brownsville were lost when the vessel sank near the mouth of the Rio Grande. Instead of "quieting the uncertainty and confusion" surrounding the South Texas land titles, the Bourland-Miller Commission created more questions. In 1937 historian Florence Johnson Scott remarked that where a tract of land had not been recommended for approval in the report issued by Bourland and Miller, it was frequently alleged that the owner had not contacted the commission and had therefore been excluded. However, the most frequent allegation was that the papers relating to a particular tract had been lost in the shipwreck of the *Anson* (Scott 151–152). What the Bourland-Miller Commission did accomplish was to create much business for land lawyers in South Texas for generations to come.

After the Bourland-Miller Commission failed to resolve the issue of all the land titles in the lands acquired in 1848, the Texas legislature appointed another commission to take up the same task, but this body was even less successful than the first. After this second attempt, the legislature decided to let the judiciary deal with the matter, and henceforth questions regarding title to Mexican and Spanish land grants south of the Nueces were decided by the district courts. This legislation (and its 1862 amendment) produced only twenty-nine title confirmations in Nueces, Webb, Zapata, Hidalgo, and Starr counties. Undoubtedly, the outbreak of the Civil War halted or delayed many of these judicial land confirmations. Galen Greaser points out that many cases initiated in 1860 or 1861 were not decided until after 1868, "with some decided as late as 1871" (*New Guide* 139). As of 1870 the Texas legislature transferred the jurisdiction to hear these land matters solely to the district court of Travis County.

The act of 1870 represented a substantial departure from the previous statutes for confirming Spanish and Mexican land grants. Not only were the venue and jurisdiction for these actions now solely with the district court of Travis County, but the proceedings "became more adversarial," according to Greaser, and claims "no longer enjoyed the presumption of validity for Spanish and Mexican grants" (*New Guide* 139–140). Perhaps these changes prompted the heirs of Antonio Zapata to file suit for confirmation of their title in the district court of Zapata County in September of 1871, but the court denied their petition, presumably because it lacked jurisdiction to hear it under the new legislation (*New Guide* 318). They would have to take their case to Austin.

The hardship of having to litigate in a distant forum did not deter the daughters of Col. Antonio Zapata in their quest to obtain state confirmation of their father's land grant. A suit against the State of Texas, seeking to have the title to Zapata's "Villa" confirmed, was filed by Petra Zapata, joined by her husband (as the law required married women to do in legal matters), Eulalio González; Rafaela Zapata and husband, Bartolo Morales; María Anna Zapata and husband, José María Coronado; and Dolores Zapata, a single woman. The Zapata daughters won a favorable decision from the Travis County district court, but the state appealed the ruling to the Texas Supreme Court, which reversed the district court decision and remanded the case to the lower court (*New Guide* 318). The Zapata heirs, like good country people, sensed from which direction the wind was blow-ing and, rather than engage in futile battles, asked the district court to dismiss the case. The court complied with their request on March 7, 1884, at the same time that it dismissed a similar suit from the heirs of Pedro Bustamante, who had received similar treatment from the Texas Supreme Court (*New Guide* 202–203).

The next legislation to quiet the still-unquiet titles in South Texas came in 1901. Under this legislation, the state attorney general challenged the Tejanos' land titles by bringing "trespass to try title suits to recover land possessed or claimed under alleged titles from Spain or Mexico where no valid evidence for such grants was found in the General Land Office" (*New Guide* 143). That the state became the plaintiff under the 1901 legislation raises the possibility that it was actively seeking to augment its landholdings. Land had always been the most valuable asset that Texas had, even before it became independent from Mexico. After 1836 the new republic rewarded its supporters with land certificates (similar to land grants) and subsequently made land equivalent to money by issuing land scrip, which is defined as "evidence of debt which was payable at a given rate of land" (Miller 59–60). Land scrip was much more liquid than the certificates given earlier to soldiers and immigrants, because scrip did not require the recipient to live in Texas, and it was negotiable (Miller 60). Land scrip was the manner in which the State of Texas paid for public projects, such as the construction of the state capitol, and how it encouraged the construction of railroads and the digging of canals. Attempting to husband this great wealth, the Texas Constitution of 1876 designated one-half of the remaining public lands for the support of public schools (Miller 62). Soon, even with an enormous expanse of land, Texas was close to exhausting this resource, and Miller states that "by 1898, the reservoir of unappropriated public lands, like Mother Hubbard's cupboard, would be bare" (62).

It is possible, then, to see a connection between the legislation of 1901 that sought to "test the validity" of Spanish and Mexican land titles in South Texas and the need of the state to get its hands on more land in order to meet its commitments. The claimants under the Spanish and Mexican land grants found it increasingly difficult under successive legislation to prove their rights to lands that had been held for a long time by their ancestors. The culmination of this legislative persecution by the State of Texas against the successors of the Original Grantees came, in Zapata County, with the state's multiple suits for trespass to try title, which were consolidated into one suit styled as *Haynes v. State*.

This case, which wound its way through the state courts for several years, was first filed in 1903 by the State of Texas in the Travis County district court against the heirs and successors in interest of Antonio Zapata, Pedro Bustamante, Jesús Benavides, and others. At this time, although the Benavides and the Bustamante heirs were able to respond to the state's claim, the daughters of Antonio Zapata were no longer involved in the suit. Time had undoubtedly taken its toll (if they were alive, the daughters would have been in their seventies and eighties), but economic necessity would have done likewise. By 1903, Zapata's "Villa" grant was in other people's hands, among them Leonard Haynes, who gave his name to the litigation.

Leonard Haynes was the son of John L. Haynes, who had been among the early wave of Anglo-Americans who came to the lower Rio Grande with Gen. Zachary Taylor and the U.S. Army in preparation to invade Mexico in 1846 and stayed on after the war had concluded. He settled in Starr County, home of Fort Ringgold, and became that county's representative to the Texas legislature. During the Civil War, he joined the Union army and helped raise a regiment of Tejanos for the Union (Thompson, *Laredo*, 115). After the Texas legislature passed an act on April 24, 1871, that provided for "obtaining and transcribing the several acts or charters [Actas de Posesión] founding the towns of [the Villas del Norte]," Haynes was appointed by the State of Texas to obtain such documentation (Scott 157). The son, Leonard Haynes, a graduate of Cornell University, became not only a prominent rancher in Zapata County but also the county engineer and surveyor (Thompson, *Laredo*, 119). Lott and Martínez mention that about 1950 Leonard Haynes was "one of the extensive landowners of the county," being in possession of the "Villa ranch . . . one of the oilfield areas of the county" (215).

At the time of the *Haynes* litigation, J. J. Haynes, Leonard's brother and the Zapata County surveyor, testified that he had located "the certificates and alternate sections" for his brother covered by Zapata's grant. (The state surveyed land in 640-acre tracts, each one being designated as a certificate.) Leonard Haynes himself testified, "I have had the lands which are shown on the map exhibited to me inclosed for as much as anyhow as three years" (Haynes v. State 85 SW 1037). As of 1900, then, Zapata's "Villa" had passed to others' hands—Haynes's, primarily—but the state now claimed the land for itself.

At issue in *Haynes v. State* was the validity of the land titles that had originated with the Guerrero municipal council in 1833. The crucial question required the court to determine when title to the land had passed—if it had passed at all—from the sovereign (the Republic of Mexico acting through the State of Tamaulipas) to the grantees. The legal title had clearly been issued too late (1848) by the then governor of Tamaulipas, but, much earlier than that, the grantees may have well acquired *equitable* title to the property, as the landowners claimed. An equitable title, according to *Black's Law Dictionary*, is "a right in the party to whom it belongs to have the legal title transferred to him." According to their argument, before 1836 the grantees had already complied with all the requirements needed to acquire title, and the governor's action had therefore been superfluous.

At trial the defendants—Haynes et al.—introduced testimony to prove their equitable titles. They introduced certified copies of the surveys made by Antonio Canales and subsequent surveyors, as well as depositions from persons who were familiar with the lands and the grantees. One of these depositions was from Andrés García, who stated that he had been a member of the municipal council of Guerrero in the 1850s and that he was acquainted with the Zapata grant "since 1829, and I know that he [Zapata] was then in possession of said land as a raiser of small stock," meaning sheep and goats (85 SW 1034).

Based on the evidence presented at trial (where the defendants lost), the Court of Civil Appeals found that both Antonio Zapata and Pedro Bustamante "first settled on said lands about the year 1822" and that both men "continued in possession thereof until the same [were] surveyed ... in the year 1835, and thereafter under claim of right and ownership" (85 SW 1035). The court, obviously quoting from the Haynes and Bustamante pleadings, inserted a stirring description of the grantees' tenacity in holding on to their land. Referring to Zapata, the court stated that he had "remained in ... possession of said land, cultivating the same, and raising his livestock ... until he died about the year 1840," adding that "during the years from 1836 until about 1852, the incursions of the hostile Indians occasionally drove him and his heirs off said land, but they always returned" (85 SW 1035).

According to the same court, Pedro Bustamante had also remained in possession of his grant, "Las Comitas," from 1822 until he died in 1855, "although there were many incursions of hostile Indians during the time from the year 1836 until about 1854 ... which caused the other settlers to temporarily leave their lands." The court continued, "Yet the said Bustamante, who had built himself a blockhouse or fort upon said land, was never driven off by the Indians and valiantly held his ground against them." Clinching matters, the court added that "some of the heirs of said Bustamante, his children and grandchildren, have never sold their interest in said Comitas tract, and have always lived and still live upon it" (85 SW 1036).

These stirring descriptions of grantees' tenacity notwithstanding, the Court of Civil Appeals ruled against their successors in all the consolidated cases. The court, having decided that equitable titles deserved the same protection as legal titles under the provisions of the Treaty of Guadalupe Hidalgo, determined nonetheless that the grantees had not complied with the requirements to acquire equitable titles to their lands. The court made this finding based on a letter dated November 28, 1847, from a municipal official in Guerrero to the office of the Governor of Tamaulipas. The letter had accompanied "seventeen titles, which contain the vacant lands denounced and surveyed from the year 1831, until that of 1835," according to the Guerrero official. The letter of transmittal concluded with the explanation that the payments made by the grantees were not included with the titles "so as not to expose the same," but that the state government should determine the mode of payment and "draw against this receiver's office" (85 SW 1034). The appellate court concluded that since the land had not been timely paid for, the grantees had not acquired equitable title and therefore had no rights to the land.

Fortunately for the grantees' successors, two years later, on March 27, 1907, the Supreme Court of Texas reversed the Court of Civil Appeals in *Haynes v. State* (100 SW 912). The court reasoned that although the municipal officials from Guerrero had not included payment with the seventeen titles sent to the state capital, this did not mean that the grantees had not made timely payment. The delay in remitting the funds to the state coffers may have been the fault of the municipal authorities and not due to any error or negligence by the grantees. These suppositions that the court took into account became necessary because the court recognized that the Tamaulipas state archives in Ciudad Victoria, the state capital, had been destroyed by the French troops "under Col. [Charles] Dupin in 1864" (100 SW 914). Since it was impossible to determine what had really happened with the grantees' payments for the land, the Texas Supreme Court decided to give their successors the benefit of the doubt: "There is not a fact or circumstance to which we have been pointed by . . . the state which would impair the force of the presumption of law that the money was collected at the time the land was surveyed and the title papers made up by the municipal authorities" (100 SW 914).

The Supreme Court of Texas having rendered its decision in the seven cases consolidated under *Haynes* in favor of the landowners, they were at long last able to enjoy quiet ownership of their property, but not for long in at least one instance—that of the heirs of Jesús Benavides, the original grantee of El Pedernal. The state, having lost its earlier challenge against the Benavides title under the *Haynes* case, now challenged the accuracy of the survey covering El Pedernal in *Benavides et al. v. State et al.* (214 SW 568). The Benavides heirs lost at the trial court and appealed to the Court of Civil Appeals, which, in its opinion, quoted (in translation) from the explanation given by Antonio Canales for his survey. Canales described El Pedernal as a trapezoid-shaped tract containing "two leagues for large stock," the pastureland being bounded "on the southwest with lands of Rio Grande, on the southeast with those adjudicated to Mier, on the northeast with the Jabali pasture lands, Charco Redondo and El Gruyo, on the northwest with the Matamos" (214 SW 569). The Court of Civil Appeals, in its 1919 decision, disagreed with the description given by the surveyor in 1835, second-guessing Canales in his calls for natural objects that he had presumably observed on the ground.

Beginning with the shape of the tract, the appellate court determined that since a trapezoid consisted of straight lines, the southwest boundary could not be the "lands of Rio Grande," which were deemed to be the porciones on the river because the backs of the porciones did not yield a straight line but more of a staircase effect. Next, the court quibbled with the landowners over the meaning of topographical terms in Spanish. Where the field notes prepared by Canales called for *la Canada del Defto Mig* as a boundary, the court rightly concluded that *Canada* was a misspelling of *cañada* and that *Defto* and *Mig* were abbreviations of *Difunto Miguel* (the late Miguel). However, whereas the landowners held that *cañada* was understood by the inhabitants of Zapata County to mean a drain or drainage area, the court insisted that it meant a valley because that was what the dictionary said: "Cañada is not a technical word, and therefore not the subject of expert testimony. Any one, though having no knowledge of the Spanish language, can ascertain its meaning by consulting a Spanish-English dictionary" (214 SW 572).

The result of *Benavides v. State* was that the court redrew the boundaries of El Pedernal to yield what the court deemed a trapezoid, in the process shaving off about half of the original grant: "The Pedernal, as claimed by the appellants, contains nearly double the quantity of land called for in that grant" (214 SW 571). Judgment was rendered, not only for the state but also for "parties who had purchased from the state for the remainder of the land described in plaintiff's petition" (214 SW 570). The state had already begun selling parts of El Pedernal, even before the court issued its ruling, so certain had been the outcome.

In spite of losing almost one-half of the land grant received by their ancestor some one hundred years before, the descendants of Jesús Benavides continued to hold on to El Pedernal (each portion getting smaller with successive generations), even to this day. The heirs of Pedro Bustamante did likewise with Las Comitas, now renamed Bustamante, which received a state historical marker in 1993. And some of the Peredas, whose improvident ancestors had sold Cerrito Blanco and Charco de la India by the 1860s, were able to reacquire part of the ancestral lands through the intercession of Cupid, as will be related in the following chapter. The heirs of Col. Antonio Zapata may not own their ancestor's land anymore, but the entire county and the county seat bear his name.

In 1951, when the town of Zapata and other ancient settlements in Zapata County faced imminent destruction from the waters of Falcon International Reservoir, the county fathers commissioned Virgil N. Lott and Mercurio Martínez to write the history of the area before it all became history. The authors called their book *The Kingdom of Zapata*, an allusion to a quip made by some political wit to describe the contrarian nature of the county that consistently elected Republican officeholders while the state was solidly Democratic (late nineteenth and early twentieth century). The term was more apt than its originator ever imagined, and it stuck. Lott and Martínez dedicated *The Kingdom of Zapata* to the pioneers of Zapata County, among them, in the forefront, Col. Antonio Zapata, as well as to the others, not as well known, but whose names still appear on the old land maps and on the headstones of cemeteries hidden in the brush country.

《 THREE 》

Grandfather's Revolution
THE HORSEMAN

According to a Laredo historian, in the summer of 1913 an unidentified bandit, posing as a revolutionary (*carrancista*), seized Guerrero, Tamaulipas, with about eighty men, sacking the town and burning ranches in the area. The bandit then shifted tactics and proceeded to collect an "export tax of $4 to $15 a head for cattle that owners tried to move across the river for safekeeping" (Wilkinson 386). Actually, during the revolutionary decade from 1910 to 1920, seizing cattle from the ranches in northern Mexico and selling them in the United States to pay for military supplies was a common practice of revolutionaries and counterrevolutionaries alike, among whom were Venustiano Carranza and Pancho Villa (in the first group) and Victoriano Huerta (in the second).

During the Mexican Revolution, the ranchers "quickly realized that, if they wanted a profit from their stock, they would have to ship their cattle into the United States" (Machado 12). The revolutionary leaders along the Rio Grande, noticing the cattle exodus, knew that they would be left without a source of money and food supplies if the trend continued. Therefore, Gen. Pablo González, Carranza's military commander of the Army of the Northeast, prohibited the exportation of cattle within the area under his control, which included the Villas del Norte (Machado 12). This prohibition came some six months after Venustiano Carranza had decreed (in October 1913) that a tax of four to ten pesos per animal would be levied on cattle exports (Cumberland, *Constitutionalist*, 76). The unidentified bandit mentioned by Wilkinson may have served as the inspiration for Venustiano Carranza, for the *Primer Jefe* (as Carranza styled himself) promptly implemented as a tax scheme what had started out as extortion.

My maternal uncle, Juan Ángel García, once related to me that his father—my grandfather Benito García—had been among those ranchers who moved their cattle to Texas to keep their stock from falling into the hands of revolutionaries and *federales* alike. However, I have trouble imagining my grandfather paying extortion or tax to move his cattle, since the García family has always seemed to me to be reluctant to part with money or property. What the Garcías had, they held on to, beginning with the first Juan Ángel García who appears in the family tree. He was born in Monterrey, Nuevo León, in 1736 and came to Revilla with his parents, Don Vicente García and Doña Josepha Gertrudis de Lizondo, at the founding of the settlement, according to the inventory of settlers prepared by Don José Tienda de Cuervo in 1757 (Cavazos Garza 114).

In 1778 Juan Ángel García married Ana Josefa Treviño, according to the parish records of Nuestra Señora del Refugio in Guerrero, Tamaulipas. By 1831, when Juan Ángel García was of an advanced age, he was shown as owning Revilla/Guerrero Porción 47 on the Río Salado, which had been awarded to his father, Don Vicente García, in 1767 by the Royal Commission of the General Visita. Don Vicente had been one of the agrimensores who had surveyed the lands granted to the Revilla settlers by the Spanish Crown during the General Visit, and Porción 47 had been awarded to him in payment for his surveying work. In 1831 Santiago Vela, alcalde of Guerrero, complying with a decree from the state governor, memorialized the land titles of the jurisdiction of Guerrero in order to have a record of land ownership since the founding of Revilla ("copiando en testimonio estos documentos para que protocolisados haya constancia de las propiedades de la primera población de esta ciudad"). The document containing this information first listed the original grantee and next gave the name of the current owner ("by inheritance or purchase") as of 1831. Porción 47 showed Don Vicente García as having been the original grantee in 1767 and Juan Ángel García as the current owner, by purchase (probably from the other heirs), as of 1831 (GLO, *General Visita*, 1767, Guerrero).

Almost a century after the first Juan Ángel García married in Revilla, his great-grandson, the second Juan Ángel, married Gorgonia Garza Pereda, the granddaughter of José Manuel Pereda, in 1876 and started his own family. I do not know how much—if any—of Porción 47 had passed into the hands of the second Juan Ángel, since the land was subdivided over the years as the heirs multiplied. Still, however much land the second Juan Ángel had, it may not have been enough to provide for his young and growing family. Ranching and dryland farming furnish a precarious living at best, and, therefore, Papá Juan (as his grandchildren called him) found it prudent to secure a government job to augment the family exchequer: he became a customs guard at the Guerrero customhouse.

Lorenzo de la Garza, in *La antigua Revilla*, relates that the *aduana*, or customhouse, was established in Guerrero on March 2, 1876, by Gen. Porfirio Díaz. This event was remarkable because at that time Díaz was, at best, an impatient candidate to the presidency of Mexico and, at worst, a fugitive whose purpose in visiting the Villas del Norte was to foment rebellion against the legally elected president, Sebastián Lerdo de Tejada. In neither capacity did he have the authority to establish customhouses, but Díaz succeeded in his quest to be president of Mexico, and he kept his promise to open aduanas in the Río Bravo/Grande settlements that had supported him.

It was in 1881, during the interregnum between Don Porfirio's first and second presidential terms, while his friend, Gen. Manuel González of Tamaulipas, kept the presidential seat warm for his patron, that Papá Juan received his government job. On September 9, 1881, President Manuel González signed the document appointing Juan Ángel García as *celador de la Aduana Fronteriza de Guerrero* (customs guard at the border customhouse in Guerrero), with a salary of eight hundred pesos a year. The appointment was retroactive to May 7. Papá Juan had just turned thirty-one years of age two days before his appointment.

In 1881 he had been married five years, and he and Gorgonia had two young sons. The oldest, born on March 21, 1879, was named Benito because he shared a birthday with the late and lamented benefactor of Mexico, President Benito Juárez, who had died in 1872. The second child, Lucio, was born on January 7, 1881. Three other children followed in the next six years: Juana, the only daughter, born in August of 1884 and named, undoubtedly, after her grandmother Juana Pereda; and José Demetrio and Guadalupe, born in 1885 and 1887, respectively. The family lived near the customhouse, on Calle Hidalgo, which made it convenient for Papá Juan to go to work, and they continued to live there after his death on September 25, 1906. He had just passed his fifty-sixth birthday some two weeks before he died. The cause of death was given as a cancerous condition of the liver, and it may have presented itself suddenly, because he had been reappointed as *celador montado de tercera clase* (mounted customs guard, third class) only the previous July.

Undoubtedly, having a job with the *aduana fronteriza* was a highly desirable situation for the inhabitants of the Villas del Norte, not only because it meant a secure income to offset the vicissitudes of ranching and farming, but also because it could provide a lifelong career: witness Papá Juan, who, at the time of his death, had held his position for twenty-five years. And even after his death the benefits of his position spilled over to his family, for in March of the following year his son Lucio was also appointed to the customs service. However, Lucio did not simply step into his father's old job. In the thirty years since the border customs service had been established, it had clearly become professionalized and systematized. When he died, Papá Juan had held the rank of *celador montado, tercera clase*, but Lucio entered the customs service in 1907, at age twenty-six, as a *celador a pie de sexta clase* (foot guard, sixth class). The customs service was also apparently somewhat of a closed shop, for Lucio's appointment reads that it was in substitution for a named guard who had been dismissed. Another difference in the son's appointment was that Lucio was posted to the aduana in nearby Mier, rather than to the one in Guerrero, although he may have been temporarily assigned to Guerrero, as indicated by an envelope from the Treasury Department (Secretaría de Hacienda) that was addressed to Lucio García Garza at the "Ada., C. Guerrero, Tamps."

It appears that Lucio took up his post in Mier sometime in 1907, and within two years he had found an additional reason for making his home there: he had fallen in love with a young woman named Concepción Ramírez, a descendant of Cristóbal Ramírez, the original grantee of Porción 17 of Revilla and other lands on the eastern banks of the Rio Grande in what became Zapata County, Texas. Lucio and Concepción were married in late December of 1909. The photograph that she gave Lucio, perhaps to mark their engagement, shows a beautiful young woman of serious demeanor, whose intense feelings for him are revealed in the dedication on the back of the photograph: "Tuya o de Nadie" (Yours or No One's).

It was this same photograph (one of multiple photo postcards, such as were in vogue then) that Lucio sent to his sister, Juana, in Guerrero on June 23, 1911, the day before her saint's day—June 24, the feast day of St. John the Baptist. On the front of the postcard he identified his wife as Sra. Concepción R. García; on the back of it, he told his sister: "Hoy te deposito la presente para que cada bez [vez] que la beas [veas] recuerdes de la que fue mi fiel esposa que estubo [estuvo] en unión conmigo 1 año, 4 meses, 24 días. Y Dios me la quitó" (I am mailing this today, so that every time that you see it you will remember the woman who was my faithful wife for one year, four months, twenty-four days. And God took her away from me). Lucio added that Concepción had died on May 14, 1911, five weeks earlier; according to family sources, the cause of death was consumption, which was so prevalent in those times. At her death she was, in Lucio's precise calculations, twenty-one years, five months, and six days old. Lucio concluded his message to his sister with his felicitations on her saint's day, but it is unlikely that his correspondence brought her any cheer.

The fall of Porfirio Diaz's thirty-year regime in May of 1911, which coincided with Concepción's death, and the election to the presidency of his challenger, Francisco Madero, in the fall of the same year brought few changes to the Villas del Norte, because Madero's goal had been to effectuate a change of incumbent with a minimum of disruption to the status quo. It was not until Madero was assassinated in February of 1913 by orders of Victoriano Huerta that the Mexican Revolution began in earnest. The revolt against Huerta's murderous regime followed almost immediately in the north, led by the governor of Coahuila, Venustiano Carranza.

The Villas del Norte were among the first military objectives of the carrancistas (who called themselves *constitucionalistas*) because of the strategic position of the Villas on the border and the revenues that their customhouses generated. However, the Villas del Norte did not willingly embrace revolution and had to be subdued by force by the carrancistas. On April 21, 1913, for example, Lt. Col. Jesús Ramírez Quintanilla and about 150 horsemen of the constitutionalist army attacked Mier, but they were driven back by 600 *rurales* (rural police) and members of the fiscal police (customs guards) who remained loyal to the federal government (*Diccionario de la Revolución* 7:69). It is most probable that Great-uncle Lucio was among the *aduanales* fighting off the revolutionaries in Mier, since he had remained in the customs service. His loyalty may have been more a matter of pragmatism than of principle, although there was probably some of each. Not only did he draw his salary from the federal government, which, even in the hands of a usurper, still paid its bills, but there was also a history of government service in the García family. Indeed, it would have been surprising if the entire family had not been staunch *porfiristas* since the 1870s, when Porfirio Díaz, by creating the border customs service, had given employment first to Juan Ángel and then to his son. Only reluctantly would the Garcías have transferred their allegiance to Francisco Madero after Don Porfirio had sailed away to exile in France in the spring of 1911, and this allegiance may not have held when confronted by a counterrevolution led not only by Victoriano Huerta but also by Don Porfirio's nephew, Félix Díaz.

More than one hundred years after Papá Juan's death, it is difficult to discover the reason why it was his second son, Lucio, who followed his father into the customs service after the patriarch's death. The most likely explanation is that in 1906 Benito, the oldest, was already married and had a child and therefore was less inclined to relocate if the job required it. In November of 1903 Benito had married twenty-three-year-old Zoila Pérez Treviño. As Benito recounted the story to his grandchildren, it had been love at first sight—at least for him—when he caught a glimpse of Zoila washing her long, blond hair through the open *portón* (double doors) of the courtyard of her aunts' house. She was an orphan who had been born on her mother's family ranch in Zapata County, Texas, and, after her parents' death, had been taken in by her paternal aunts in Guerrero. Benito was instantly smitten by her and maintained his devotion throughout their marriage. "¡Qué mujer tan bonita tengo yo!" (What a pretty wife I have!) he would exclaim, even in old age.

Zoila was less demonstrative of her affections, in general, but she could not have been insensitive to the attentions of the attractive young man whose dark good looks harkened back to his paternal grandmother, Juliana Rodríguez, known in the family as La Morita, for her Moorish appearance. Photographs taken when Benito was middle-aged, after he had eventually followed his father's footsteps into the Resguardo Aduanal (Customs Service), show him strong and confident in his khaki uniform, a Sam Browne gun belt stretched diagonally across his broad chest. Above the full mouth, his luxuriant mustaches curved upwards, like twin scimitars.

In addition to his physical attractiveness, Benito was clearly also a determined suitor, for having been love-struck by Zoila after one glance, he made his feelings known to her and proposed marriage without delay. His message was conveyed in a letter composed and written, most likely, by a professional scribe, if we judge by the fine copperplate penmanship and the flowery sentiments expressed: "Respetable señorita . . . La vida sin una compañera . . . es imposible. . . . Esta compañera es la esposa. . . . Suplicándole una contestación que espero me hará el más dichoso . . . de los hombres. Respetuosamente . . ." (Life without a companion is impossible. . . . This companion is one's wife. . . . Begging of you a reply that will make me the happiest . . . of men. Respectfully yours . . .). And so she married him—whether because she reciprocated his feelings, or because she was an orphan, already past twenty and living in her aunts' house and desired a home of her own, she never said.

The month after Mier was attacked by the revolutionaries, it was Guerrero's turn. On May 12, 1913, constitutionalist colonel Lucio Blanco sent troops to occupy Guerrero and put the municipal authorities—Huerta supporters—to flight. Many Guerrero inhabitants followed suit, taking whatever possessions they could, including their cattle. It was perhaps then that it was decided—in a family conclave or maybe in the midst of chaos—that Benito should take his wife and their three children, as well as his mother and his sister, and their cattle (not necessarily in that order), across the Rio Grande. They would go to Las Escobas, Zoila's birthplace in Zapata County, where her aunts, uncles, and cousins still lived and where she still owned land with her two brothers, and they would wait there until the violence had subsided across the river.

The cattle would be forded at some low-water crossing in the Rio Grande near Guerrero. There were several such spots: El Paso Chaveño, near Uribeño (present-day San Ygnacio); Lopeño Crossing; and Falcón, or Ramireño de Abajo (George 49–53). Grandfather Benito, on horseback, would have herded the cattle, perhaps with the help of his brothers, and crossed the livestock into Texas. The women and the children, though, had to be transported across the river by a *chalán*, one of the flat-bottomed square boats manned by four oarsmen—one poling at each corner— that plied the Rio Grande along the stretch between Laredo to Brownsville, where there were no bridges. Felipita, my grandparents' oldest child (named after her maternal grandmother, Felipa Treviño), was eight or nine years old at the time and retained as her most vivid memory of the river crossing the image of her mother sitting on the chalán, wearing a hat, as if she were on a festive outing. The situation was clearly unusual, and Felipita found it—particularly the hat—very comical. Her mother, however, did not share her daughter's amusement and scolded her.

Once on dry land, the family still had to travel some thirty miles from the river to reach Las Escobas, most likely by wagon pulled by mules or oxen. Arriving at Las Escobas, they would have found there a settlement that reproduced Guerrero in miniature. In some respects people are like turtles that carry their homes on their backs. When the Treviño brothers— Leonardo and Teodoro—had left Guerrero around 1870 to settle the land purchased by their father, Don Alejandro Treviño, some thirty years before, they had replicated in their Texas home the sandstone houses they had left behind. They had placed them side by side, with common walls, flush against the narrow street that bisected the two rows of structures. They were all one-story buildings, except for Leonardo Treviño's house. My grandmother's grandfather had constructed a two-story dwelling, or *casa fuerte*, where the inhabitants could take refuge in case of danger. The second story of this house could be reached only by a ladder, and during attacks by Indians or other marauders, the compound residents would pull up the ladder once everyone was safely upstairs. On the flat rooftop, the parapet around the perimeter was punctured every so often by *troneras*, or gunports, through which the defenders could fire on the attackers.

Returning to her birthplace, where her maternal clan still lived, was undoubtedly a happy occasion for Grandmother Zoila, in spite of the sad circumstances that had precipitated the return. On the other hand, her mother-in-law, Great-grandmother Gorgonia, may have had a very different reaction on arriving at Zoila's birthplace, the Rancho Las Escobas del Borrego. Although relieved at having reached safety, Gorgonia must have still found it a difficult pill to swallow to have become a guest in the place that would have been hers—if her predecessors had not sold it—and that one day would belong to Benito and Zoila's children. In a place where lineage was traced through land ownership, Gorgonia's grandchildren would claim their birthright through the Treviño line rather than through the Pereda.

Gorgonia Garza Pereda was well aware that the origins of Las Escobas lay in the land grant of Cerrito Blanco, which had been awarded to her grandfather, José Manuel Pereda, in 1810 by the Spanish Crown. José Manuel's daughters and sister, however, had sold their interests in the land to various purchasers, among whom had been Don Alejandro Treviño, Zoila's great-grandfather, who had bought half of the Cerrito Blanco Grant from Josefa Pereda, José Manuel's sister, some seventy years earlier. Don Alejandro, however, had delayed the settlement of Cerrito Blanco for some thirty years, which subsequently led to serious title complications for his sons.

We can only speculate about the reasons for this delay, but Don Alejandro's age and the turbulent times he lived through may have been the deciding factors. In 1843, when Josefa Pereda conveyed the land to him, Don Alejandro was fifty-three, and he may have felt already too old to start a new venture across the Río Bravo. However, he had two sons in their twenties, and he may have bought the land with them in mind. Teodoro Treviño was twenty-seven when he married in 1843, the same year that his father bought half of Cerrito Blanco, but he was widowed by 1863, when he married for a second time. Leonardo Treviño, three years younger than Teodoro, married Andrea Gutiérrez in 1847. Both men had large families, whose births spanned from the 1840s until almost 1870. Perhaps it was those young families that kept Teodoro and Leonardo in Guerrero, where there was greater access to necessary services, such as midwives, and postponed their departure for Zapata County until 1872.

Political events in both countries—the United States and Mexico—may also have played a part in the delayed move. From 1835, when Don Alejandro had first contracted to buy land in Cerrito Blanco, to the 1870s, when his sons actually settled there, the land grant was part of a territory claimed by five jurisdictions, in turn: Mexico, the "So-Called Republic of the Rio Grande," the Republic of Texas, the United States, the Confederacy, and, again, the United States. While the 1840s and 1850s were chaotic and filled with strife in Mexico, particularly as a result of the invasion by the United States and the resulting loss of half of the Mexican territory, the early 1860s were equally turbulent in both countries. In 1861 France sent troops to occupy Mexico (in preparation for the arrival of the puppet emperor Maximilian), and the American Civil War broke out. It was clearly not the right time to undertake a major move.

The Civil War in South Texas played out very differently from the way it unfolded in the rest of the country. The Civil War along the lower Rio Grande consisted primarily of a number of skirmishes and guerrilla activities, often between groups of Tejanos of different political persuasions. The Tejanos—as the descendants of the original settlers came to be known, to distinguish them from their Mexicano kinsmen across the river—really had "no dog in the fight" in the American Civil War, since it was rare for them to own slaves. However, the dislocations brought about by the secession of Texas from the Union exacerbated political factionalism as well as both the latent and the overt Anglo hostility against the Tejanos. It was this hostility that precipitated the so-called Cortina War on the eve of the Civil War and launched a persecution of Mexicanos and Tejanos alike in South Texas.

The raids in South Texas by Juan Nepomuceno "Cheno" Cortina and his followers merged into the general climate of violence and unrest immediately preceding and following the declaration of war between the Union and the Confederacy and blurred the battle lines. Webb, Zapata, and Starr counties had voted, along with the rest of Texas, to secede from the Union, but most of the voters in those counties were Anglos who sympathized with the Confederacy, and the opinion of Tejanos in the matter probably carried little, if any, weight. The Anglo Confederates, however, were quick to brand Cortina and his followers as Unionists so as to paint them doubly evil.

Although most of the Tejanos abstained from voting on the secession issue, those who sided with the Confederacy came mainly from among the remaining large landowners and merchants, such as Zapata County judge Ysidro Vela and the powerful Benavides family of Laredo. Jerry Don Thompson, in *Vaqueros in Blue and Gray*, draws a clear contrast between Cheno Cortina and Santos Benavides, saying, "While the latter represented the more aristocratic Tejanos, or those who had been able to retain much of their land and wealth[,] . . . Cheno Cortina had become the leader to the poor vaqueros, campesinos, and the generally illiterate persons of Mexican descent on both sides of the Rio Grande" (13).

However, not all Tejanos remained passive on the issue of secession. Opposition to the Confederacy soon flared up in Zapata County, where some forty armed Tejanos under Antonio Ochoa marched to Carrizo, the county seat, "seeking to prevent any of the county officials from taking the oath of allegiance [to the Confederacy]" (Thompson, *Vaqueros*, 15). The Zapata County rebels were defeated and several killed by Confederate forces; however, Antonio Ochoa escaped across the river to Guerrero, where he joined forces with Cortina in order to invade Zapata County. Thompson describes the panic that followed: "[M]any ranchers and sheepmen ... fled their homes for the more secure environs of the larger towns. From Roma northward to Laredo, the only villages that remained occupied were Carrizo and the small settlement of San Ygnacio" (*Vaqueros* 18).

Under such circumstances, it was clearly not advisable for Teodoro and Leonardo Treviño to set out from Guerrero to establish a new homestead in the hinterlands of Zapata County. Instead, they waited until the Civil War had concluded with the defeat of the Confederacy in 1865. Perhaps they even waited until the unpleasant aftermath of Reconstruction had passed as well. There is no agreement as to exactly when the Treviño brothers arrived in Zapata County, whether it was in the late 1860s or the early 1870s. In the 1980 issue of the *Texas Family Land Heritage Registry*, the only entry for Zapata County is Escobas Ranch, founded by Teodoro and Leonardo Treviño (83). The historical comments included under this entry contain the information that "Teodoro and Leonardo Treviño came to Zapata County in 1872 and 1876, respectively, to take possession of land which their father had earlier purchased" (83). However, Jo Emma Bravo Quezada, in her study of Escobas and surrounding ranches, states that it was in the 1860s that Teodoro and Leonardo Treviño, "sons of José Alejandro Treviño, came to South Texas to take possession of their father's land." Quezada adds that the first home was built in 1872 by Teodoro Treviño and that Leonardo built a two-story house in 1876 (85). In any case, it seems likely that the Treviño brothers' arrival in Zapata County would have preceded the building of their houses by at least several months, and this may explain the discrepancies in the dates given in the two narratives.

But what made the founding of Las Escobas Ranch different from that of neighboring ranches (and perhaps clouded its origins in Cerrito Blanco) was a twist of luck—bad luck, for it turned out that the Treviño brothers had built their houses, corrals, ponds, and other improvements on the wrong land. They had settled on land to the southeast of Cerrito Blanco. This story has become part of family lore and is related by Rosalinda Treviño, a descendant of Teodoro's and the daughter of one of the current ranch owners, in *Zapata County Folklore, 1984*: "Several years after the locations of homes and ponds... the Treviños [learned] from land surveyors they had located some three miles south of the original survey of Cerrito Blanco" (44). Jo Emma Quezada explains the serious miscalculation and its repercussions in her study as well: "Because of the lack of precise markings to show the boundaries, what was thought to be their [the Treviños'] property was actually M. A. Hirsch's.... [The Treviños] negotiated to exchange 2 acres of land in Cerrito Blanco for 1 acre of land that would later become known as Escobas Ranch" (85).

Eventually, Leonardo and Teodoro Treviño, as well as several of their children, bought additional land, some directly from the State of Texas, as evidenced by the appearance of their names on several square-mile state surveys as original grantees. All the land that Teodoro and Leonardo inherited from their father, as well as what they and their children acquired on their own, became known as Las Escobas del Borrego. The name "Escobas" was supposed to have been suggested by the broomweed that abounded in the area (*escoba* is a broom), and the possessive "del Borrego" clearly referred to the family's main occupation—sheep raising.

Mrs. Teodora Treviño Mendenhall, Teodoro's granddaughter, used to recount that when Leonardo and Teodoro came from Guerrero to take possession of their father's land, they came herding ten thousand head of sheep, anticipating Benito's cattle fording by some fifty years. Hearing "Auntie Dora" tell the story, I would imagine an undulating sea of wool advancing across the grassy savannas that, at that time, covered what later became the brush country (perhaps as a result of overgrazing). The story narrated in the *Texas Family Land Heritage Registry* recites that "at one time, over 10,000 head of sheep were being raised on the Escobas Ranch" (83). The same source also mentions that the Treviño sheep were sheared twice a year and that the wool was sold in Corpus Christi (83).

Of course, the Treviño clan was not unique in raising sheep in Zapata County. Sheep had been numerous on the plains of the lower Rio Grande since the founding of the Villas del Norte. By 1877, sheep and goats outnumbered cattle in Zapata County by more than nine to one, according to historian V. W. Lehmann (27), and in time the increasing sheep production seriously depleted the grassland (113). The range deterioration, coupled with the depredation of the flocks by predators (coyotes, primarily), bad weather, and disease, hastened the decline of sheep raising. By the late 1800s, cattle had supplanted sheep in the Rio Grande Plains as a more profitable crop, and the Treviños followed suit. In January of 1881, for example, Teodoro Treviño sold thirty-eight steers to H. Nein, according to the cattle sales tabulated by Armando C. Alonzo in *Tejano Legacy: Rancheros and Settlers in South Texas, 1734–1900* (299). Las Escobas del Borrego dropped the reference to sheep from its name and became simply Las Escobas.

When the Guerrero contingent arrived at Las Escobas, seeking refuge from the Mexican Revolution, Grandmother Zoila found at least a dozen aunts and uncles, plus numerous cousins, all working at making the settlement a paying concern. Although they now focused on raising cattle, sheep and goats were still around. My uncle, the third Juan Ángel García, recalled having often seen his maternal great-aunt Francisca Treviño wearing a sunbonnet, her work boots peeping out from under her long skirts, herding a flock of goats that produced for her the equivalent of the American farmwife's "egg and butter money."

Life at Las Escobas was more rustic than that recounted by Jovita González in *Life along the Border*. In her book, González described living conditions in Cameron, Starr, and Zapata counties in somewhat romantic terms, saying that women there, in the early twentieth century, lived "if not in luxury, at ease" and that the landowner "did not do any of the manual labor himself" (81). Las Escobas was a self-sufficient settlement where the landowners—men and women—worked side by side with the hired help. These landowners did their shopping for staples in the family store and schooled their children in their own schoolhouse, taught by a teacher paid by them. According to the U.S. Census of 1880 (the year of Grandmother Zoila's birth, when the ranch had been in existence less than ten years), the one-room schoolhouse at Las Escobas was presided over by a teacher named Joshua Armstrong, and the total ranch population was 132 people.

When death came, all these people, owners and employees alike, were buried in the Escobas cemetery that still remains today, with headstones going back more than one hundred years. The dead lay buried within sight of the living as the latter went about their daily labors. And because life was so uncertain, and death could strike at any moment and for myriad reasons, at times taking young adults who left young families behind them (like my great-grandparents Antonino Pérez and Felipa Treviño), children developed a stoic attitude toward death. In a letter written on February 26, 1967, by Mrs. Teodora Treviño Mendenhall to her cousin María Elena Pérez, Mrs. Mendenhall replies to María Elena's questions about her grandparents, Antonino and Felipa: "This couple and their children lived here at Escobas with Grandpa Leonardito and Grandma Andreíta and my mother—Juanita. When Aunt Felipita died they all stayed together.... In 1892, when Grandma Andreíta died, Alfredo [María Elena's father] was just a little boy [and] cried, hearing the women do that. Zoila [Alfredo's older sister] tried to console him, telling him we all had to die. He answered, '¿Y después quién llola [llora]?' [And who is left behind to cry?]."

Orphans, like my grandmother and her siblings, were cared for by their grandparents or aunts and uncles, if they were fortunate. If relatives were not available, friends or neighbors would take them in. Lott and Martínez remark in *The Kingdom of Zapata*—perhaps more sentimentally than realistically—that "on the ranches on this frontier there were no orphans, for if a child were unfortunate enough to be deprived of both parents, it was at once taken into the home of any ranchman who arrived first, and, whether legally adopted or not, became a member of the family" (25). Sometimes, even if one or both of a child's parents were alive, the child would be given for rearing to friends or relatives who were childless, and the child would grow up with two sets of families. Such was the case with my grandmother's uncle Félix Treviño and his wife, Ildefonsa Garza, who raised Lina Rodríguez, a neighbor's child, as their own, to the extent of giving her an elaborate wedding reception at Las Escobas on November 30, 1912.

El Demócrata Fronterizo, a Spanish-language weekly newspaper from Laredo that focused its coverage on the lives, deaths, and doings of Mexicanos in South Texas, reported extensively on that wedding in its issue of December 4, 1912. The story, with a dateline of Randado, Texas (apparently the most important settlement in the vicinity), announced in rather gushing tones the marriage between Mr. Pedro Garza, son of Martiniano Garza, a rancher and farmer of Zapata and Brooks counties, and the "virtuous and esteemed señorita Lina Rodríguez," adopted daughter of Mr. Félix Treviño, a merchant (Félix and Ildefonsa owned the Escobas general store), and "legitimate daughter" of Mr. José Rodríguez, who was present at the event with his two other children.

The list of guests at the wedding read like a local who's who and included members of the de la Garza family from El Randado Ranch, which had been founded in the 1830s. Also reported present were Félix Treviño's brother, Evaristo, and his wife, Francisca Treviño (they were first cousins), and their daughter, Inocente, with her husband, Fernando Cuéllar. Adopted children probably provided the unintended benefit of renewing the gene pool in these isolated communities, where marriages between first cousins were difficult to avoid. In the Treviño clan, for example, there was, at that time, another instance of such a marriage, consisting of Manuel Treviño, son of Teodoro, and Juana Treviño, Leonardo's daughter.

The writer from *El Demócrata Fronterizo* reported that the "civil ceremony" had taken place at eight o'clock in the evening, but did not mention a religious service. The absence of a priest at a Catholic wedding was unusual, since christenings, weddings, and funerals were—and still are—the most religiously (in every sense of the word) observed milestones of a person's life in the Hispanic world. According to Jovita González in *Life along the Border*, Mexican men might be anticlerical in their views, but they went to church "three times in their lifetime, and of the three they were taken there at least twice by women: when they were baptized [and] when they were married" (85). The most likely explanation for the absence of the priest on this occasion was the distance of the ranch from town and the shortage of priests in that part of South Texas, which resulted, according to González, in the small communities' being neglected, although "from time to time, as often as possible, the missionary priest made occasional visits to the ranches" (85). The priest who would have visited Las Escobas at this time was a missionary from Roma, Texas, in Starr County, who rode circuit, like the old judges. A resident of modern-day Zapata County related that at the end of the nineteenth century the Oblates of Mary Immaculate would send a priest on horseback out of Roma to tend to the spiritual needs of the scattered communities in the area (Flores 47).

After the civil ceremony at Lina and Pedro's wedding there commenced, according to the newspaper report, a "sumptuous dance" ("dio principio un suntuoso baile"), which did not end until seven of the following morning. Rather than an instance of riotous living, though, the late—or early—conclusion of the festivities was most likely dictated by safety concerns, since it would have been dangerous for the guests to return home over lonely roads and *senderos* (paths) in complete darkness. Refreshments were served throughout the night by the young people present, the reporter added. Undoubtedly, they were also served breakfast before departing for home.

Describing dances that were probably similar to the one held at Las Escobas on this occasion, Jovita González stated: "The dances given by the owners of the ranches marked the social feature of the year. To these functions were invited all the landed aristocracy from the surrounding country as well as from the towns" (83). González, writing in the late 1920s, perhaps waxed nostalgically over a way of life—a Tejano antebellum—that was never as glorious as her depiction of it when she added that the ladies would arrive at the dances "in the family coach, escorted by mounted cavaliers who rode by the side of the carriage" (83). The families most likely arrived in mule-drawn wagons, rather than carriages, although the young men probably did take the opportunity to show off their horsemanship before the friends and neighbors present.

Among the members of the house party present at the wedding at Las Escobas was Jesús M. Montemayor with his family, which consisted of his wife, Gregoria Treviño, daughter of Teodoro, and their adoptive son, Víctor. If Lina Rodríguez was an adoptive child who knew and maintained contact with her biological family, this does not appear to have been the case with Víctor, of whose family nothing is known. Víctor, a strikingly attractive man, was undoubtedly the focus of many feminine eyes at the "sumptuous dance," without apparently much effect on him. Not until the following year, when the Guerrero relations arrived, were his affections engaged, and then not by a dewy-eyed maiden but by a forceful young woman on the verge of spinsterhood at age thirty.

Almost two years after Lina and Pedro's marriage, Las Escobas Ranch was the site of another wedding. In the fall of 1914, Gorgonia Garza, Viuda (Widow) de García, announced the upcoming marriage of her daughter, Juana, to Víctor Montemayor. In keeping with the Mexican custom, the wedding announcement was issued jointly by the parents of both the bride and the bridegroom. The recipients of the announcements were also invited to the religious ceremony that would take place at the home of the bride in Las Escobas, Zapata County, Texas, on October 2, 1914, at "3 a.m." I have wondered if perhaps the time, which was inserted by hand in the printed invitation, was in error; but when I consulted with Mrs. Adela F. Etcharren, originally from Monterrey, Nuevo León, she informed me that various members of her family, including her grandmother who lived in Villaldama, Nuevo León (not far from the border), had also been married at that unusual hour. Mrs. Etcharren also shared with me her grandparents' wedding invitation, which recited that the wedding would take place on July 11, 1911, the civil ceremony (required in Mexico) to be held at the bride's home at 8:30 p.m., to be followed by the religious services in the parish church at "3 a.m." of the following day. According to Mrs. Etcharren, the weddings in Villaldama were still being held at three and four in the morning as late as 1939 and 1942, according to other wedding announcements in her family. The reason for the unusual hours may have been religious or merely practical, and herein may lie a topic for further study at another time.

The wedding at Las Escobas was performed by Father Tomás Villarreal, who signed the marriage license issued by the Zapata county clerk, and at some point during the festivities the bride and groom had their picture taken. The wedding portrait shows Víctor and Juana in the typical pose of the times—he, sitting, while she stands by his side, her right hand resting proprietarily on his shoulder. He is clean-shaven and fine-featured, with a light complexion, and looks at the camera with an air of confidence tinged with a hint of arrogance. She is tall, with a proud carriage and a no-nonsense expression, a handsome, rather than pretty, woman with the swarthy complexion of the Garcías. She wears a floor-length gown with a wide lace collar and elbow-length white gloves. In her left hand she holds a wedding bouquet. Perhaps because the ceremony had taken place "at the home of the bride," she does not wear a veil and is bareheaded, revealing—surprisingly—short, black, wavy hair rather than the long tresses that tradition decreed were a woman's "crown of glory," a hint, perhaps, of Juana's independent nature.

Several months after Juana's wedding, sometime in 1915, her sister-in-law, Zoila, gave birth to her fourth child, a boy whom the parents named Benito, after his father (his older brother was the third Juan Ángel García). However, unlike his father and his two sisters and brother, the baby was blond and blue-eyed, like his mother, according to family stories. Possibly because he was the baby or because he looked like her, little Benito was supposed to have been Zoila's favorite. One reason for this preference may have simply been the child's fair hair and complexion. Although racial discrimination had been outlawed in Mexico for a hundred years (since the abolishing of the casta system in 1813), in reality there was a bias against dark-skinned persons, and parents usually hoped for—whether realistically or not—fair-skinned offspring.

In spite of the contentment engendered by joyous occasions such as weddings and births, the worsening situation in Mexico cast a pall over the García family in Las Escobas, particularly over Mamá Gorgonia, who had left behind three sons there. In 1915, Mexico had no government—or, rather, it had too many governments. After having been complicit in the assassination of President Francisco Madero in February of 1913, the American ambassador, Henry Lane Wilson, had anointed Madero's murderer, Victoriano Huerta, as the next president of Mexico while the incoming American president, Woodrow Wilson, stood by impotently until his inauguration on March 4. Upon taking office, Wilson promptly disowned the Huerta regime, which now found itself repudiated both at home and abroad. Wilson's government, however, would not recognize the legitimacy of Venustiano Carranza's constitutionalist movement either and refused to sell arms to all Mexican combatants. Finally, in the summer of 1914, Huerta's regime, weakened by constant pressure from the forces under the constitutionalist umbrella and starved of arms by the American embargo, collapsed. However, once the common enemy was defeated, it became clear that neither Pancho Villa nor Emiliano Zapata would accept Venustiano Carranza as their leader, and the revolutionary army split into three major factions: the Constitutionalists under Carranza, the Northern Division under Villa—both operating from the north—and the Zapatistas in the south. The bloodiest stage of the Mexican Revolution had begun.

As long as Huerta had maintained the semblance of a central government, we can surmise that Great-uncle Lucio García remained at his post with the customs service on the border. It is uncertain what the two younger brothers, José and Guadalupe, did at this time, although from family recollections it appears that José, who was married and had several children, had remained in the vicinity of Guerrero. One of José's children, who was an infant at the time, later recalled what José's wife had related about his travails in 1914 or 1915. According to the family story, José had been out on horseback in the vicinity of their ranch near Guerrero when he was taken prisoner by an armed detachment of horsemen. This group forced him to remain with them and fight with them until, at some point, an injured José ended up in a Mexico City hospital, where he recuperated before finding his way back home.

In spite of gaps in the narrative, we can fill in what likely happened by referring to known events. From the fact that it was Carranza's troops that occupied or attacked Guerrero, we can infer that it was the carrancistas who abducted Great-uncle José García. It could have also been the Huerta government troops but for one scrap of recollection repeated to me by my sister. She recalled hearing Aunt Felipita (who would have been ten or eleven years old at the time) say that Mamá Gorgonia's greatest fear during the Revolution had been that her two sons—Lucio and José, presumably—would meet in battle and kill or wound each other. The most logical inference to be drawn from this recollection is that each son was part of an opposing group, and since Lucio served in the federal customs service and as such was obliged to defend the government, then José must have been with the revolutionaries. In addition, it seems probable that if José ended up in Mexico City, it would have been with the carrancistas since their army occupied the capital in the summer of 1914 and held it until November of that year, when they evacuated the city at the approach of Villa and Zapata. From 1914 until almost 1917 the three armies plunged Mexico into a bloodbath, a situation that undoubtedly caused Mamá Gorgonia ceaseless anxiety in Texas.

In the meantime, the community of Las Escobas experienced its own personal tragedy, as if to show that South Texas was not immune to violence. Approximately on November 8, 1916, Jesús M. Montemayor, Juana's father-in-law, was shot to death on his ranch, El Potrero, some three miles away from Las Escobas. *El Demócrata Fronterizo* of Laredo did not report the incident until December 2, because it wanted to ascertain all the facts before doing so, according to its explanation. The sequence of events leading to the shooting had begun on Sunday, November 5, in the afternoon, when Mr. Montemayor left his home at Las Escobas to work on building a sendero at El Potrero, accompanied by a servant named Doroteo Hernández. The following Wednesday, November 8, his wife, Gregoria Treviño, sent their son, Víctor, with some provisions and garbanzos for planting. Víctor returned to Las Escobas that evening, leaving his father and Doroteo working together, apparently on good terms. Upon his return, Víctor conveyed to his mother his father's message to expect him back Thursday afternoon.

However, Jesús Montemayor did not return on Thursday, and early Friday morning a frightened cowboy arrived at Las Escobas with the news that he and four other men had gone to El Potrero while searching for a stray calf. There they had noticed that the door of the *jacal*, or hut, was open, and, upon entering, they had found the ranch owner lying on his back in the middle of the room, a *morral*, or hemp sack, hanging from his right arm. He had been shot in the stomach and was dead. The worker, Doroteo Hernández, was missing, as was the weapon. The conclusion reached by the authorities was that Mr. Montemayor had been killed on Wednesday, presumably after Víctor's departure, because the mule team that was to pull the plow for planting the garbanzos had not been fed or watered, according to the ranch hands who found the animals.

Jesús Montemayor was buried at Las Escobas on Saturday, November 11, at ten o'clock in the morning, according to *El Demócrata Fronterizo*. The reporter was unable to give any information as to the whereabouts of the suspected killer but provided, instead, an extensive biography of the victim. Jesús M. Montemayor had been born in 1861 in a small town near Monterrey, Nuevo León, where he attended school and studied bookkeeping. He had eventually made his way to Laredo, working at various commercial establishments before going into partnership with Félix Treviño in a store at Las Escobas, where he married Félix's cousin Gregoria in 1887. At some point he had left the partnership and devoted himself to ranching and farming. Whether he had purchased land of his own or worked his wife's is not clear, although his name appears on the old land maps of Zapata County.

The reporter for *El Demócrata Fronterizo* lamented the untimely death of Jesús M. Montemayor, a man who had many important friends in Laredo, as well as in the neighboring counties. The writer added that Americans, too, had held Montemayor in high esteem because he was a true gentleman ("Todos los americanos que trataron con él lo apreciaron mucho, porque era todo un caballero"). The last statement speaks volumes about the tension-filled relations between Anglo-Americans and Mexicans (as both the Mexican- and U.S.-born were called) in South Texas. That South Texas Anglos did not usually hold Mexicans in high esteem is what the writer from *El Demócrata Fronterizo* was clearly indicating.

By the end of 1916, hundreds of Mexicans had been killed in Texas by Anglo vigilantes, self-styled militias, and Texas Rangers in a period of violence known as the Bandit War of 1915, a period reminiscent of the Cortina War of 1859–1860. Although there appeared to be no connection between Montemayor's killing and the anti-Mexican violence prevalent at the time, neither was there much effort expended in finding his killer—Doroteo Hernández or someone else. The case remained unsolved, for the authorities were probably content with attributing the killing to the Mexican hired hand, a case of one Mexican killing another, as thousands were doing across the river.

There is no denying that the violence of the Mexican Revolution had spilled over across the Rio Grande in various forms. Cattle were stolen and smuggled out of Mexico to be sold for weapons and ammunition in Texas, and the armaments were then smuggled into Mexico. Mexican and Anglo-Americans living in Texas took sides with the various factions fighting in Mexico and offered aid and comfort to their favorite faction or persecuted those they opposed. Sometimes bullets flew across the Rio Grande—in both directions. That a state of war existed between the two neighboring countries, even if war had not been declared, was the conclusion reached by a Texas court after an international skirmish.

Lott and Martínez recount that on June 15, 1916, a troop of the Fourteenth Cavalry was camped in San Ygnacio, in Zapata County, when it came under attack by "so-called bandits" from Mexico. There were seventy-five men in the attacking force, and they killed six soldiers, later escaping across the Rio Grande, except for four who were captured and put on trial in district court. The prosecutor was the district attorney for Webb and Zapata counties, John A. Valls, who claimed that the attackers were carrancistas. Lott and Martínez remark that this allegation was to be expected "from one who had been close to Don Porfirio all of his life and who regretted deeply the overthrow of the president" (121). As a matter of fact,

Valls was so close to Porfirio Díaz that he was a godson of the former president, and as such was ready to believe the worst of the carrancistas (Worley 53-54).

The four captured men were tried for murder, convicted, and sentenced to death. The sentence was appealed, and the Texas Court of Criminal Appeals reversed the sentence of the district court. It turned out that the district attorney had shot himself in the foot by insisting that the four men were carrancista soldiers rather than common outlaws, for as soldiers, the court reasoned, the defendants were prisoners of war and should be repatriated to their country. They were therefore delivered to the Mexican consul in Laredo and escorted to Nuevo Laredo, much to the chagrin of district attorney Valls (Lott and Martínez 121-122). The authors add that the court went "to great length in proving that the United States was at war with the de facto government of Mexico, although there had not been a declaration of war" (123).

However, the match that turned the smoldering hostilities between Mexicans and Anglos in South Texas into a conflagration was the uncovering of the purported conspiracy known as El Plan de San Diego. The so-called plan allegedly called for an uprising by Mexicans in the Southwest, from Texas to California, to take back those lands by killing all the Anglo males over the age of sixteen. Other oppressed minorities, such as African Americans and Native Americans, would also have claims to their own homelands under the plan.

The plan came to light in January of 1915 with the arrest of a man named Basilio Ramos in Hidalgo County, Texas. Ramos was subsequently indicted by a federal grand jury in Brownsville, Texas, on the charge of conspiring to steal U.S. property, "to wit, the states of Texas, Oklahoma, New Mexico, Arizona and California" (*US v. Basilio Ramos, Jr., et al.*, as cited in Harris and Sadler 218). According to Charles Harris and Louis Sadler, a sign that the American authorities took neither Ramos nor his plan very seriously was the reduction of his bond from $5,000 to $100 by the federal judge in charge of the case, who commented that Ramos belonged more in a hospital than in a jail (218). The judge may have had a lenient attitude because February 20, the date fixed by the plan for the uprising, had come and gone with no sign of rebellion. Ramos, however, gave every sign of sanity by doing what so many defendants along the border have always done—jump bail and flee across the river.

The uprising called for by the Plan de San Diego never materialized. However apocryphal the Plan may have been, the sentiment behind it had a basis in the reality of the oppression and injustices experienced by the

Mexicans in South Texas, and once again, as during the Cortina War, Mexicans were reported raiding and attacking towns and ranches in Willacy, Cameron, Hidalgo, and other counties where the Anglos were dominant. The Anglo response was swift and violent. "What ensued," according to Harris and Sadler, "was what Anglos called the 'Bandit War,' a savage struggle involving a lot of racial profiling, with bullets raining on the just and the unjust alike" (248). Beginning in the summer of 1915, South Texas Anglos, with the help of the Texas Rangers, formed posses to capture the raiders and mete out summary justice by hanging or shooting any Mexican suspected of being an irredentist.

Charles Cumberland quotes a story from the *San Antonio Express* issue of September 11, 1915, that describes the public reaction to the killings in deep South Texas, saying that the "finding of dead bodies of Mexicans, suspected of being connected with the troubles, has reached a point where it creates little or no interest. It is only when a raid is reported, or an American is killed, that the ire of the people is aroused" ("Border Raids" 300).

The "people" referred to in the newspaper were, of course, the Anglo-Americans, for the Mexicans did not count. Mexicans were nonpersons, game on whom open season had been declared and whose dead carcasses were dragged by ropes through the brush, actions that were captured in the photographs of Robert Runyon, one of which "circulated the nation as a picture postcard" (Samponaro and Vanderwood 88). This famous postcard showed three mounted Texas Rangers, each posing with his human trophy, a dead body on the ground still attached to the rope with which the man had been dragged through the brush—whether before or after death is not clear.

In their book on Runyon's photographs, Samponaro and Vanderwood also describe a scene captured by Runyon of the crowds that thronged the international bridge as they tried to cross from Brownsville to Matamoros on foot, on horseback, and on mule-drawn carts, as a result of "the turmoil" that caused "thousands of Mexicans and Mexican-Americans under harassment and worse by the Texas Rangers and others" to flee to Mexico and leave their property behind. The authors add that it was estimated that "7,000 people like these crossed the International Bridge in search of sanctuary" (97). Many of those people rushing across the bridge had probably sought sanctuary in Texas just a short time before, when the Mexican Revolution had entered into its third and bloodiest act, in the fall of 1914. Others had been born in Texas and had been forced to abandon lands they had inherited from their ancestors, the Original Grantees. Many of those latter emigrants undoubtedly returned when "the troubles" (in the words of the San Antonio newspaper) died down, but as Samparo and Vanderwood point out, since "few possessed the funds necessary to defend their holdings in court, they lost everything to Anglo entrepreneurs anxious to develop the rich, well-irrigated land, now tied to a broadening national communications network" (97).

These same entrepreneurs, who in 1915 had been anxious to clear the land of undesirable brush and Mexicans, soon found that the land needed workers to exploit it, and by 1916 they were asking Mexicans to come back. On March 18, 1916, the *Brownsville Daily Herald* reported that "a big demand for labor in Hidalgo County in connection with farm work, development, land clearing and other improvements has caused a heavy amount of immigration through the port of Old Hidalgo." The paper was quick to assure its readers that although the number of immigrants from Mexico was large, "no diseases have developed [because] the usual precautions against typhus fever are being taken with fumigations, gasoline baths and other precautions." Two days later the same newspaper carried a related story, informing that immigration officials would henceforth be posted at Roma and Rio Grande City, after an absence of six years, and explained that the decision had resulted "from the unusually heavy immigration into the United States at the border ports and also to prevent the possible entry of contagious diseases." The newspaper added that although there were no bridges at either port, "crossings are made by means of ferry lines" (March 20, 1916).

During the so-called Bandit War, the Treviño clan probably remained unmolested at Las Escobas, since the violence was mostly confined to south of Starr County. Furthermore, Las Escobas was located some thirty miles away from the banks of the Rio Grande, where the incidents occurred most frequently. In addition, all of Zapata County was remarkably isolated. Jovita González, writing about this area in the 1930s, found it a backwater and prefaced her description of the county by saying: "If the happiness of a country depends upon its having no history, Zapata County should then, by rights, hold first place in this; for nothing of interest or importance has ever been recorded of its history" (60). She continued her rather unfair remarks, rubbing salt in the wound: "[A] county thoroughly Mexican and rural, it has been untouched by progress and development. The people continue living their placid existence becoming only aroused when Americans try to buy or lease their land" (60).

Considering the consequences suffered by Mexicanos and Tejanos in Starr County (González's birthplace) and counties to the south of it as a result of the "progress and development" brought by the Anglo immigrants to South Texas, it is not surprising that the inhabitants of Zapata County were touchy when "Americans" showed interest in their land. The residents of Las Escobas were undoubtedly grateful to lead "placid existences," marked only by their own personal tragedies. Jo Emma Bravo Quezada, in her work on Las Escobas, enumerates among those buried in the cemetery there two children of Manuel and Juana Treviño who died within two years of each other: nineteen-year-old Cristóbal (July 1913) and seventeen-year-old Juanita (October 1915). From those years at Las Escobas, my uncle Juan Ángel García recalled hearing his father remark, after a visit to Manuel Treviño's house, that Juanita was very sick and declining rapidly. It was my uncle's impression that the illness had been typhoid fever, caused by bad drinking water. Another untimely burial in the Escobas cemetery was the stillborn child delivered by Great-aunt Juana García from her marriage to Víctor Montemayor.

These losses undoubtedly marred the apparently placid lives of the residents of Las Escobas, but they were part of the cycle of life and death—however untimely the latter. Other events, though, were more unpredictable, such as Great-aunt Juana's divorce. The loss of their first child, coupled with the murder of Víctor's father, must have put a great stress on the marriage, and it may have been that Víctor's response to this stress was to engage in extramarital dalliances. Juana certainly felt that his conduct had been such that she could not overlook it or condone it, and she sued for divorce, an almost unheard-of step in that culture at that time. Víctor must have pleaded with her to forgive him, and her family must have counseled her to relent and take him back, but her reply became a family by-word: "Ya dije que no y es no" (I said no, and I mean no).

When the García family returned to Guerrero after the violence had abated, Juana returned as she had left—as a single woman. She left behind in Texas her former husband and her dead child and picked up her old life in Guerrero, a sadder but wiser woman. She continued living with her widowed mother in the family home on Hidalgo Street until Great-grandmother Gorgonia Garza Pereda died in the first days of 1925 at age seventy-three. Juana García, known to the younger generation as Tía Juanita, never remarried, and neither did her brother Lucio, who had been widowed in 1911. The two of them set up joint housekeeping and remained together until his death in 1968.

It was probably sometime in 1917 that Grandfather Benito moved his cattle back across the Rio Grande, and Grandmother Zoila, now with four children, and her mother and sister-in-law made the return trip to

Guerrero on the chalán from Zapata. It must have been a good time to be a ferry operator on the lower Rio Grande, as refugees from the Revolution returned home to Mexico, hopeful that the worst was over, while the Mexican-Texans in Mexico went home to Texas, trusting that the violence there was likewise at an end. The Anglo landowners in South Texas were again clamoring for Mexican labor, reconfiguring the image of the former enemy from villain to vassal.

When Tía Juanita was in her nineties, she would recall the dismay that her family had felt when they returned to Guerrero after a three-year absence to find their home wrecked. Soldiers had been quartered in their house, she said, and had even stabled their horses inside with them. Guerrero was a ghost of its former self, so many families having left for good, their houses now standing empty.

But the García siblings and their mother were together again in Guerrero, all safe from the Revolution. Zoila was also glad to be reunited with her older brother, Gilberto, who had remained in Guerrero throughout the violence. However, just as life seemed to be returning to normal, Gilberto and his wife, Ana Muzza, suffered the painful loss of their young son Enrique, who died in November of 1917. A photograph of the child's funeral cortege is identified by the caption: "Funerales del niño Enrique Pérez Muzza. C. Guerrero. 11–7–1917." An unknown photographer captured the pathetic procession led by a horse-drawn wagon covered with a white canopy that sheltered the small coffin. The wagon was followed by a long line of children, the girls dressed in communion white and carrying bunches of flowers, the boys in their Sunday clothes. The adults lined the sidewalks, their eyes fixed on the young mourners who accompanied their departed friend to the cemetery.

Grandmother Zoila surely grieved the untimely death of her young nephew, but a harder blow awaited her the following year of 1918, when her own child, three-year-old Benito, died as well. She used to recount to her children, later on, how one hot August day she had dressed him in a little sailor suit and taken him to church with her. When they returned home, the child came down with a fever, and the frantic parents had watched as the frail body quickly lost the battle with death. Stunned, they had sought an explanation for their son's rapid decline and came up with the usual reason given for sudden illnesses: *el mal de ojo*, or the evil eye. The child had looked so angelic, with his blond curls and dressed in his sailor suit, that someone had coveted him and, by doing so, had cast the evil eye on him. The doctor who had attended him, though, knew the reason to be otherwise and, on the death certificate, listed the cause of death as typhoid fever. Little Benito died on August 10, 1918, the day before his oldest sister, Felipita, turned fourteen.

In times of strife there are not only winners and losers; there are also many who "win some and lose some," simply by making the best of changing circumstances. Grandfather Benito had removed his family to safety in Texas and had managed to preserve the family cattle as well by doing so. However, his brother Lucio, who had remained in government service even when the government was in the hands of usurpers, was surely out of a job when that government fell in 1914. The post of customs guard, which had remained in the family for over thirty years, would have certainly passed to another family who had not backed the wrong side, except for the strong sense of family solidarity that prevails in the Latin culture, which the Anglo-Saxons dismiss as nepotism.

Some families are fortunate to produce at least one member who—like Joseph in the Bible, who helped his brothers and his people—comes to the aid of his relatives. The Pérez and the García families were blessed with one such benefactor. Grandmother Zoila had a first cousin named Enrique Medina, the son of one of the paternal aunts in whose house she had been raised. Enrique was a lawyer who had been educated in Matamoros, where he made the acquaintance of other young men who became prominent in the revolutionary movement in Tamaulipas, among whom was Emilio Portes Gil. Portes Gil became governor of the state in the 1920s and interim president of Mexico in 1928, and where Portes Gil went, he took his friend Enrique with him (*Diccionario de la Revolución* 7:145).

Undoubtedly, the restoration of the Guerrero customhouse to its prerevolutionary importance in the 1920s was due in large measure to the influence of the illustrious son *licenciado* Enrique Medina. And, surely, the merit of his efforts on behalf of his native place was not diminished by the fact that, in helping Guerrero, he also benefitted his extended-family members. Foremost among these was his first cousin Gilberto Pérez Treviño, who became the civilian administrator of the aduana. Gilberto, in turn, did his familial duty by facilitating the employment of his brother-in-law Benito García Garza, in the Resguardo Aduanal, which provided Grandfather Benito with many years in the saddle as a mounted guard, following, at last, his father's example.

My recollections of Papá Benito (as I called him) are from a time long after he had left the customs patrol. He was at least seventy when I first remember him, but he still sported the luxuriant mustache (now white) that he had in the old photographs. He invariably wore khaki shirts and trousers, which was the work uniform for the ranchmen, and boots were the everyday footwear that marked him as a horseman, as did the clinking of spurs that announced his approach. My most vivid memories of him always link him to his horse, a golden palomino named El Sable (Saber). I remember my grandfather feeding Saber oats from a nose bag around the horse's head—as a reward, no doubt, for the long trek from the ranch to town—as he unsaddled him.

One of those treks—from town to the ranch—was the most exciting journey I have ever taken. One summer afternoon shortly after my father's death, when I had achieved the sad status of being completely orphaned (my mother had died some four years earlier), Papá Benito took me to the ranch, where my grandmother waited for us. He picked me up and put me in front of him in the saddle atop of the tall palomino, and we began our journey by crossing the bridge over the Río Salado and were soon trotting along a narrow sendero cut in the midst of the thick brush. I was a little fearful, especially as darkness fell, wondering how we would find our way home, but I said nothing. Finally, the moon appeared in the darkening sky and bathed the brush—the mesquites, the chaparros, the tasajillos—with a silvery light. There were occasional scurrying noises underfoot from varmints or the occasional coyote that only magnified the silence that surrounded us. Then, seeming to sense my anxiety, my grandfather began to sing "Allá en el rancho grande," and the silence no longer frightened me. I felt safe now. Confidence flowed to me from Papá Benito's calloused hands on the reins and from the muscular arms that held me secure in the saddle. It did not even matter that he could not carry a tune, for neither could I. It seems that I inherited that from him.

《 FOUR 》

Grandfather's Revolution
THE HISTORIAN

Toward the latter part of 1911 my grandfather Lorenzo de la Garza engaged in a flurry of correspondence with the men who had emerged victorious in the struggle to end the thirty-year rule of Mexican president Porfirio Díaz. The most important of these communications—all composed on his indispensable Underwood typewriter—was a letter of congratulations to the recently installed president of Mexico, Francisco I. Madero. The new president, with commendable promptness, acknowledged my grandfather's good wishes within the same month of his inauguration—November—on his personal stationery. The reply read: "Correspondencia particular del Presidente de los Estados Unidos Mexicanos" (Personal correspondence of the President of the United States of Mexico), followed by the text of the note: "Francisco I. Madero, Presidente Constitucional de los Estados Unidos Mexicanos, agradece a Ud. Su atenta felicitación" (Francisco I. Madero, Constitutional President of the United States of Mexico, thanks you for your courteous letter of congratulations). The note concluded by reciting the place and date: México, Noviembre de 1911.

The words are perfunctory and were undoubtedly repeated in response to hundreds, if not thousands, of well-wishers throughout the country. Nevertheless, the communication is significant because it reveals that Grandfather Lorenzo, like many others in Mexico, was conscious that a new era had begun in 1910 with the uprising that had led to the end of the Porfiriato, as the thirty-year rule of Porfirio Díaz was known. After all, Grandfather had not seen the need to write letters of congratulations during Don Porfirio's multiple reelections. Although my grandfather was a prolific letter writer who usually retained copies of his correspondence, no letters to Don Porfirio were found among his papers.

That fall of 1911 *todo México* (all of Mexico), including Madero and his circle of revolutionaries, was amazed—and not a little apprehensive—at the enormous feat that Madero's followers had accomplished by toppling the political edifice of the Porfiriato. Men in their early forties, like Grandfather Lorenzo, scarcely remembered a time when the stern visage of Don Porfirio had not stared at them out of the official portraits that hung in schools and public buildings. It was, indeed, difficult to believe that Don Porfirio was gone, when a scant fourteen months earlier, in September of 1910, he had posed for photographs surrounded by his cabinet as he received the foreign dignitaries and emissaries who had come to burnish the celebration of one hundred years of Mexican independence and thirty years of "Order and Progress" under the presidency of Porfirio Díaz. And yet, nine months after the centennial celebrations, in May of 1911, Don Porfirio had boarded the steamship that carried him to exile in France. Mexico's Man of Iron had become from one day to the next just another eighty-year-old grandfather taking his first trip to Europe, albeit a trip from which he would not return.

My paternal grandfather, Lorenzo de la Garza—or, in the style of Guerrero, Papá Lorenzo—was born in 1867 and was therefore nine years old when Porfirio Díaz achieved his goal of becoming president of Mexico by toppling the incumbent, President Sebastián Lerdo de Tejada. Grandfather and his contemporaries grew up in the atmosphere of the Porfiriato, which subordinated individual rights and political beliefs to domestic order and economic progress. Papá Lorenzo was born in Agualeguas, Nuevo León, but his parents, Blas María de la Garza and Francisca Garza, moved their family in early 1872 to Guerrero, Tamaulipas, where Don Blas María engaged in commerce, dealing in agricultural products such as cattle, hides, cotton, and other crops.

Lorenzo, the youngest son, attended school in Guerrero, most likely that founded by Don Sabás Vázquez, a fellow countryman from Agualeguas (who may have been a relative, since Francisca's full name was Garza Vázquez) who had migrated to Guerrero in the early 1860s. When he finished his studies in Guerrero, Lorenzo was apprenticed in his father's business, and when he reached a suitable age, he was taken on as a partner. From early on, Lorenzo manifested a civic-minded nature that led him to participate in a variety of community activities. For example, among the family papers collected in a small trunk, I found an old theater program announcing that on July 31, 1887, the Teatro Benavides of Ciudad Guerrero was to present a performance of *El jorobado* (*The Hunchback*) with a cast of local actors that included twenty-year-old Lorenzo de la Garza.

Another memento of his civic involvement in the life of Guerrero was dated November 10, 1895; it was an invitation from the local school board (La Junta de Instrucción Pública), signed by the board president, Manuel Vela Ramírez, who also served several terms as mayor, and by Lorenzo de la Garza, board secretary. The invitation requested the public's attendance at a ceremony to present prizes to students at the Boys' School (Plantel de Varones, no. 1).

However, already in the 1890s the Pax Porfiriana that had nurtured my grandfather's generation was coming under attack, ironically enough from the same region where Porfirio Díaz had launched his conquest of Mexico—the northern frontier, specifically, Brownsville, Texas. Catarino Garza was a border journalist, a critic of the Díaz regime who had allied himself with Dr. Ignacio Martínez, a former general and a disillusioned Díaz supporter from Monterrey. In late 1890 both men entered Mexico from Carrizo (present-day Zapata), Texas, and engaged in some skirmishes near the border but were driven back to Texas. By 1891 both Garza and Martínez had established themselves in Laredo, Texas, and from there continued to publish anti-Díaz literature until one day, as he walked on the streets of Laredo, Dr. Martínez was assassinated. The order to kill Dr. Martínez allegedly came from Gen. Bernardo Reyes, the governor of Nuevo León and one of Díaz's most loyal satraps (Benavides Hinojosa 219). Later that year Catarino Garza attempted another unsuccessful rebellion and engaged in a battle at Las Tortillas, a ranching community near Guerrero, from where he was beaten back to Texas. Faced with relentless opposition, Garza departed for New Orleans, where he embarked for exile in Central America (*Diccionario de la Revolución* 7:104). Pax Porfiriana was reestablished along the Rio Grande for the time being.

After his marriage in 1896 to Esther Peña, Lorenzo continued his civic activities in Guerrero, a prominent one being serving as secretary of the 1906 committee to celebrate the centennial of the birth of Benito Juárez. The Juárez centennial was observed throughout the country, in accordance with a decree issued by his onetime student and later rival, Porfirio Díaz. The most lasting accomplishment of this committee in Guerrero was the erection of a statue of Benito Juárez, which was placed on the central plaza and which today occupies a similar place in the new town (Guerrero Nuevo).

The Juárez centennial festivities stretched from March 20 to the end of the month, beginning with a fair on the main plaza and the inauguration of an acetylene gas light plant to illuminate the plaza. On March 21, the day of Juárez's birth, the centennial committee unveiled the statue of Juárez, followed by the official address read by the committee secretary, Lorenzo de la Garza, and by additional speeches, patriotic songs, and fireworks. According to the official program (which I unearthed from the small tin trunk), the remaining festive days included horse races, cockfights, livestock exhibits, dramatic presentations, and stalls of food and drink. The program also reminded the townspeople to clean and beautify the exterior of their houses, as well as to sweep the streets, in order to contribute to the "splendor of the festivities."

A curious footnote to the Juárez centennial celebration was the involvement in it of the Central American republic of El Salvador, which erected a bust of Juárez and placed it on the prominent Avenida Independencia of its capital, where it joined the existing bust of Gen. Porfirio Díaz. The Guerrero committee somehow learned of the Salvadoran gesture and sent a letter of appreciation, enclosing copies of their own program of events. The president of the Republic of El Salvador replied to the Guerrero committee secretary, effusively thanking "Don Lorenzo de la Garza" for his letter detailing the celebrations in Ciudad Guerrero. The Salvadoran president signed himself "P. José Escandón." Herein, perhaps, lies the reason for the correspondence between the Guerrero committee and the president of El Salvador: he may well have been a descendant of the founder of the Villas del Norte, Don José de Escandón (L. de la Garza, *La antigua*, 28–29).

But in the midst of the patriotic fervor and the climate of optimism that accompanied the Juárez centennial celebrations of 1906, other, less happy events, were taking place in Mexico in that year—an ominous example being the strike by miners in the town of Cananea, Sonora, on the border with Arizona. Among the changes to land laws made by the Díaz government was a significant alteration to the long-established rule of mineral ownership in Mexico. Going back to Spanish law, the ownership of the minerals had always resided with the sovereign, who would grant concessions to individuals, provided that the sovereign received a stipulated part of the production called a royalty. But in 1884 and 1887 the Mexican Congress, at the direction of President Díaz, passed new codes of mining law that gave the owners of the surface also ownership of the minerals underneath. A law of 1892 further strengthened the new rule, conferring "unquestioned title to whatever subsoil deposits there might be beneath the surface," upon the purchase of private property. John Mason Hart points out that these changes in the Mexican legal framework spurred U.S. interest in Mexican mining, to the extent that American mining concessions went from 40 in 1884 to 13,696 in 1904, involving almost a quarter of a million hectares (142). One of the American mining operators was the Greene Cananea Copper Company, jointly owned by William D. Greene and John D. Rockefeller's Anaconda Copper Company and located in Cananea, Sonora, where unfair working conditions for the Mexican miners led them to strike.

One of the organizers of the miners' strike in Cananea was Lázaro Gutiérrez de Lara, who is described as an intellectual precursor of the Mexican Revolution by James D. Cockcroft (127) and by Juan Fidel Zorrilla and Carlos González Salas (*Diccionario* 225). Lázaro Gutiérrez de Lara was born in Monterrey, Nuevo León, into the family that had produced the two *hermanos héroes*, Col. Bernardo Gutiérrez de Lara and Father Antonio. According to Zorrilla, Lázaro graduated from the National School of Jurisprudence in 1898 and became a judge in Chihuahua in 1902, at the same time that he edited a weekly newspaper. In the early years of the twentieth century, he joined the Partido Liberal Mexicano (PLM), which must have spelled the end of his judicial career, since the Díaz government controlled all government appointments and quickly disciplined critics and opponents, of which the PLM was one (Zorrilla and González Salas 225).

The Cananea miners' strike began in an orderly fashion with the workers demanding shorter work periods and higher wages and ended in a riot that left the company store manager dead and the store in ashes. The state government then stepped in, breaking up the strike and ordering the miners back to work (Hart 66–68). The strike leaders were imprisoned, although Gutiérrez de Lara escaped. He sought refuge in Los Angeles, California, where he came into contact with other political exiles who were followers of the Flores Magón brothers, the founders of the PLM (Zorrilla and González Salas 225).

Gutiérrez de Lara returned to Mexico after his stay in California, accompanying American journalist John Kenneth Turner in 1908 and acting as his guide and interpreter. The result of this trip, particularly their visit to Yucatán, was Turner's book, *Barbarous Mexico*, a scathing exposé of the slave labor practices in the *henequén* (hemp) plantations of Yucatán—practices that were abetted by the Díaz government—and of the brutal repression meted out by that government to its opponents.

Turner's book came out in 1910 (coinciding with both the independence centennial and the outbreak of the Revolution), two years after the publication of the pivotal Creelman interview with Díaz and one year after Francisco I. Madero published *La sucesión presidencial en 1910* (*The Presidential Succession in 1910*), the two works that helped precipitate the Mexican Revolution. In 1908 President Díaz had granted an interview to a journalist from the United States named James Creelman in which he announced that he would not seek reelection in 1910, citing two reasons for his decision: the first was his age (he would be eighty in 1910), and the second was his belief that the Mexican people were now ready to change governments at election time in a peaceful manner. Perhaps Díaz was sincere in 1908 when he expressed his wish to retire from the presidency, or perhaps he just wanted to see who popped up as political rivals. In either case, the response to his announcement was not long in coming (Benavides Hinojosa 285).

Gen. Bernardo Reyes had served as governor of Nuevo León for twenty years with unswerving loyalty to the president who had placed him in office. Under Reyes's stewardship the state, and particularly Monterrey, the capital, had become a center of commerce and industry, and the local elites were his staunch supporters. Soon after the Creelman interview, Reyista clubs were formed to promote his candidacy for president, or for vice president, should Díaz decide to run one more time. No one expected Díaz to last more than one additional term in office—if that long. Therefore, this time the choice of vice president was of crucial importance. General Reyes was content to be the heir apparent; as vice president he would be only a heartbeat away from the presidency. Moreover, the current vice president, Ramón Corral, was singularly unpopular and unsavory; however, it was Corral who held the inside track in the race for number two (Benavides Hinojosa 291).

Another hopeful for the presidential sash emerged in 1909 from outside the Díaz inner circle but from within the wealthy elites of the north. He was Francisco I. Madero, whose book on the presidential succession had made him known throughout Mexico. He became the standard-bearer of the Anti-Reelectionists as he toured Mexico in the middle part of 1909, calling for political reform under the old Díaz slogan of *Sufragio efectivo, no reelección* (Effective Suffrage, No Reelection), and he was moderately successful in attracting followers to his cause, which did not include revolution. Madero had set out to be a presidential candidate, not a revolutionary. People of his class did not engage in revolutions. Anita Brenner described the large Madero family in *The Wind That Swept Mexico* as more of a clan, numbering 172 male members who owned about "a million and a half acres in cotton, lumber, rubber, cattle; besides mines and smelters competing with the Guggenheims; besides wine and brandy distilleries, mortgages and real estate and provincial banks" (21).

The Díaz government was good to the rich, and the Maderos, being rich, did well under that regime, although not as well as richer rivals, such as the Guggenheims, who were not only richer but also foreign, giving credence to the saying that Mexico was a mother to foreigners but a stepmother to Mexicans. Nonetheless, the Maderos were part of the ruling class and were not happy with "Panchito's" political activities. In 1909 both Madero's father and grandfather tried to dissuade him from pursuing his candidacy. Madero's grandfather Don Evaristo, in particular, foresaw the repercussions of his grandson's ambition, warning him: "You are far from knowing the country in which we live" (Cumberland, *Genesis*, 88). Indeed, Madero perceived the change he sought only in political terms—free elections that would, somehow, also solve the social and economic problems that plagued Mexico. And in early 1910, with his popularity growing, it seemed as if Madero actually had a chance of achieving his goal of succeeding Díaz.

Díaz decided that it was time to put a stop to Madero's electioneering and arrested him in Monterrey in June of 1910 on trumped-up charges of having incited rebellion earlier in San Luis Potosí, where he was then sent to be incarcerated. Madero was released on bail the following month on condition that he remain in the city, but he did not. Madero's imprisonment, although of short duration, seems to have been the turning point in his political development. Up to his arrest, he had apparently believed that President Díaz would bow to public opinion and allow free elections. However, during his confinement in jail Madero witnessed Porfirio Díaz and the despised vice president, Ramón Corral, imposed once more on the Mexican people through the usual farce of reelection. Francisco Madero, his brother Gustavo, and other close allies began thinking of armed revolt as the only option for change.

September 16 of 1910 marked the centennial of Mexican independence. September 15, when independence celebrations traditionally commence, was also Porfirio Díaz's birthday. Born on the eve of Mexican independence and after thirty years at the helm of his country's destiny, how could Díaz not have come to identify himself with the Mexican State? Like Louis XIV, he *was* the state. Porfirio Díaz, who had been refused recognition as president by foreign powers when he had seized the office more than thirty years before, had by now been consecrated as the savior of Mexico by those same powers. He had been awarded a multitude of decorations by those governments that had snubbed him earlier, receiving, among others, the Grand Cross of the Legion of Honor from France and the Grand Cross of the Order of the Bath from Great Britain (Godoy 206–207). He displayed these decorations like a constellation of glittering stars on his chest in the official portraits that presided at all the government buildings. The medals also photographed well in the widely circulated color postcards of

Don Porfirio, such as the one I remember seeing in a plush-covered picture album that once belonged to my paternal great-aunts. In September of 1910, apparently at the apogee of his power, while celebrating both the independence centennial and another reelection, Díaz posed with his cabinet of *científicos*, his inner circle of experts, for a photograph described by Anita Brenner: "Round him, like cherubim and seraphim in a religious picture . . . a group of courtly, elderly men" (7).

Meanwhile, away from the festive capital, a group of younger men plotted to dethrone the aging heavenly host as Madero planned his flight to the United States. He had managed to elude his watchers in San Luis Potosí, and in early October of 1910 he boarded a train for Laredo, disguised as a workman. From the border city he continued his trip to San Antonio, Texas. Francisco Madero was there to organize the uprising that was now inevitable.

The United States would seem an unlikely haven for Mexican revolutionaries, in light of its long-standing hostility toward Mexico (since before the Mexican War) and the sporadic outbursts of violence against Mexicans, especially in Texas. Soon after Madero's arrival in San Antonio, for example, a young Mexican ranch worker named Antonio Rodríguez was arrested in Rocksprings, Texas, near San Antonio, for allegedly killing an Anglo woman. Rather than waiting for a trial, a mob abducted him from the jail where he was held and burned him at the stake (*La Crónica*, November 12, 1910). However, the revolutionaries of 1910, like others before them, had little choice of escape routes, and so they fled north.

Plotting the overthrow of a friendly government while in the United States was a violation of the neutrality laws, and earlier foes of the Díaz government had been prosecuted by American authorities. Turner, in *Barbarous Mexico*, related that the Flores Magón brothers, founders of the PLM, had been imprisoned in the Los Angeles County jail and in the federal penitentiary in Florence, Arizona, from 1907 to 1910 for plotting to overthrow the government of Porfirio Díaz, even if only through the elective process. Lázaro Gutiérrez de Lara, Turner's guide in Mexico, was imprisoned too in 1907 after the failed Cananea strike, under direct instructions from the attorney general of the United States, and was held for over three months on a fabricated charge (Turner 290–293).

Madero and his family members, though, moved about the United States with relative ease. In early 1911 the Madero family held a conclave in Corpus Christi, Texas, to discuss the financial repercussions of Francisco's political activities. A short while earlier Madero had unsuccessfully tried to launch invasions into Mexico through Eagle Pass, Texas, and from New

Orleans while Gustavo Madero traveled to Washington, D.C., attempting to raise funds for the incipient Revolution (Cumberland, *Genesis*, 131). For a time, while the Maderos dithered, it seemed as if the Revolution would be stillborn. Finally, in February of 1911, Francisco Madero, under increasing pressure from opposite sides—his own supporters and the American authorities—returned to Mexico. He crossed the border at El Paso on February 14, just ahead of an order for his arrest from the United States government. On the other side of the border, the revolutionary forces were concentrated in Chihuahua, waiting for his arrival.

Northern Chihuahua figured prominently in Madero's strategy for a successful uprising. According to Cumberland, Madero's plan of campaign "envisaged the capture of some smaller towns in northern Chihuahua, the isolation and defeat of small units of the federal army . . . and the ultimate capture of the border city [Ciudad Juárez]" (*Genesis* 130–131). The battle of Casas Grandes on March 6, 1911, which Madero lost, is the best-known example of Madero's northern strategy. However, there was an earlier battle on March 4 in the small town of Santa Rosalía, Chihuahua, on the rail line from Ciudad Juárez to Mexico City, a battle that marked the appearance of one of Madero's most loyal supporters, Pancho Villa. This incident at Santa Rosalía is one of the earliest, and perhaps least-known, raids led by Villa. Although these early encounters were not a success, Enrique Krause believes that they revealed "Villa's tactical genius" and that, at Santa Rosalía, Villa, "with a small group of loyal and well-armed men[,] . . . distinguished himself" (*Mexico* 308–309).

Santa Rosalía was merely a footnote to the Mexican Revolution, but it was probably Papá Lorenzo's first brush with the bloodbath that was to follow. On March 5, 1911, *La Prensa*, an afternoon daily from Monterrey, carried on its front page the story of an attack launched against the municipal buildings of Santa Rosalía. According to the newspaper, the attacking force consisted of four hundred rebels "al mando del cabecilla Francisco Villa" (under the command of the ringleader Francisco Villa). In spite of the large attacking force, the assault was described as an *escaramuza*, or skirmish, and only six of the *revoltosos* (troublemakers) were reported killed, as well as Pancho Villa's horse. Rather than emphasizing the revolutionary activities, though, *La Prensa* focused on the regrettable deaths of local officials and well-known persons, among whom were "Lic. Lorenzo M. de la Garza, don Desiderio Flores, alcaide de la cárcel, [jail warden], el Sr. Ramos, secretario del juzgado [court clerk]," and others whose names were unknown.

La Prensa devoted most of its report to the death of the lawyer (*licen-*

ciado) Lorenzo M. de la Garza, who was described as a very well-known person in Monterrey, having attended secondary school (Colegio Civil) and law school in that city. Furthermore, de la Garza belonged to a "distinguished family" who resided in nearby Laredo. The writer added that he had had the pleasure of seeing de la Garza in Monterrey during the centennial celebrations of the previous September.

Lorenzo Manuel de la Garza was my grandfather's nephew (as well as his namesake), the oldest son of his older brother Cándido and his wife, Prudencia Benavides, who had married in Guerrero in August of 1880 before moving to Laredo. According to documents in the possession of Lorenzo Manuel's great-nephew José Carlos de la Garza Tamez, Lorenzo Manuel had run into trouble with Gen. Bernardo Reyes in 1903 by joining other law students in protesting Reyes's government. As related by a Reyes biographer, students from the law school in Monterrey participated in an anti-Reyes demonstration on February 5, 1903, which led to arrests and to a much larger protest two months later on the Plaza Zaragoza—the main square—that ended with gunfire from the police (Benavides Hinojosa 264–267). After this later protest, which happened on April 3, Lorenzo Manuel wrote to his father at the family ranch near Bruni, Texas, describing the police attack on the unarmed protesters, as they lay on the ground: "Caímos al suelo unos sobre otros . . . y así la policía nos disparaba." Lorenzo Manuel concluded his letter by assuring his father that he was safe but in hiding and warned him to stay away from Monterrey.

Among my grandfather's papers there was, in addition to the March 5, 1911, issue of *La Prensa* (the story of the attack highlighted), a business card introducing Lorenzo M. de la Garza as attorney-at-law, respectfully offering his services in Chihuahua as of July 1910: "Abogado, respetuosamente se ofrece a las órdenes de Ud., Chihuahua de 1910." And among the documents located by José Carlos de la Garza is a copy of the decree printed in the official publication of the State of Chihuahua, dated July 13, 1910, whereby Lorenzo M. de la Garza was authorized to take the *examen professional de abogado*, the equivalent of the bar exam, on July 4, 1910. Apparently, he passed the exam, and immediately afterwards he had his professional cards printed and circulated among family and friends.

Although the seven years between 1903 and 1910 are unaccounted for, the most likely scenario is that Lorenzo Manuel felt it prudent or necessary to distance himself from the wrath of Bernardo Reyes and left Monterrey. He eventually settled in Chihuahua, where he finished his legal studies and hung out his shingle. He had been practicing law for less than a year before he died.

The exact particulars of his death do not emerge from the newspaper story, but they can be pieced together from other surviving documents. In his family research, José Carlos de la Garza found an *esquela*, or obituary, that was published by the family of Cándido de la Garza, announcing that on February 28, 1911, their son Lorenzo M. de la Garza had passed away at the age of twenty-nine years and eight months in Ciudad Camargo (perhaps a new name for Santa Rosalia, since that name appears on old maps but not on recent ones for the same location), Chihuahua. The obituary was dated March 5, 1911, the same day that the story of the raid appeared in *La Prensa*. However, that story apparently contained an error, since my grandfather had outlined, with blue pencil, the paragraphs relating to his nephew's death and had placed a large "X" at the end of that section.

The obituary did not give any details of how Lorenzo Manuel had died. This information comes, instead, from the official death certificate issued on March 1, 1911, by the judge of the civil court in Ciudad Camargo, Chihuahua. The certificate read: "[A]yer a las 12 p.m. falleció el señor Licenciado Lorenzo M. de la Garza, de consecuencia de *Heridas*," fixing Lorenzo Manuel's death at noon of the previous day, as a result of "wounds," the last word inserted by a different hand. How the wounds were inflicted is not specified (most likely during the *villista* attack), in contrast to the information provided in the death certificate for Faustino Ramos, the court clerk, who survived the attack only to die the same day at six in the afternoon, "a consecuencia de haber sido fusilado por los rebeldes" (as a result of being executed—by firing squad—by the rebels).

The death of Lorenzo Manuel in Chihuahua was a link in the chain of family misfortunes that had begun with the death of the patriarch, Blas María de la Garza, in early January of 1910. Papá Blasito, as his grandchildren called him, had been born in 1821, the year that Mexican independence was consummated (as opposed to declared) and died in 1910, when the republic sought to be reborn in revolution. Perhaps it was a kindness that he did not live to see his grandson die as a result of that rebirth, nor the death of his own son, the young man's heartbroken father, which followed two months after Lorenzo Manuel's death.

By 1910 Lorenzo and Esther's family included four children—two boys and two girls. Their older son, Lorenzo Jr., completed the fourth grade that year in Guerrero at the Colegio Bernardo Gutiérrez de Lara para Niños (a boys' private school), as his report card recorded. His younger brother, Fabio, was most likely also a student there, as a photograph of the two boys in school uniform would seem to indicate. The two girls were still toddlers at the time. On the first day of April of the following year, less than a month after the tragic news of Lorenzo Manuel's death, Lorenzo and Esther welcomed the arrival of a third daughter, whom they named Octavia Amelia. There had been an earlier Octavia, the first daughter, who was born in 1900 and lived only for thirty-two days, so the name would seem to have been a family favorite, except that the second Octavia was always called Nela. Perhaps it was a diminutive for "Amelia," or, more likely, it came from "Marianela," the eponymous heroine of the novel by Benito Pérez Galdós, a Spanish novelist much admired by Lorenzo.

Within weeks of Nela's arrival, the age of the Porfiriato came to an end, dying "not with a bang but a whimper." Madero had followed his early March defeat at Casas Grandes with the capture of Ciudad Juárez two months later. This victory spurred rebellions throughout the country, and the Man of Iron wavered. Not only was Don Porfirio eighty years old then, but at the crucial time he was in great pain from an abscess of the jaw. He turned in his resignation on May 25, 1911, leaving the government in the hands of Francisco León de la Barra, who had been the ambassador to Washington until his appointment to the Díaz cabinet two months earlier.

My de la Garza great-aunts' admiration for Don Porfirio was undoubtedly shared by their brothers, even if the men did not keep his picture postcard in a plush album, as the women did. I once heard Nela remark that her father had considered Madero a traitor to his class for instigating the Revolution. However, Grandfather Lorenzo was clearly a pragmatist who conformed his actions to the adage of *Al mal tiempo buena cara* (In bad times—or bad weather—put on a good face). Thus, he began to explore what good could come from the changed national circumstances, as soon as the change was clear. In spite of his respect for Don Porfirio, Papá Lorenzo must have been aware that under Díaz's rule few avenues for career advancement had been open to the younger generation, even those belonging to the provincial elites. Cumberland, in his book on the Madero revolution, quotes Manuel Calero y Sierra, a contemporary critic of Díaz, lamenting that Díaz had a "horror of injecting new blood into the governmental organism" (8). My grandfather's firstborn son, Lorenzo Jr., was thirteen years old in 1911, and for him my grandfather now envisaged a career in the diplomatic service. A new regime meant new opportunities, and Grandfather Lorenzo set to work to make those opportunities a reality for his son.

Francisco León de la Barra was merely a caretaker president, but he had earlier held the second most important position in the foreign ministry, as ambassador to Washington. Therefore, on September 14, 1911, Grandfather Lorenzo wrote a letter to him on his business letterhead, which identified him as a general trader in business since 1895 ("Lorenzo de la Garza, Negociante en General. Casa Establecida en Negocios desde 1895"). In this letter, Grandfather respectfully informed the interim president that he had a son whom he wished to guide into the diplomatic service, and inquired whether the government sponsored a course of study in this area. Whatever shortcomings politicians of that era had, lack of manners was not among them, and within a week, on September 20, President León de la Barra responded on his personal letterhead to Grandfather's query, informing him that special exams were given by the foreign ministry and that a list of the subjects covered by the exam was available from the department in charge of that area.

There is no indication of whether Papá Lorenzo was discouraged by this example of polite "passing the buck" or if he decided to wait until after the elections before pursuing the matter of his son's career. Political events in Mexico were still very much up in the air and without certainty as to what the approaching elections would bring. Madero's election was not really in dispute, but, as in the previous year, the question of the vice president was troublesome. Early on, Francisco Vázquez Gómez, one of the original Anti-Reelectionists, had been the front-runner for that position, but after various disagreements with Madero, Vázquez Gómez lost Madero's support. At the party convention in late August of 1911, Madero's new choice of running mate, José María Pino Suárez, who had presided at the party convention the previous year, was chosen as the vice presidential candidate.

The choice of Pino Suárez left Vázquez Gómez and his supporters understandably unhappy, and to complicate matters, a direct challenge to Madero's own candidacy arose shortly before the election: Gen. Bernardo Reyes, whom Díaz had dispatched to Europe to quell his political ambitions, was back in Mexico, probably kicking himself for not having stayed home to pursue his own presidential calling. However, upon his arrival, he had assured Madero that he had no political ambitions, only to "succumb" a few weeks later to the pleas of his supporters who wanted him as president. Then, in an about-face, he withdrew his candidacy a few days before the October 1 election. He then left for San Antonio, Texas, the usual preliminary step to launching a rebellion (Cumberland, *Genesis*, 166–168).

General Reyes knew that he had a following in Texas. In San Antonio, a welcome committee of three hundred persons awaited his arrival, according to one biographer (Benavides Hinojosa 335–336). In Webb County, Sheriff Amador Sánchez was a stalwart supporter who risked prison for the *reyista* cause. American federal officials, who had been tracking the reyistas for some time, uncovered in November of 1911 a cache of arms stored in the Webb County jail in Laredo, as well as horses, saddles, weapons, and ammunition in various locations in the city. Reyes was in Laredo at the time, and both he and Sheriff Sánchez were arrested for violation of the Neutrality Act, only to be later released on bail (Wilkinson 382–383). Sheriff Sánchez was subsequently indicted in federal court, pled guilty, and was convicted of the charge. He was sentenced to pay a fine, which he did, and was later pardoned by outgoing President William Howard Taft on February 21, 1913 (B. de la Garza 90). General Reyes, on the other hand, jumped bail and crossed into Mexico to start his revolution.

Meanwhile, in Mexico City the electors who had been elected on October 1, in their turn, chose Francisco I. Madero as president and José María Pino Suárez as vice president of Mexico on October 15, 1911, as Henry Lane Wilson, the ambassador from the United States, had predicted they would do (Cumberland, *Genesis*, 169). My grandfather had come to the same conclusion as Ambassador Wilson and sent Pino Suárez a letter of congratulations dated October 14, the eve of the election. Papá Lorenzo, though, played it safe, congratulating Pino Suárez for his earlier election as governor of Yucatán and wished him well in his "arduous government tasks" as the nation entered a "new democratic era, a glorious product of the triumphant Revolution," words that applied equally well to the presidential election of the following day.

Pino Suárez replied from Mérida, the capital of Yucatán, with a promptness that spoke well not only of his courtesy but also of the efficiency of the mail service. His letter was dated October 30, 1911, and was on his personal letterhead. Pino Suárez understood my grandfather's "double-duty" congratulations and thanked him for his good wishes on the occasion of his election to the governorship of Yucatán and subsequently as vice president of Mexico.

The presidential inauguration took place on November 6, rather than on the appointed date of December 1, because the interim president, León de la Barra, who had come in second in the vice presidential race, resigned before his appointment ended. Grandfather duly sent his congratulations to the new president of Mexico, Francisco I. Madero, and received President Madero's thanks in return. But Papá Lorenzo was not done with letter writing yet. Pursuing the goal of launching his oldest son in a diplomatic career, Grandfather also sent his good wishes to Manuel Calero, the new secretary of foreign relations, although he made no mention in his letter of the ulterior motive that undoubtedly motivated his letter. Calero, too, replied with his thanks, as did several recently elected state governors who had also been the recipients of Grandfather's good wishes, among them the governors of San Luis Potosí, Estado de México, and Aguascalientes. The latter signed himself "afmo. Amigo y S.S. A. Fuentes" (affectionate friend and *seguro servidor*, which would translate as "obedient servant"). Perhaps Grandfather was, indeed, personally acquainted with Governor Alberto Fuentes, who was photographed with Madero, Pancho Villa, and Venustiano Carranza in early 1911 near Ciudad Juárez and who, like them, would later be assassinated by political enemies.

It does appear that Papá Lorenzo counted at least one of the Maderos—Ernesto, the president's uncle—as an acquaintance or perhaps even a friend. On November 25, 1911, Ernesto Madero, who became secretary of the treasury (*secretario de hacienda*) in his nephew's cabinet, wrote a letter on black-bordered notepaper, thanking his *estimable amigo* (esteemed friend) Don Lorenzo de la Garza for his letter of condolences. In the reply there was no reference to the particular death that was mourned, although it must have been a close family member, as indicated by the stationery.

Grandfather Lorenzo could have met Ernesto Madero at the Casino Monterrey, the gathering place of the northern elites. The Casino Monterrey had been founded as a social club by Monterrey merchants in the 1860s, but it did not really take off until twenty years later. It was exclusive, with only some fifty members at its start, but later it grew, although slowly and selectively. The Maderos had their family seat in the neighboring state of Coahuila, but they also maintained a home in Monterrey, where they had important investments. In *The Monterrey Elite and the Mexican State, 1880-1940*, Alex M. Saragoza lists Ernesto Madero as a member of the governing board of the Casino Monterrey in 1910 (75). Although my grandfather was not a regular member of this club, he held temporary membership in it on the various occasions when he visited the city. In December of 1893, for example, he received a membership card that allowed him club privileges for one month. Again, in July of 1896, he was given temporary membership under the sponsorship of a regular member. The president of the Casino Monterrey that year was the governor of Nuevo León and the proconsul for Porfirio Díaz in northern Mexico, Gen. Bernardo Reyes.

Fifteen years later, in 1911, General Reyes was neither governor of Nuevo León nor president of the Casino Monterrey. He was on the run, plotting to topple the duly elected president and launching an abortive invasion from Texas, as his old mentor, Porfirio Díaz, had done almost forty years before. Reyes had even coined a plan, as did all revolutionaries. This one had a poetic name, El Plan de la Soledad, which was not a meditation on solitude but the name of the hacienda in Tamaulipas where he composed it. The name was prophetic, because the general found himself almost alone, searching for an army that never materialized. He and his small group of followers were, instead, captured on Christmas Day of 1911 near Monterrey and taken as prisoners to Mexico City.

The attempt by General Reyes to cast himself as the successor caudillo to Porfirio Díaz had failed, but Madero had little cause to rejoice with this victory. His problems were only multiplying. In the south, in the state of Morelos, Emiliano Zapata, frustrated with Madero for not initiating land tenure reform, issued his Plan de Ayala to implement this goal, in defiance of the president. In the north, in Chihuahua, one of his early supporters, Pascual Orozco, feeling that his contributions to the Madero uprising had not been suitably recognized, joined with the disgruntled Vázquez Gómez brothers and took over the state government. Madero now found himself at war with his former supporters, and to fight them, he turned to military holdovers from the Díaz regime (Cumberland, *Genesis*, 196).

Madero did not seem to realize that he was trying to maintain the Porfiriato without Don Porfirio, an approach that lost him the respect of his early supporters but did not gain him friends among the reactionaries. A world in which *maderistas* and *porfiristas* could coexist had a very short life expectancy and was in its death throes in the summer of 1912. "The last gala of the Porfiriato" (*la última fiesta del Porfiriato*) was how Horacio Casasús (the son of Joaquín Casasús, one of Don Porfirio's inner circle) described the wedding of his sister Margarita (Margot) to Manuel Sierra (the son of Don Porfirio's secretary of education, Justo Sierra), according to Carlos Tello Díaz in his family history. Among the wedding guests present at the Casasús mansion were Francisco Rincón Gallardo, Don Porfirio's son-in-law, as well as other prominent porfiristas, such as Enrique Creel, Pablo Escandón, and Tomás Braniff. From the maderista camp there were Gustavo Madero, brother of the president, as well as Vice President Pino Suárez and Juan Sánchez Azcona, President Madero's personal secretary and the bride's uncle (Tello 86). But attitudes were hardening at the extremes, and if Madero thought that maderistas and porfiristas could forget their differences and lie down together like the lion and the lamb, he was living in a fool's paradise.

Perhaps my grandfather shared Madero's wishful thinking that the "triumphant Revolution" would herald a new benevolent age, because, for the first time, he participated as a candidate in the state elections of 1912. Under the auspices of the local party, the Partido de Guerrero, Grandfather Lorenzo was elected *diputado suplente* (alternate representative) to the Tamaulipas state legislature. The *escrutinio*, or canvassing, of the election results showed that Papá Lorenzo had received 1,247 votes. There was no mention of opposing candidates. The elections of February 1912 were statewide and were an attempt to restore state governance, which had practically disappeared under Porfirio Díaz, who had appointed all state governors. The most important position chosen was, of course, that of governor, although in Tamaulipas the interim governor, Matías Guerra, was kept in his post because the earlier front-runner, the candidate of the Partido Liberal de Tamaulipas, died shortly before the election.

For Papá Lorenzo the prolongation of Guerra's tenure in office was most fortuitous because Governor Guerra was a native of Guerrero, and taking advantage of this circumstance, Grandfather hoped to obtain government sponsorship for the publication of *Dos hermanos héroes*, his dual biography of Guerrero's most famous sons, the Gutiérrez de Lara brothers, who had led the Mexican independence movement in Tamaulipas. This work must have taken my grandfather several years of laborious research and writing, for he must have done it in the time he could snatch from his business and family commitments. However, I was not able to find among his papers any notes or rough drafts of the manuscript. Finally, in the fall of 1912, he had his manuscript ready and, amidst the new climate of political optimism, he submitted it for publication by the state government press. But since he was a novice, for the most part, in the ways of government bureaucracy, he failed to formally submit a request for its publication, and Governor Guerra informed him of this oversight. It may have been of some consolation to my grandfather that the governor personally wrote to him and addressed him as *muy estimado y fino amigo* (my very esteemed fine friend) in order to give him the disappointing news. Still, in due course my grandfather undoubtedly submitted the required application, and the publication of *Dos hermanos héroes* was scheduled to occur in the fullness of time.

However, dark clouds continued to threaten the political horizon in Mexico. Old porfiristas may have come to embrace the "triumphant Revolution," as my grandfather had, or they may have become lukewarm maderistas, as Governor Matías Guerra did (under Díaz, Guerra had been interim governor in 1901), but one critical institution had never accepted Madero: the army. Again, Madero did not fully grasp this hostility, which manifested itself in the revolt of Félix Díaz in October of 1912. Madero's misguided desire to maintain continuity had extended to retaining the old dictator's nephew, Félix Díaz, as military commander of Veracruz. Not surprisingly, Díaz staged a rebellion, which was eventually suppressed by government troops, and Díaz joined Gen. Bernardo Reyes in prison in Mexico City. Now the supporters of the ancien régime had two of its representatives together in one place to rally round.

On the home front, 1912 brought Lorenzo and Esther a family tragedy from an unexpected quarter: Texas. On August 14 their brother-in-law, Manuel Gutiérrez, and his father, Don Francisco Gutiérrez Garza, were killed on their ranch in Webb County, north of Laredo, by their tenant, Alonzo W. Allee (B. de la Garza 15–21). The killing of the two men left two widows, the younger one being Francisca Peña, Esther's older sister, and the older a first cousin to the two sisters, as well as seven orphans, for, with Manuel's death, Francisca became the sole parent of seven children, the oldest of whom was only sixteen. In addition to the shock and grief felt by my grandparents because of the killings, they probably also felt uneasy at the increasing anti-Mexican feeling in Texas, where they might have to seek refuge if the situation in Mexico worsened.

By February of 1913 Mexico City was boiling over with plots against the government, but Madero seemed confident of overcoming them, as he had the Díaz and Reyes rebellions. What developed instead was a barracks revolt that unleashed on the capital a reign of terror that came to be known as *la decena trágica* (the tragic ten days). Beginning on February 9, mutinous troops stormed the prisons where Bernardo Reyes and Félix Díaz were held and released them. General Reyes then insisted on leading the charge on the National Palace, against the pleas of his son Rodolfo, who accompanied him. The National Palace was defended by troops who had remained loyal to the government, under the command of Gen. Lauro Villar. According to a Reyes biographer, Rodolfo tried to hold the reins of his father's horse to halt the old man's charge, warning him that he was likely to get shot, and the old man had replied, "But not in the back," as he drew his gun. Shots rang out, and Gen. Bernardo Reyes fell from his horse, mortally wounded (Benavides Hinojosa 352).

From Madero's perspective, the worst outcome of the attack on the National Palace was that General Villar was seriously wounded and had to be relieved of his command. Madero then sealed his own fate by entrusting the defense of his headquarters to Gen. Victoriano Huerta, unaware that Huerta had already betrayed him. Huerta pretended to protect Madero while he and his co-conspirators (chief among them Félix Díaz) "brought death and destruction to the capital as part of a deliberate plan to sicken the populace to the point of demanding Madero's overthrow to put an end to the carnage" (Cumberland, *Genesis*, 234).

While the people of the capital, suffering daily artillery barrages, may have been excused for calling for Madero's head as the price of peace, there was something almost indecent in the alacrity with which Madero's downfall was first received along the border. By February 14 Nuevo Laredo had fallen to "a large number of rebels headed by Col. Andrés Garza Galán, Nicanor Valdez and Pascual Orozco, Sr., [who] took Nuevo Laredo . . . this afternoon," according to a telegram sent by Webb County sheriff Amador Sánchez to Texas governor O. B. Colquitt. The sheriff's telegram, reproduced in the February 15 issue of the *Laredo Times*, continued: "The garrison composed of about 250 volunteers and 150 federal soldiers joined Garza Galán [in] proclaiming General Treviño as president of Mexico." The reference was to Gen. Gerónimo Treviño, who had been brought out of retirement by Porfirio Díaz to replace Bernardo Reyes in 1909 as military commander of the Nuevo León zone. Madero had retained General Treviño in his post, just as he did with Félix Díaz and Victoriano Huerta.

However, Nuevo Laredo was not alone in abandoning Madero at the first opportunity. On February 17 the *Laredo Times* reported that Matamoros had fallen into the hands of rebels "at five o'clock this morning without a single shot being fired or any bloodshed," adding, "It was a peaceful capitulation." In Guerrero, too, the immediate effects of the rebellion against Madero must have been minimal. Among the family papers there is a photograph of twenty-two little girls—first graders—in their Sunday best, and their two teachers. Standing in the back row, in white, is my aunt, Ofelia de la Garza, who was six years old at the time. The caption at the bottom of the photograph reads, "1er. Año escolar," and the date, "2-15-1913." As of February 15, life was apparently continuing its course in Guerrero, including the taking of class photographs.

During the days of the *decena trágica*, the *Laredo Times* alternated between publishing upbeat reports about the preparations for Laredo's annual Washington's Birthday celebrations and items dealing with "numerous rumors regarding the crucial situation in Mexico" (Monday, February 10, 1913). On February 15, for example, the *Times* announced that President Madero had resigned, or "abdicated," on the previous evening and had been succeeded—as Porfirio Díaz had been two years before—by Francisco León de la Barra. The newspaper added: "The news appears to have had a relieving effect universally through Northern Mexico."

But Madero had not resigned, although U.S. ambassador Henry Lane Wilson pressured him to do so, as did the ambassadors from England, Germany, and Spain, at Wilson's behest. Losing patience, Victoriano Huerta and Félix Díaz determined to remove the president by force and notified

Ambassador Wilson of their plans. Wilson then cabled Washington that the government had fallen, anticipating by several hours the arrest of the president and the vice president, which occurred on February 18. Wilson then summoned Huerta and Félix Díaz and dictated to them the composition of the next Mexican government: Huerta was to be provisional president, although his cabinet would be chosen by Félix Díaz, advised by Rodolfo Reyes (Cumberland, *Genesis*, 236–238).

The next question to be decided was what to do with Madero and Pino Suárez. Huerta consulted on this point with his mentor, the American ambassador, but Wilson, emulating Pontius Pilate, washed his hands of the matter, merely telling Huerta that he should do "what was best for the peace of the country" (Cumberland, *Genesis*, 240). Until now the possible fates that had been discussed for Madero had been exile — the traditional solution for deposed leaders — or commitment to the lunatic asylum (a novel approach). On February 21 the *Laredo Times* attempted to reassure queasy readers by writing: "Ambassador Wilson wires that Madero will neither be thrown into a madhouse nor summarily executed, but will be given a fair trial, and that his worst possible fate will be exile." But on the same day that the *Times* assured its readers that Madero would receive a fair trial, plans were set in motion to assassinate him and Pino Suárez, and they were shot late that night by army officers acting under Huerta's orders.

If Henry Lane Wilson believed that permanently removing Madero was best for the peace of the country, he was soon disabused of this idea. No sooner had Huerta usurped the presidency than rebellions exploded. As early as February 19, when Huerta, with Wilson's blessing, proclaimed himself president, the rebels in Nuevo Laredo objected, and the *Times* reported that "the Rebel Leaders in Nuevo Laredo, Gen. Pascual Orozco, Sr., military commander, and A. Galán, civil governor, refuse to recognize government under Huerta." There was no mention of the would-be president of Mexico, Gen. Gerónimo Treviño.

Madero's assassination galvanized previously tepid maderistas into action, among whom the governor of Coahuila, Venustiano Carranza, was the most notable. By the end of February, the Coahuila legislature had authorized the governor to declare the state independent of the central government, and the struggle to avenge Madero's death had begun. Like other rebels before him, Carranza issued a political manifesto, the Plan de Guadalupe — named after his hacienda — to legitimate his cause. Within days of the plan's publication, the state government of Sonora, represented by Adolfo de la Huerta, adhered to it as well (Krause, *Carranza*, 38). However, the state government of Tamaulipas did not do so, and its governor, Matías Guerra, lost no time in assuring Victoriano Huerta of his support (*Diccionario de la Revolución* 7:114).

According to Krause in his study of Carranza, the preparatory stage of the rebellion against Huerta lasted six months, from March to August of 1913 (38). However, its effects on the border were almost immediate. For example, in late February the federal (Huerta) government attempted to starve out the rebel forces in Nuevo Laredo under Garza Galán (who was in the unenviable position of having repudiated both Madero and Huerta) by closing the port of Nuevo Laredo. The effect of the closing, according to the *Laredo Times*, was to paralyze the import and export business: "Wholesale and retail establishments on both sides of the line are now subjected to great loss as a result" (February 27, 1913).

The battles followed soon after. On March 17 the *Laredo Times* headlines screamed: "Fierce Battle Raged in New Laredo This Morning." The subhead elaborated: "Rebels and Federals Fought for Nearly Two Hours, Rebels Being Repulsed Three Times." The rebels, having been "repulsed" in Nuevo Laredo on March 17, had no better luck in Guerrero in early April. The *Laredo Times* reported on April 8 that the rebels had been "repulsed by the brave citizens" of Guerrero. The story read: "Advices received here today convey the intelligence that a big battle between rebels and citizens of Guerrero, seventy miles down the river from this city, took place last night." The newspaper explained, "[T]here are no Mexican federal soldiers at that place[;] consequently, the only protection the town had was through its own citizenry." The "brave citizens" of Guerrero who "repulsed" the anti-Huerta rebels on their own apparently did so without help from their mayor, for he resigned on the same day that the rebels arrived. According to Lorenzo de la Garza, in *La antigua Revilla* (1952 edition), Sinecio Gutiérrez had taken office as mayor on January 1, 1913, to serve the customary one-year term, but he resigned on April 7, "when the revolutionaries entered the town" (*que entraron al pueblo los revolucionarios*) (42).

The rebels, who were known as the Constitutionalists, persisted in their attacks on the federal forces along the Tamaulipas border, and on April 21, 1913, they attacked Ciudad Mier, which was defended by approximately six hundred men from the Rurales, the old rural mounted police organized by Porfirio Díaz, and the customs patrol, or Resguardo Aduanal. The Constitutionalists took the city after four hours of combat but were unable to hold it and abandoned it the same day. A few weeks later, on May 12, the Constitutionalists returned to attack Guerrero, and this time they succeeded, after the "Huertista authorities" fled upon the arrival of forces sent by Constitutionalist colonel—later general—Lucio Blanco (*Diccionario de la Revolución* 7:69). Two days earlier, on May 10, Blanco's troops had taken Reynosa, which was defended by eighty volunteers and a handful of federal troops and Rurales, and executed the mayor (Herrera, *Visión*, 73).

The constitutionalist attacks that had begun in mid-March in Nuevo Laredo and had proceeded down the river to Guerrero, Mier, and Reynosa had had Matamoros as their ultimate goal. This they captured on June 4, 1913. Control of Matamoros gave the Constitutionalists access to the receipts generated by the busy customhouse there, which filled their coffers and advanced their cause. However, the war against Huerta was far from over, and the end of 1913 again saw the *huertistas* entrenched in Nuevo Laredo and the Constitutionalists preparing to take it from them. The second battle for Nuevo Laredo commenced on New Year's Day of 1914 and continued throughout the following day until Gen. Pablo González, Carranza's commander in Tamaulipas, ordered a retreat down the river after learning that federal reinforcements were on the way (*Diccionario de la Revolución* 7:151).

The withdrawal of the Constitutionalists undoubtedly came as a relief to the inhabitants of Nuevo Laredo who had not already fled across the river, as well as to those on the Texas side who had watched the fighting from an uncomfortable proximity. According to Wilkinson, in his history of Laredo, "Both Mexican generals tried to keep their men from shooting toward the left bank of the river, and ... they were fairly successful in their efforts.... A few shots, however, did fall in Laredo, and one man was killed and a few wounded." The commander of Fort McIntosh also took the precaution of closing the international bridge during and after the battle to prevent "the passage of spies, smuggled ammunition, and *sightseers*" (387; emphasis added).

In late March of 1914 the Constitutionalists, under the command of Gen. Jesús Carranza, brother of the *Primer Jefe*, attacked Guerrero, which was now under the control of *huertista* general Gustavo Guardiola (who had been a mere colonel during the battle of Nuevo Laredo). The battle in Guerrero raged for the entire day of March 23. Guardiola had 1,400 men, plus two cannons and several machine guns, and the Constitutionalists numbered over 1,000 men and also had artillery (*Diccionario de la Revolución* 7:69). According to Guerrero historians Lilia Treviño Martínez and Eduardo Treviño de León, Gen. Jesús Carranza had positioned his cannons on the south side of the Río Salado, across from Guerrero, on a promontory known as Las Lomas de la Piedra de la Virgen, for the red stone hills that had provided the materials for building the church of Nuestra Señora del Refugio. Guardiola commanded another high point referred to by the locals as La Loma del Degüello, which may have been a place of execution or slaughtering, for that is the meaning of the word. Guardiola certainly put the site to a sinister use, bombarding Carranza's troops from there. The latter returned fire from their own position, both groups raining shells and bullets over Guerrero (Treviño Martínez and Treviño de León 56). At six in the evening General Guardiola finally called it quits and ordered a retreat toward Nuevo León, although some of his men opted for crossing into Texas rather than following him (*Diccionario de la Revolución* 7:69).

By 1914, Treviño Martínez and Treviño de León relate, a great many of the local families had already abandoned their homes and property in Guerrero and fled across the Río Bravo, seeking safety in Texas (56). Undoubtedly, the first revolutionary attacks in 1913 had sent an unprecedented shock through Guerrero and its habitants. The *guerrerenses* had not experienced comparable violence in almost forty years, and it spurred among them an exodus across the river, turning them into refugees. A survivor of one of those refugees is quoted by Lori B. McVey in *Guerrero Viejo: A Photographic Essay*; relating that his family had camped with others on the banks of the Río Bravo, he remembered that "the old people went down to the edge of the water and wept when the cannon began [to fire]" (45).

Papá Lorenzo had most likely sent Mamá Esther and the children to stay with his brother Irineo and his family in South Texas in 1913, after the first attacks on Guerrero. The decision would have been prompted not only by the growing violence, but also by Mamá Esther's pregnancy. Her youngest child, Rafael, was born on February 27, 1914, in the Rio Grande Valley.

As Victoriano Huerta's grip weakened, the objectives of his military commanders shifted from taking and holding towns to destroying them as they abandoned them. This happened in Nuevo Laredo. After the Constitutionalists took Monterrey, General Guardiola, in Nuevo Laredo, sensed the coming debacle and ordered his troops to evacuate the town. Before leaving, though, they set fire to it on April 24, 1914 (*Diccionario de la Revolución* 7:151). By mid-July Huerta had been forced to resign, and he left the country as the Constitutionalists began their march on the capital. It was "The Collapse of a Tyranny," as a Mexico City newspaper announced on July 16, 1914 (Cumberland, *Constitutionalist*, 143).

But the collapse of tyranny did not end the war. It was only the end of the second act of the drama of the Mexican Revolution. The third act began after the defeat of the common enemy. Now the three main factions under

Carranza, Villa, and Zapata fell to fighting among themselves to decide which group and leader would prevail. By the beginning of 1915, Mexico found itself in the embarrassing—not to mention chaotic—situation of having at least three presidents at the same time. They were Venustiano Carranza, who claimed the presidency by virtue of being *Primer Jefe*, or first among equals, of the anti-Huerta forces; Eulalio Gutiérrez, the compromise choice of Villa and Zapata at the Convention of Aguascalientes in the fall of 1914; and Roque González Garza, president of the convention, who had taken charge when Gutiérrez fled to escape the wrath of Pancho Villa (Cumberland, *Constitutionalist*, 190–192).

The year 1915 marked perhaps the nadir of the revolutionary decade. Cumberland says of that year that "food shortages were endemic throughout the nation all during 1915, with the situation critical in Mexico City, Monterrey, Guadalajara, Chihuahua, Hermosillo, and many other centers of population" (*Constitutionalist* 209–210). Guerrero chronicler Fernando Garza González attributes the food shortages there to the sacking of the previously well-supplied stores by individuals who, under cover of the Revolution, profited from the looting (16). As of 1911 Papá Lorenzo had described himself as a *negociante en general*, or general businessman, but it is doubtful that there was anything left to trade in 1914. He may as well have left town with his wife and children, except that his mother was elderly and ailing and could not be moved. She was in the care of her two daughters, Juana, a widow, and Petra, a spinster; and Lorenzo probably felt obligated to stay and protect the womenfolk.

Great-grandmother Francisca Garza died in that year of 1915 at the age of eighty-three. Even after this, my grandfather, as well as Juana and Petra (always known by their diminutives as Juanita and Petrita) stayed on in what must have been a ghost town, apparently unmolested, although the great-aunts did experience one frightening incident that became part of family lore. According to the story handed down, one day a young man in military uniform came knocking at their door, demanding to see Doña Juana de la Garza, Viuda (Widow) de Caso. Juanita, no doubt burdened by the guilty knowledge of the plush-covered album that cradled the portrait of Don Porfirio, concluded that she was about to be led to the firing squad. But demonstrating the stern stuff of which she was made, she replied: "It is I." Upon hearing her reply, the young officer threw his arms around her, calling her "Madrina" (Godmother). The identity of the officer was forgotten, but it is likely that it was someone whom she had not seen since childhood, probably not since she had held him at the baptismal font, and who was now fully grown into a revolutionary.

Papá Lorenzo, having been put out of business by the Revolution, had to find other means of making a living, as well as finding a way of staying alive. The year of 1915, with the various factions engaged in a war without quarter, was not the time to remain uncommitted. Guerrero had been carrancista territory off and on since 1913 and remained so in 1915, although a party of villistas made at least one foray into the vicinity of Guerrero in March of 1915 (*Diccionario de la Revolución* 7:177). For Papá Lorenzo, therefore, it was a matter of choosing the known devil. He signed on with the carrancistas for a job probably more dangerous than one in the front lines: he became their tax collector.

Since early 1913, when Carranza disavowed the Huerta government and rose against it, he began to do what all governments do—levy taxes. According to Cumberland, Carranza depended on export taxes, particularly on cattle but also on the petroleum products exported from Mexico. However, taxes on the latter were difficult to collect, because the oil companies were foreign owned and claimed to be exempt from taxation. In addition, the chaotic state of the country made all tax collections irregular at best, as Carranza later admitted: "In many cases it was necessary to leave tax collecting at the disposition of the military authorities" (Cumberland, *Constitutionalist*, 76–79).

The military authorities, in turn, often delegated the tax collecting to civilians in their jurisdiction, as was probably the case with my grandfather. A railroad pass, dated August 21, 1915, and signed by the commander of the Guerrero garrison, P. J. Guerra, allowed my grandfather free travel on the "constitutionalist" railroads to Ciudad Victoria, the state capital. Grandfather was identified as "Citizen Lorenzo de la Garza, state tax collector, who travels to that city [Victoria] on official business." Victoria, however, had been occupied during the first half of 1915 by the villistas, who had declared a tax holiday for the poorer classes (*Diccionario de la Revolución* 7:87). The carrancistas were now in control of the state capital, but tax collectors must have been as popular as the plague. Even as late as December of 1916, taxpayers in Tamaulipas were reluctant to pay their taxes. According to *El Demócrata Fronterizo*, a Laredo weekly paper, the state government was warning delinquent taxpayers that it would foreclose on their properties and auction them off if they did not pay their taxes (December 2, 1916).

As 1915 marched forward, so did the constitutionalist army, headed by Venustiano Carranza's chief lieutenant, Alvaro Obregón. Emiliano Zapata's forces were marginalized in the south, precluding him from linking up with Pancho Villa, who was decisively defeated by Obregón in Celaya, Guanajuato, in April of that year. By 1916 it was clear that the Constitutionalists had emerged as the prevailing force, although the country was far from being pacified and still suffered the ravages of hunger and disease. Nevertheless, Carranza attempted to "begin the process of returning to a 'legal order,'" according to Cumberland. Carranza therefore decreed that municipal elections should be held on the first Sunday of September and that newly elected municipal councils would serve from October 1 of that year until December 31, 1917. Eligibility for municipal office, however, was limited to civilians who had not "aided with arms or by serving as public employees those governments or factions hostile to the Constitutionalist cause" (*Constitutionalist* 326–327).

In Guerrero this decree meant that Anastacio García Treviño, who had served as mayor since 1914, resigned his office on July 29, 1916, and turned it over to Régulo Flores, who was duly elected to that post and served until the end of 1917, according to de la Garza (*La antigua* 68). Contemporary accounts describe Régulo Flores as a conscientious mayor and a compassionate person. José M. de la Garza—a grandson of Irineo de la Garza, my grandfather's older brother—related an example of the mayor's compassion. Recalling the time that he spent in Guerrero between 1916 and 1917, when he was six years old, José said that people there had had some food, such as beef and milk, because they had some cattle, but they had no staples like coffee, flour, or beans. Fortunately for the townspeople, "once a week a wagon pulled by oxen came to town; [and] a wealthy man named Regulio [sic] Flores bought it and gave it free to anyone who needed" (McVey, *Guerrero Viejo*, 47).

However, by the first half of 1916, the guerrerenses who had remained in the deserted town, like Papá Lorenzo and his sisters, or who had already returned began to feel that peace was beginning to return to them. Undoubtedly, the greatest outrage committed against the town during the various occupations would have been the desecration of the church by troops of any of the factions involved. Troops had been quartered—along with their mounts—in private homes and public buildings, which must have included the church. Therefore, in order to cleanse the sacrileges committed in a holy place, the Catholic organizations of Guerrero issued invitations to the faithful to attend the blessing of the church devoted to Nuestra Señora del Refugio. The blessing ceremony was conducted by the bishop of Tamaulipas, Dr. José de Jesús Guzmán, on June 14, 1916, at eight in the evening. At eight on the following morning, the bishop officiated at a Mass of thanksgiving and a prayer service for peace. One of my greataunts (most likely Juanita, being the older sister) received an invitation to be a *madrina*, or sponsor, of the blessing. Fortunately, the invitation was preserved among the family papers and survived to inform us of this little-known event.

By 1917, order had been sufficiently restored in Mexico that émigrés began to return, and on December 1 of that year the Laredo weekly, *El Demócrata Fronterizo*, reported on the exodus of Mexicans from Texas: "La prensa de Texas vuelve a dar noticias de grandes caravanas de mexicanos que regresan a México, después de haber vivido en Texas por muchos años. Regresan con sus familias, sus carros, sus muebles y con todo lo que tienen" (The Texas press again reports on the large caravans of Mexicans returning to Mexico, after having lived in Texas for many years. They return with their families, their cars, their furniture, and everything they own).

Just as there is no record of the precise date when Mamá Esther and her children left Guerrero to escape the revolutionary violence, there is no record either of the exact time of their return; however, it can be safely assumed that they were back home by 1917. A possible clue is found in a photo postcard that is addressed, "A mis queridas tías, Juanita y Petrita de la Garza" (To my dear aunts, Juanita and Petrita de la Garza) and signed, "Your nephew, Rafael de la Garza." The message, in adult handwriting, adds the age of the child in the photograph as three years and six months. The postcard, bearing no postage (an indication that it had been enclosed in a letter or hand-delivered), gives no address except the city, "C. Guerrero, Tamps.," and the date, "Sep. 1 1917," is rubber-stamped. On the reverse the photograph shows a little boy perched on a chair wearing a light-colored suit and holding a matching sun helmet in his hand. As an aside, it is interesting to note that photographic postcards, also known as real photo postcards, were all the rage during the first decades of the twentieth century, and the inhabitants of the Texas-Mexican border obviously succumbed to the photo fever, if we judge by the prevalence of these items. Rafael de la Garza's portrait may have even been taken by Robert Runyon of Brownsville, Texas, who left a prodigious collection of images of the people of the lower Rio Grande on real photo postcards during the years of the Mexican Revolution (Samponaro and Vanderwood 3).

Although the date on the postcard—September 1, 1917—is not conclusive proof that Mamá Esther and the children were back in Guerrero by then, there is evidence that one family member—Lorenzo Jr.—was already in Guerrero at the time of the independence festivities in mid-September of 1917. A surviving program of the events is dated September 14 and is signed by the president of the organizing committee, Gilberto Pérez (my maternal great-uncle), and the secretary, Lorenzo de la Garza, Jr., is also listed on the program as delivering a patriotic speech. In 1917 Guerrero, although still under military occupation, was attempting to return to normalcy as the organizing committee of the festivities (La Junta Patriótica), "in conjunction with the civil and military authorities," prepared to celebrate the 107th anniversary of Mexican independence with a two-day event (September 15 and 16) that began and ended with musical serenades on the main plaza. The marathon-long program on September 16 started at four in the afternoon in front of the Palacio Municipal (City Hall) in the presence of the civil authorities, public employees, garrison troops, children from both the public and private schools, and the general public. There were thirty-six numbers on the program, including official speeches, patriotic recitations, and musical numbers by children from the public school (*escuela oficial*) and girls from the private school named after a heroine of the independence movement, Leona Vicario.

Whether Mamá Esther and the younger children were present to hear nineteen-year-old Lorenzo's patriotic speech on September 16 or returned later to Guerrero is not known, but a sign that by the end of that year Lorenzo needed "a new family car" to accommodate his growing brood in Guerrero is found in a receipt for the purchase of a *tartana* (buggy) and a *guarnición* (harness). Lorenzo paid fifty pesos "en oro metálico mexicano" (in Mexican gold) on December 4, 1917, to Emeterio Flores in Nuevo Laredo for both items. We do know that by 1919 Mamá Esther and little Rafael were certainly in Guerrero, since that year they posed for a passport photograph that was stamped with the date by the Mexican immigration office. Papá Lorenzo finally had his family back home.

The decade between 1910 and 1920 had convulsed the country and left no family unscathed. In those years my grandfather had built up his hopes for giving his oldest child a career in the diplomatic service and had seen that possibility vanish with the assassination of President Madero and the bloodbath that followed. He had lost a nephew and namesake during a villista attack in the early days of the Revolution. And he had almost seen his intellectual offspring literally go up in smoke.

In the early part of 1915, when the villistas had occupied the state capital, they claimed many victims, among them the state government press that had just published *Dos hermanos héroes*. In the introduction to the biography of the Gutiérrez de Lara brothers (finally published in 1939), the then governor of Tamaulipas, Marte R. Gómez, explained that "the excesses inherent to the Revolution" had brought about the destruction of the first printing run of one thousand copies of *Dos hermanos héroes*.

The books were lost, he added, in "one of the many fires that lit our internal war" (en uno de los muchos incendios que alumbró nuestra guerra intestina) (L. de la Garza 5–6). Ciudad Victoria did seem prone to be set afire by vengeful occupiers, if we remember that Col. Charles Dupin and the French *contre-guérilla* had set fire to the state archives in 1864 and destroyed many titles to land belonging to residents of Guerrero (see chapter 2). In addition to the printing run of one thousand books, the villista conflagration apparently also consumed the original manuscript submitted by my grandfather, since it was not among his papers. However, *Dos hermanos héroes* was not completely reduced to ashes. One advance copy, already in the author's possession, remained to see the light again in the years to come. The fruit of Papá Lorenzo's historical research and writing did, after all, survive the devastation of the Revolution, as did, also, the Gutiérrez de Lara papers. With the memory of the press conflagration undoubtedly still fresh in his mind, my grandfather sought a place of safety for the most important sources for *Dos hermanos héroes*—Don Bernardo's journal and his letters—and between 1918 and 1920 he conveyed these documents to the Texas State Library and Archives, where they still repose today.

Flag of the Republic of the Rio Grande, on display at the Republic of the Rio Grande Museum in Laredo, Texas. Vertical background for stars is red, bottom band is black, and top band is white. Courtesy of Joanna F. Fountain.

Historical marker at the Capitol of the Republic of the Rio Grande, Laredo, Texas. Courtesy of Joanna F. Fountain.

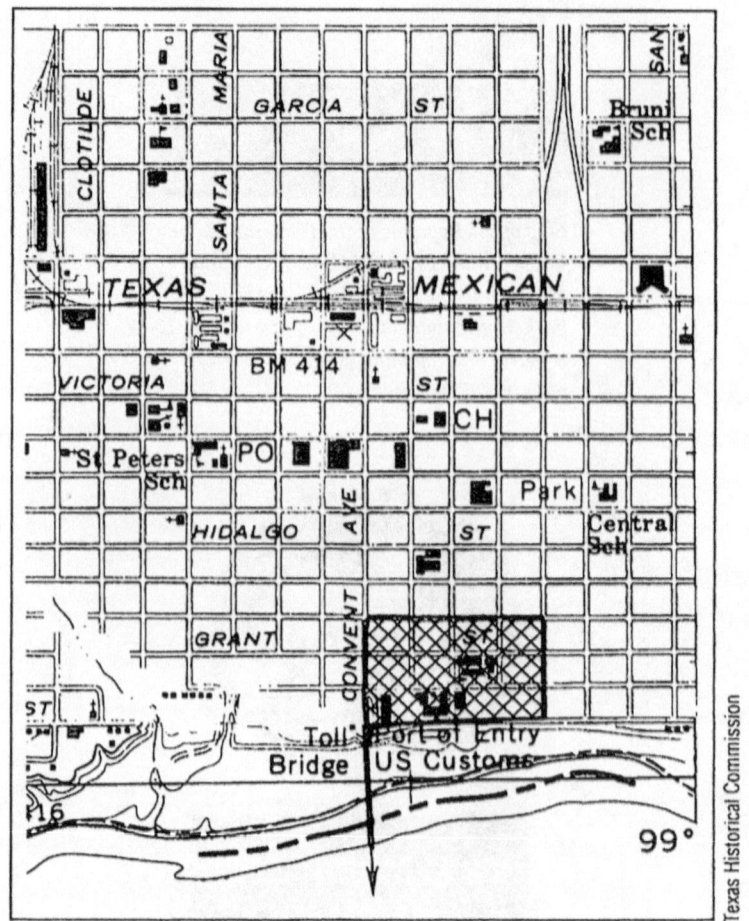

San Agustín de Laredo Historic District, Laredo, Texas (the streets of Laredo). Courtesy of the Texas Historical Commission.

San Agustín Cathedral and Plaza, Laredo, Texas.

Juan Francisco Farías (1807–1870), secretary of the Republic of the Rio Grande. Courtesy of George Farías.

Restored Capitol of the Republic of the Rio Grande. Courtesy of Joanna F. Fountain.

Laredo, Texas, circa 1890. Note the early bridge.

San Agustín Parochial School. Courtesy of Webb County Heritage Foundation.

Lucio García Garza and his mount in Nuevo Laredo, Tamaulipas, January 8, 1914.

Wedding portrait of Juana García and Víctor Montemayor in Las Escobas, Zapata County, October 1914.

Leonardo Treviño home, built in the 1870s, in Zapata County, Texas. Note the tronera (gunport) near the roofline.

Wedding invitation of Juana García and Víctor Montemayor, ceremony to be held at the bride's home in Las Escobas on October 2, 1914, at 3 a.m.

Wedding invitation of María R. Muñoz and Juan Ugarte, the religious ceremony to be held in the parish church of Villaldama, Nuevo León, July 5, 1911, at 3 a.m. Courtesy of Adela F. Etcharren.

Fabio de la Garza (far right) and cousins in Donna, Texas, 1925, dressed for a costume party.

Left to right: *Esther, Ofelia, and Nela de la Garza sitting atop their brother Fabio's car in Raymondville, Texas, circa 1930.*

Nela de la Garza standing by the sign at the city limits of San Perlita, Texas, circa 1930.

A child's funeral cortege in Guerrero, Tamaulipas, November 1917.

Horsemen on parade around the plaza in Guerrero, Tamaulipas, September 1926.

Picnic at "Las Brisas" on the Río Salado, Guerrero, Tamaulipas, May 1927.

Graduating class of the Ladies' Sewing Academy, Guerrero, Tamaulipas, 1928.

Lorenzo de la Garza (right) with his father-in-law, Juan Martín Peña, Guerrero, Tamaulipas, circa 1905.

Lorenzo de la Garza (left) with a visitor in the de la Garza home, Guerrero, Tamaulipas, circa 1945.

Nela de la Garza in front of a window of the de la Garza home, Guerrero, Tamaulipas, circa 1945.

Palacio Municipal (City Hall), Guerrero, Tamaulipas, circa 1950.

Beatriz Eugenia de la Garza (far left) and friends in front of the Church of Nuestra Señora del Refugio, celebrating the Guerrero bicentennial in October 1950.

Ofelia and Nela de la Garza in front of the ruins of their house in Guerrero Viejo, circa 1975.

Church of Nuestra Señora del Refugio and Plaza Vicente Guerrero, Guerrero, Tamaulipas, circa 1950.

Ruins of Nuestra Señora del Refugio Church. Guerrero Viejo, Tamaulipas, circa 2000.

《 FIVE 》

The Prodigal

On May 17, 1922, my paternal grandmother, Esther Peña de la Garza, wrote a letter from Guerrero, Tamaulipas, to her second son, twenty-year old Fabio Lorenzo, in South Texas. (Having been born on August 10, on his father's birthday and the feast day of San Lorenzo, it was practically inevitable that he should have that middle name, although his older brother was already Lorenzo Jr.)

In the letter, Esther laments that Fabio has been gone from home for some time and that she still cannot become accustomed to his absence: "Ya tienes tiempo de estar lejos y no puedo acostumbrarme." She adds poignantly: "Miro a mis hijos y veo que me falta uno. Eres tú" (I look at my children and notice that one is missing. It is you). Gently chiding him, she reminds him that he had promised to visit his family in Guerrero during the month of May and that he was to bring his cousin Neíto" (Irineo de la Garza Jr.) with him, but in his latest letter he had made no mention of the visit. She makes excuses for them, though, remarking that they are probably too busy to make the trip. Esther is also philosophical about the reason for Fabio's absence, saying that she knows that he needs to be where his work is. At least she is reassured that he is with family members: "Estoy conforme, sé que estás con los de tu familia."

Fabio was indeed with family members in South Texas, the family of his uncle Irineo de la Garza, and, specifically, he was working for—or with—his cousin Irineo Jr., whose business letterhead identified him as "Comerciante en Mercancías Generales" (proprietor of a general store) in Donna, located in Hidalgo County. Mamá Esther and her six children had spent the most difficult years of the Mexican Revolution—from 1913 until 1916 or 1917—with her brother and sister-in-law in South Texas, and when she returned to Guerrero, Fabio may have stayed behind with his uncle's family. However, it is more likely that all the children returned to Guerrero with their mother because the year 1916 saw a surge of violence against Mexicans in South Texas instigated by Anglo vigilantes and Texas Rangers in response to unfounded irredentist plots alleging that Mexicans planned to take back Texas. In addition, the following year, 1917, brought the entrance of the United States into World War I and with it the possibility of Mexican males being conscripted to fight in Europe. Both situations would have hastened the self-repatriation of Mexican refugees, and Mamá Esther would have been loath to leave either of her older sons in Texas under those circumstances.

It is most likely that Fabio returned to Texas after 1918. Some surviving holiday cards indicate that he was living in Texas in 1920, for he sent New Year's greetings in January of 1921 to his youngest sister, nine-year-old Nela, whom he addressed rather formally by her seldom-used first name, Octavia, wishing her "muchas felicidades te desea tu hermano en el año nuevo" (best wishes for the new year from your brother). In contrast, he addressed his baby brother informally, as Rafaelito, and hoped that the new year would be a very happy one for him and that God would keep him well, together with the "auto" (obviously, a toy car) that Fabio had sent him for "Cristmas," a gift that Rafaelito had yet to acknowledge. Neither holiday postcard carried postage, so perhaps they were enclosed in a letter to his parents.

Although Lorenzo and Esther were undoubtedly grateful and relieved that they and their family had survived revolution and exile, life for them and for most Mexicans in the aftermath of the Revolution did not pick up where it had left off before the uprising. Many people who left Mexico during the Revolution did not return afterwards, and those who did found a different Mexico when they came home. In the Villas del Norte, where ranching was the principal livelihood, families like my grandparents on both sides were able to reclaim their ranches when the violence had subsided and began the task of reconstruction. Grandfather Lorenzo, though, did not, or could not, resume his commercial activities, which had been the buying and selling of agricultural products, perhaps because the agricultural sector had been too disrupted by almost ten years of violence. Still, the ranch remained the focus of family activity, and Esther, in her letter to Fabio, brought him up-to-date on the doings there. She reported that heavy spring rains had filled the stock pond, and now they worried whether the dam would hold. Also, the family was preparing to move to the ranch for the summer vacation: "Tu papá quiere que en las vacaciones vayamos al Rancho." In a long postscript, Lorenzo, too, reiterated his plans to spend part of the summer at the ranch to see which projects he could accomplish while there: "Yo pienso ir . . . a pasar las vacaciones en el rancho y ver que trabajo realizo estando allá la familia."

However, the ranch could not provide a livelihood for the sons, as well as for the parents and the younger children; therefore, the older boys had to make their own way. Fabio was to follow the family tradition of commerce begun by his grandfather Blas María de la Garza, but in Texas, not in Mexico, with his cousin Irineo Jr., the fifth of Irineo de la Garza's eight children. There was, perhaps, as great an age difference between Neíto and Fabio as there was between their fathers—some fifteen years—but that age gap covered very different experiences for the cousins. In 1916, for example, Fabio was still a fourteen-year-old boy while Irineo Jr. was already a widower. In 1913 Irineo Jr. had married Otila Villarreal in Zapata County. Otila, a cousin of my maternal grandmother, Zoila Pérez, was born in 1895 and was a twenty-one-year-old bride when she died in childbirth with her child. Her widower never remarried, and perhaps to alleviate his loneliness, he took his young cousin Fabio under his wing and mentored him in his business.

Fabio's association with his cousin, though, may have been intended only as a preliminary step before the younger man would establish his own firm, and he may have already been on his own in the spring of 1922, according to his mother's letter. Esther's letter refers to an earlier one from Fabio to his sister Ofelia in which he had mentioned his new address, not in Donna, but in the neighboring town of Mercedes: "Ayer recibimos tu carta para Ofelia. Cambiamos tu dirección a Mercedes, creyendo recibas la correspondencia más pronto." As a result of the letter to Ofelia, his parents had noted the new address and sent the letter of May 17 there, hoping that he would receive it quicker. The inference drawn from the mention of the town of Mercedes is that Fabio was exploring the various communities in the Lower Rio Grande Valley for possible locations for a store. The postscript from his father confirms this supposition, for in it Lorenzo tells his son that he is in agreement with Fabio's suggestion that, after the period from July to September (when Lorenzo and the family would be at the ranch), he (Lorenzo) should travel to South Texas to see if Fabio could establish himself in one of the Valley communities—if the business situation improved ("si se componen los negocios").

Both father and son recognized that, for the time being, the main obstacle to Fabio's plans was the bad economic situation in the United States and, particularly, its impact on the Mexican population in the Valley, who would constitute Fabio's customers. The size of this population in the

United States, and particularly in Texas, ebbed and flowed according to the prevailing political and economic conditions in both countries. There had been a large influx of immigrants into Texas, refugees from the Mexican Revolution, especially from 1913 to 1915. This population flow was reversed after 1915, in the wake of the Bandit War, which allegedly heralded the takeover of Texas by Mexicans but resulted instead in their persecution. However, the entry of the United States into World War I in 1917 increased the demand for agricultural products and for the workers who harvested them, at the same time that Mexicans began returning home. American growers then increased their efforts to recruit Mexican agricultural workers, until the end of the war in 1918 and the return of American soldiers made Mexican workers redundant. In addition, economic activity in the United States declined in the aftermath of the war. "Southwestern farmers were going bankrupt [in 1921], and out of work Mexicans were stranded in remote hamlets without food or means of returning to Mexico," is how one writer describes the situation in the postwar period (Metz 375).

Against this economic background, Fabio's plans for starting his own business did not seem practicable, at least not then, but he obviously believed that his future lay in the "Magic Valley," as it was called by its promoters. In 1922 the Lower Rio Grande Valley did indeed seem magical, since in twenty years it had blossomed from brush country into plantations and orchards. Ten years later—in 1932—the *McAllen (TX) Monitor*, a weekly newspaper, reprinted a paean to the area from the *Telegraph World*, the official publication of the association of Western Union employees, summarizing the history of the area: "On July 4, 1904, the first railroad... came into Brownsville, the most southerly city of the U.S. Irrigation and citrus fruit came later.... In less than twenty years, a quarter million acres of grazing land has been converted into highly productive fruit and vegetable land." The writer then proceeded to enumerate the assets of the area: "6,000 citrus trees are now producing. Half a million acres... are yet available to irrigation." The writer seemed to be describing the Promised Land: "The Magic Valley extends upstream through 70 miles of intensively cultivated land, dotted by beautiful modern homes.... Paralleling the river, 16 cities almost connect their outskirts along the 70 miles of shady avenues" (December 9, 1932).

The seventy-mile stretch of shady avenues was bracketed by the city of Brownsville in the south and upstream by Mission, "the city of grapefruit fame," as the enthusiastic telegrapher labeled it. These two cities, and the other fourteen between them, had been carved out of the old porciones and other lands granted by Spain or Mexico to the early settlers from

1767 to the mid-1830s, according to Florence Johnson Scott. Mission, for example, was founded on part of Porción 56 of the Reynosa jurisdiction, while Donna was located on La Blanca, a Mexican grant, and Mercedes on the Spanish Llano Grande Grant (168–169). In the second half of the nineteenth century, the ownership of these land grants had begun to pass from the Original Grantees or their descendants to Anglo-Americans who came to South Texas after 1848 and, particularly, after the Civil War. These new owners acquired interests in the old land grants by legal and extralegal means and established ranches, becoming part of the ruling class, sometimes by marrying into Mexican landowning families, as was the case with Mifflin Kenedy, who married Petra Vela (Alonzo 115). However, the arrival of the railroads to the Lower Rio Grande Valley at the turn of the twentieth century brought a different type of immigrant (as they were called) to the area. These newcomers were land speculators, large-scale growers, and small farmers, and they changed the physical and human landscape of the Rio Grande Valley (Montejano 159).

An example of the new type of Anglo immigrant to South Texas was Thomas Jefferson Hooks, who in 1902 established La Blanca Agricultural Company after buying twenty-three thousand acres of land fronting the river (the original grant of the same name had contained twenty-four thousand acres). Part of this land Hooks gave to his divorced, twenty-one-year-old daughter, Donna Hooks Fletcher, who established the Alameda Ranch and ran "a successful butter business." A town was founded in 1904, which in 1907 became a depot for the St. Louis, Brownsville and Mexico Railway and was given the name Donna, after Hooks's daughter, who also became its postmistress (Garza, "Donna," 2:678).

However, to the Mexican population of the area, the town of Donna was named after a woman called Doña Beatriz. In 1986, when Lori B. McVey interviewed my kinsman José de la Garza in Weslaco, Texas, he recollected that in 1916, when he was six years old, his uncle had lived "near us in Doña Beatrice [sic] (today known as Donna, Texas)" (McVey, *Guerrero Viejo*, 47). It appears that both versions of the name are accurate, for by 1912 the town had been divided into Donna and East Donna, and East Donna, "the Mexican side of town[,] had a post office named Beatriz, after Beatriz Hooks, from 1912 to 1916" (Garza, "Donna," 2:678). This partition of Donna into a Mexican side and an Anglo side was not unique but was repeated in other Valley communities. However, in Donna it also raised the interesting possibility that "Doña Beatriz" was Hooks's Mexican (second) wife and that the two Donnas represented his bifurcated domestic life.

This pattern of divided towns into Mexican and Anglo sectors was described by David Montejano, using Weslaco as an example. Weslaco had allocated the area north of the railroad tracks to "industrial complexes and Mexican residences and business establishments while that to the south was reserved for the residences and businesses of the Anglos" (167). This was the ugly side of the Magic Valley, the imposition by the newly arrived Anglos of a rigid separation between the two ethnic groups that relegated Mexicans to agricultural labor and to the "wrong side of the tracks." On the other hand, the Anglos did not constitute a completely homogeneous group. There were poor and rich among them, large-scale growers and small and even tenant farmers; and each segment had a slightly different attitude toward the native population of South Texas, even if they all looked down on the Mexicans. To the large growers the Mexicans were undesirable but necessary to pick their crops, while to the poor Anglos, who tried to make their living as tenant farmers, the Mexicans were undesirable competition. Only the merchants had any incentive to view Mexicans in a favorable light. Montejano describes this relationship between the two groups, saying: "The merchant-customer relation moved Anglo merchants to behave in a friendly manner in their everyday contact with Mexicans.... Mexicans, in short, were a clientele to be protected and sheltered" (240).

Irineo de la Garza Jr. had inserted himself into this economic arrangement and, perhaps, had stirred up animosities among the Anglo merchants with whom he competed for Mexican customers. Nevertheless, Fabio wanted to follow in his footsteps. The promise of economic growth must have been great for Irineo and Fabio to undertake such thorny ventures. The Valley, as it was simply called, certainly seemed so fertile as to need only the scattering of financial seed to bring forth the irrigation that would make the desert bloom. It was a simple formula to create new, prosperous communities, as a representative of the railroads told the readers of the *Laredo Times*. All it needed, he said, was for some local people to "get together for a stock company, purchase a large tract of land, put in a large irrigation plant, then cut up the land in different acreages and announce to the world that [the land] was for sale." He further predicted, "This will be the nucleus of big things to follow" (February 12, 1913). In spite of the postwar slump, the South Texas brush country was already blooming as a result of irrigation projects and immigration from the northern United States, and the de la Garza cousins were among the few natives of the region who seemed poised to benefit from the prosperity that was just around the corner.

In the meantime, while Fabio waited for business to rebound in South Texas, his father struggled to adapt to the difficult economic situation in northern Mexico. The revolutionary decade between 1910 and 1920 had devastated the cattle industry there, and efforts to restock the ranches, which began after 1920, were hampered by several factors mentioned by Manuel A. Machado Jr. in *The North Mexican Cattle Industry, 1910–1975*. These factors included "continued though reduced incidence of revolutionary activity, smuggling and bandit depredations" (29–30). Additionally, there was the fear of expropriation of land by the government, since one of the driving forces of the Revolution had been the breakup of large holdings, or *latifundios*, and the redistribution of land. These difficulties did not destroy ranching in the Villas del Norte, for ranching was a way of life there rather than purely an economic activity. However, it added another degree of uncertainty to an already uncertain livelihood.

Grandfather Lorenzo was a rancher by marriage (his wife had inherited half of her father's ranch), not by tradition. Perhaps because of this, his approach to ranching had always been more rational than instinctual. For example, among his books I found a treatise on breaking horses, a skill that most ranchers acquired by practice and not by reading. He also kept a scrapbook of newspaper articles on agricultural topics, such as the benefits of various kinds of forage. By this same intellectual process he realized that ranching had to be supplemented by other sources of income, such as commerce. In the new economic landscape of Mexico in the 1920s, he became a veritable one-man international conglomerate, dealing in insurance, banking, and energy—on a small scale, of course.

For example, the insurance business that Grandfather dealt in was the sale of life insurance policies issued by the Woodmen of the World of Omaha, Nebraska. The company's full name was "Sovereign Camp, Woodmen of the World," and the policyholders were each addressed in correspondence as "Esteemed Sovereign," unless they held a higher rank. The Guerrero "camp" was designated as "Hidalgo, number 7," and Lorenzo de la Garza was the "Cónsul Comandante." My maternal great-uncle Gilberto Pérez was the "Sovereign Secretary," undoubtedly in charge of correspondence. Both men, who were close friends, apparently sold policies and collected premiums, which they remitted to John T. Yates, company secretary, in Omaha. They also handled transactions for the local policyholders, such as loans against the policy value. The company was structured as a fraternal organization, and members signed their correspondence "Fraternally yours." When a policyholder died, his beneficiaries received the proceeds of the policy, as well as a grave marker made of stone carved to resemble split logs and stumps. Even today, when visiting the cemeteries of the old and the new towns (Guerrero Viejo and Guerrero Nuevo), one still comes across these distinctive headstones that mark the resting places of those insured by the Woodmen of the World in the 1920s and 1930s.

The decision by the Woodmen of the World to sell life insurance policies in Mexico in the 1920s was proof either that the company possessed extraordinary optimism or that Mexico had surmounted the era of violence and was now open for business again. The latter view was perhaps premature. In the decade between 1910 and 1920 Mexico's population had dropped by nearly one million (from 15.2 to 14.3 million). According to Adolfo Gilly, revolutionary violence had not been solely responsible for the population decline. Contributing factors had been a decrease in the birth rate, the refugee exodus to the United States, and the influenza epidemic of 1918 to 1919 (333–334). Still, revolutionary violence had not been completely stamped out yet in the 1920s. It flared up again in 1923 with the short-lived rebellion of Adolfo de la Huerta, the former interim president of Mexico (following Carranza's assassination in 1920), who revolted against Alvaro Obregón, his old comrade in arms who had won the presidency in 1920 but refused to anoint de la Huerta as his successor.

In addition to lingering political instability, in the 1920s Mexico had to cope with economic woes that mirrored the postwar slump in the United States, with the added complications of government debt resulting from the prolonged Revolution. In northern Mexico there was only one bright spot in the business community, according to Alex M. Saragoza, and it was Mexico's first brewery, the Cervecería Cuauhtémoc of Monterrey, Nuevo León, and the bottle factory that serviced the brewery (127). The de la Garza brothers were apparently adept at spotting opportunities for financial security. Vidal, Lorenzo's older brother who had studied medicine and had opened a medical practice and a pharmacy in their old hometown of Agualeguas, Nuevo León, had a son who had followed in his father's footsteps in medicine. Instead of being a country doctor, though, Vidal's son had established himself in Monterrey, where he held the position of medical inspector at the Escuela Politécnica (Polytechnic School) sponsored by the brewery's Department of Physical and Intellectual Culture for the children of its employees.

However, away from a large city such as Monterrey, with its opportunities for professional employment, Lorenzo did the best he could for his own children. In addition to helping Fabio establish himself in South Texas, Lorenzo was instrumental in finding a position for his oldest son, Lorenzo Jr., with the customs service in Guerrero, where the young man became the post accountant. It was surely no coincidence that the chief administrator at the aduana was Don Gilberto Pérez, Papá Lorenzo's friend, the "Esteemed Sovereign Secretary" of the local "camp" of the Woodmen of the World and the young Lorenzo's godfather. Godfathers were supposed to look after their *ahijados*, and Don Gilberto did right by his.

Still, as remote from the centers of power and finance as he was, Lorenzo somehow managed to participate, even if on a small scale, in the areas that were changing Mexico in the 1920s, such as banking and finance. Lorenzo had maintained for some time an account with the venerable Banco de Londres y México; British-owned, it was one of the few banks that had survived since the 1860s to the second decade of the twentieth century (Hart 139). During that time, it had come to be one of the nation's largest creditors and, by default, Mexico's national bank. After the Revolution, as Mexico's leaders tried to put the nation's financial affairs in order, it became imperative to establish a central bank to issue a national currency with which to pay foreign claimants and make modern economic life possible. Once again, the Mexican government turned to the Banco de Londres y México and asked it to serve as the issuer of shares in the newly created Banco de México, and it did so.

On September 1, 1925, the Banco de México became a reality, and on the following September 24, Lorenzo wrote to the Banco de Londres y México in Mexico City in reply to its letter of September 18. Responding to the bank's offer to purchase for him "Acciones clase 'B' del Banco de México, S.A." (Class B shares in the Banco de México, Inc.), he enclosed a check for $495.00 (in U.S. dollars) drawn on a bank in Laredo, Texas, undoubtedly the First National Bank, where his nephew José Guadalupe de la Garza (Cándido de la Garza's son) was employed. In his letter, Lorenzo added that he estimated the sum in dollars to be the equivalent of one thousand pesos in Mexican gold. With that amount, he instructed the Banco de Londres y México to purchase ten Class B shares in the new Banco de México and to mail the share certificates to him.

Lorenzo continued his correspondence with the Banco de Londres y México throughout the 1920s and into the early 1930s, usually on matters relating to interest payments on his deposits there or on bonds issued by that institution. The correspondence reveals that the amount he had invested through the bank was substantial for the times. In the year 1922, for example, he had acquired six *certificados primitivos* (original certificates) issued by the bank. In August of 1931 he wrote to the bank, itemizing amounts of unpaid interest that he claimed were owed to him since 1922. The total sum involved principal and interest and amounted to 13,400.00 pesos in bonds of the Deuda Bancaria, or foreign debt repayment bonds, on which both the bank and the government paid interest.

By investing in the Deuda Bancaria, Lorenzo undoubtedly felt that he was doing his patriotic duty, as well as putting his money safely to work. By 1920, when Alvaro Obregón assumed the presidency, Mexico's economy was in shambles, especially after the chaos of 1914–1915, when "contending military factions precipitated military disorder by uncontrolled issues of currency" (Gilly 336). Foreign investors, especially from the United States, demanded compensation for losses they had suffered during the 1910–1920 violence in mining, oil, railroads, land, and bonds (the last now worthless). They pressured the U.S. government to withhold recognition of the Obregón government unless they were compensated for their losses. Obregón's government, in turn, needed funds to reestablish a functioning country and did not have them.

Obregón therefore needed foreign recognition to secure foreign loans to restart the country, and the only way to obtain both — recognition and loans — was to begin a long process of negotiations with the foreign investors, who were led by Thomas W. Lamont of J. P. Morgan (Hall 84–85). These negotiations led to an agreement known in Mexico as the Acuerdos de la Huerta-Lamont (the "Huerta" after Adolfo de la Huerta, Obregón's then finance minister and later rival), by which Mexico recognized its foreign debt and agreed to repay it (Pazos 119). The Mexican government, acting through banks like the Banco de Londres y México, then issued bonds bought by Mexican citizens to help their country pay its debts to foreign investors. Placing funds with the government may give an investor a sense of security, but it can also be difficult to retrieve one's money from the government's coffers. In August of 1947, Lorenzo attempted to collect on his last coupon of the Deuda Bancaria by writing directly to the Treasury Department (Secretaría de Hacienda y Crédito Público), which responded some six weeks later and, in typical bureaucratic fashion, returned his coupons, saying they could not pay on them because Lorenzo had failed to submit the bonds themselves. If he did so and managed to collect, it may have been one of the last things he did, for he died in January of 1948. After his death, there still remained among his papers stubs evidencing his shares of the Deuda Bancaria.

The Banco de México, being a national central bank, soon opened branches throughout the important population centers of the country, including Nuevo Laredo, Tamaulipas, and Lorenzo, not surprisingly, transacted much of his business there. Soon he was acting as a *corresponsal*, or correspondent, in Guerrero for the Nuevo Laredo branch, as well as receiving dividends from the same bank. A letter from him to that branch, dated January 18, 1928, makes reference to "collections that you have placed in my hands" (*cobros que se han servido encomendarme*) from local merchants, as well as inquiring about payment of the previous year's dividends. His connection with the Banco de México was sufficiently tangible that he felt justified to mention it on his letterhead. His business letterhead in the 1920s read: "Lorenzo de la Garza, C. Guerrero, Tamaulipas. Casa Establecida en Negocios Desde 1890. Corresponsalía del Banco de México, S.A." (Business Firm Established Since 1890. Correspondent of the Banco de Mexico).

Lorenzo's interest in banks extended to smaller, regional institutions, such as the Banco de Coahuila, which, unfortunately for Lorenzo, was in liquidation on April 2, 1928, when he wrote to inquire about his dividend. However, the bank must have reorganized, because I remember my aunts (Lorenzo's daughters) still receiving minuscule dividend payments from it in the 1970s.

I do not know if my grandfather's interest in banking led him to collecting coins and currencies of all sorts, but it appears that his banking activities put him in the way of receiving currency as part of enacting government regulations. It was in connection with this function that he received (and preserved) a decree from President Plutarco Elías Calles, dated June 27, 1928, regarding the withdrawal from circulation of silver and bronze coins minted from 1918 to 1920. Those coins were to be exchanged for "current currency" (*moneda actual*) by the Banco de México at any of its branches, including, presumably, the correspondent houses, such as Lorenzo's. The copy of the decree is stamped as having been received and acknowledged on July 16.

Perhaps Lorenzo's stint as a tax collector for the Carranza government during the chaotic 1915–1916 period led him to accumulate not only silver coins minted and restamped by the various revolutionary factions— which at least had the intrinsic value of the metal—but also the worthless *bilimbiques*, or paper currency, issued by Carranza's forces before they prevailed. Perhaps my grandfather kept the paper chits as a curiosity—when most people could not wait to get rid of them—or as a reminder that political chaos produces worthless money. The second view would explain why he also collected a large number of paper bills issued by various German government entities during that country's hyperinflation of the 1920s. On the other hand, Lorenzo seemed to be a natural collector, for he also collected stamps, and among his letters was a carbon copy of one sent to London, England, inquiring about a particular album and individual stamps, offering to provide in exchange some samples from Mexico.

However, during this hectic political period of the 1920s, Papá Lorenzo's primary business activity was not banking but dealing in oil concessions. Ever since the enactment of the Mining Law of 1884 had reversed the centuries-old rule that reserved the mineral rights for the sovereign, foreign investors had flocked to Mexico to exploit its vast mineral resources. With the turn of the twentieth century, oil became increasingly important for military and industrial purposes, and British and American investors began exploring for and producing Mexican oil, mostly along the coast of the Gulf of Mexico. Exploration activity, though, also occurred inland, including around Guerrero. References to the Compañía Carbonífera y Petrolera de Ciudad Guerrero appear among Lorenzo's papers, indicating that the company had signed a lease with area landowners to explore a tract known as La Bola as far back as May 22, 1909. However, the revolutionary turbulence of the following decade halted exploration in the area near Guerrero. When the oil prospectors returned, they faced the risk, not of armed rebellion, but of a change in the laws under which they operated.

In 1917, Mexico had adopted a new constitution that caused consternation among oil and mining companies because of its Article 27, under which ownership of the minerals reverted to the nation and put all the previous leases and concessions in doubt. Additionally, under a decree issued in 1918 by President Venustiano Carranza, "[p]rivate parties were required to apply for a government concession if they wished to continue drilling" (Hall 19). This rule applied whether the leases in question dated from before May 1, 1917—the date when the constitution became effective—or from later.

These legislative actions by the Mexican government upset American oil investors but did not completely deter them from continuing to look for oil in Mexico. One of these prospectors even showed up in Guerrero, trying to revive the old lease of the Compañía Carbonífera y Petrolera in La Bola tract. The prospector was a John Robert Porter from Peabody, Kansas, and he later leased additional land in Porción 13 on the Río Salado near Guerrero. Porter, undoubtedly realizing the legal and linguistic obstacles that he faced in acquiring and maintaining oil leases in Mexico, sought the help of local facilitators. These turned out to be Lorenzo de la Garza and his close friend Rafael San Miguel, a former school inspector known as Profesor San Miguel in the Guerrero and Zapata, Texas, areas, where he was highly respected, having married into the prominent landowning Cuéllar family and having developed oil leasing expertise. Throughout the 1920s Papá Lorenzo and Profesor San Miguel submitted petitions to validate their client's oil claims to the appropriate authorities in Mexico City or visited the capital to plead in person on his behalf. In today's terms, they were lobbyists representing American oil interests. However, it must be clarified that they represented independent prospectors and not major oil companies. In addition, the two men also found themselves representing the landowners who had signed leases with Porter, since Porter's loss would also be theirs, should the government decree that the minerals belonged solely to the nation and not to individuals, as it eventually did in 1938.

In the twenty years leading to the Expropiación Petrolera of 1938 (the nationalization of the petroleum industry), various laws were enacted, attempting to reconcile the rights acquired by private entities with Article 27 of the Constitution of 1917. In this climate of legislative uncertainty, Lorenzo and San Miguel mobilized all their persuasive skills on behalf of their client. To be in close touch with the center of power, Profesor San Miguel installed himself in Mexico City for months at a time at the imposing Hotel Regis, which retained its cachet until it was destroyed by the catastrophic earthquake that struck Mexico City in 1985. The hotel stationery, of which the professor made free use for his correspondence with his partner in Guerrero, boasted in Spanish and English that it was located "in the heart of the city" and that it had 300 rooms and 280 baths, "with every other modern convenience," and stated definitively that it was "the Place for Foreigners."

San Miguel would report from the capital to Lorenzo in Guerrero on the status of their projects, which usually moved at glacial speed through the various government departments. The term *demora*, or "delay," appears frequently in their correspondence, as in a letter from San Miguel to Lorenzo dated May 6, 1930, from the Hotel Regis, in which San Miguel remarks that a change in personnel at the federal petroleum offices, particularly in the legal department, would cause "una perjudicialísima demora en el despacho de los negocios" (a most prejudicial delay in the transacting of business). However, having friends in high places, or at least in the right places, could speed up matters, as San Miguel explains in the same letter. Their file, according to San Miguel, might get an expedited review in the hands of a good friend, although the friend, with all his good will, was still "un poquito flojo" (a little lazy).

Occasionally, and in spite of the various activities — personal and business — that kept Lorenzo in the Guerrero area, he felt compelled to travel to Mexico City to better represent his clients, especially if he was acquainted with a helpful government official. Such was the case in June of 1929, when Lorenzo carried a letter of introduction from Felipe Canales, the undersecretary of the department of Gobernación (Internal Affairs) to the secretary of Industria, Comercio y Trabajo (Industry, Commerce and Labor), which oversaw petroleum-related affairs. The letter read that "el señor Lorenzo de la Garza, buen amigo mío" (Mr. Lorenzo de la Garza, a good friend of mine) wished to discuss a certain matter with Secretary Ramón P. de Negri, and he (the writer) would greatly appreciate it if the secretary would help Mr. de la Garza inasmuch as it was in his power to do so. The business matter is not specified, and it could have been related to the same Porción 13 that occupied his partner, San Miguel, and John Robert Porter, but it could also have related to a client that Lorenzo represented by himself, the Watchorn Oil and Gas Company of Oklahoma City. The company had been founded by Robert Watchorn, an Englishman, who was its president. Coincidentally, John Robert Porter was "Vice-President and Superintendent" of the Watchorn Company, and it may have been he who had pointed the company in the direction of the Guerrero drilling prospects by conveying some of his rights there to Watchorn.

Lorenzo's dealings with this company encompassed both acquiring drilling rights from the landowners as well as lobbying government officials to maintain those rights, in light of changing laws and regulations. In addition, he scouted the Guerrero area for available acreage and took leases from landowners and disbursed payments to them, as a telegram from the company, addressed to him and dated October 27, 1926, illustrates: "Kindly draw drafts covering rentals on our leases in Mexico and we will honor them." It was signed by Frank Harper, identified on the company letterhead as secretary-treasurer.

Harper was Lorenzo's contact person at Watchorn, and the two maintained a copious correspondence dating approximately back to 1926. Lorenzo's letters were usually in Spanish, and Harper's communications invariably in English, and in this bilingual fashion they exchanged information for five or six years, the language issue cropping up only when Harper suggested that Lorenzo visit the company's headquarters in Oklahoma City. Originally, Lorenzo had suggested (in a letter of January 26, 1928) a personal meeting in Guerrero or Oklahoma that would allow him to present a report about the lands around Guerrero that Watchorn had under lease ("para suministrarles los informes . . . sobre las tierras de esta Jurisdicción, que tiened Uds. contratadas para exploraciones y explotaciones del subsuelo"). Harper replied on April 21, 1928, proposing: "It will . . . be well if you will come to Oklahoma City at your convenience . . . although I am sorry to say that I do not speak any Spanish." He then added offhandedly, "It may be that you will know how to overcome this difficulty." Lorenzo, however, took the language barrier more seriously, replying on

April 26: "Me preocupa lo que me dice Ud. de no saber nada del idioma español, y como yo nada sé del inglés, respecto de pronunciarlo, ese obstáculo me detiene de realizar dicho viaje" (What you say about not knowing any Spanish worries me, and since I know nothing about spoken English, this obstacle holds me back from making the trip). The inference drawn from Lorenzo's comment is that he was able to read and write English but not speak it, although his estimate of his English abilities was rather optimistic, judging by the letters that he wrote in English, which are a literal translation of Spanish.

Frank Harper eventually solved the language problem by finding "a gentleman who can speak English as well as Spanish." That gentleman had the added advantage of a lawyer father in Mexico City who "might be able to help us regarding our leases, as he is quite familiar with Mexican laws" (May 2, 1928). According to his correspondence, Lorenzo did indeed travel to Oklahoma City in June of 1928, where he met with Harper and, undoubtedly, the interpreter. When he returned to Guerrero, Lorenzo pondered on the best course to follow in order to salvage the leases that Watchorn was at risk of losing, and in subsequent letters he communicated his ideas to the company.

He suggested drafting petitions to be signed by the landowners and submitted to the Department of Industry, Commerce and Labor, asking that the leases be allowed to stand. These petitions would subsequently also be sent to the president of Mexico. This step was not a mere pro forma appeal to the ultimate authority but rather an attempt to tap the goodwill of a fellow Tamaulipan. Due to the residual violence of the Mexican Revolution, Alvaro Obregón, who had been reelected president in June of 1928 (after having previously served from 1920 to 1924), was assassinated a few days after the election. The outgoing president, Plutarco Elías Calles, then arranged for the Congress to name an interim president, and this was the secretary of Internal Affairs and former governor of Tamaulipas, Emilio Portes Gil. Lorenzo was no doubt acquainted with him, and more particularly with his attorney general, Enrique Medina, who was from Guerrero.

The following October, Lorenzo returned to Oklahoma City. On the way there, he mailed home a postcard from Fort Worth, Texas, to Lorenzo Jr., reporting that he had arrived in Fort Worth "a las 8 a.m. y prosigo hoy mismo mi viaje a Oklahoma City" (at 8 a.m. and continue my trip today). He added that San Antonio had been all decked out to receive the visit of ten thousand Legionnaires ("San Antonio estaba engalanadísima ayer con la visita de 10 mil Legionarios"). The trip, as described by Lorenzo, would have taken him from Laredo to Oklahoma City, via San Antonio and Fort Worth, on the International and Great Northern Railway, which traveled from Saint Louis, Missouri, to the border. The trip clearly stirred in him a desire for greater travel in the United States, a yearning that he was able to satisfy a few years later.

Ultimately, the appeals to the Mexican government to recognize the leases owned by Watchorn around Guerrero proved fruitless, due to Watchorn and Porter's earlier failure to make timely application to preserve their rights. It was this very failure that had prompted them to contract with Lorenzo for assistance, but he was unable to resurrect leases that had already expired by action of law. However, in 1929 Watchorn still had hopes to drill on its leases near Guerrero, although these hopes were pinned on one remaining tract, known as the Botello tract, which lay some three miles from a well being drilled by two companies—Emmex and Tamaulipas—on a site known as La Loma del Ajo (Garlic Hill). According to a letter from Lorenzo to Harper on July 8, 1929, there was "great animation" in the area in response to the commencement of drilling by the two companies, the Tamaulipas Company being, in effect, Humble of Houston. Machinery was being transported to the area, and a drilling rig was being erected, Lorenzo informed Harper. Large tanks to hold oil were also being constructed, which implied great optimism for the outcome.

Apparently, the Humble Company of Houston, Texas, had not encountered the legal difficulties with their Mexican oil leases that had plagued Watchorn. However, they must have encountered technical difficulties in drilling this well, because although Lorenzo had reported to Harper on January 27, 1930, that the well on the Loma del Ajo had reached a depth of 2,500 feet and that drilling was to proceed 1,000 feet deeper to find out if there was any oil in that horizon ("para cerciorarse si hay o no petróleo en esta demarcación"), Harper was still asking Lorenzo on November 11, 1930, to "try to find how deep the Humble Company is on the well which they are drilling, and also whether they have any showings of oil or gas at any time." During the following four months, the Humble Company, as well as the Watchorn principals and the population of Guerrero, were on tenterhooks while various contradictory reports floated around the works on the Loma del Ajo: after reaching 8,000 feet in depth, the drillers had found gas, or water, or oil, or nothing. Several times it appeared that the well was to be abandoned and the drilling equipment removed, only to have drilling recommence. Finally, in a letter dated April 6, 1931, Lorenzo confirmed the earlier rumors of work stoppage on the Humble well. The derrick was being dismantled, and twenty-two large trucks with heavy machinery were en route to Texas by the road to Laredo, since the suspension bridge between Guerrero and Zapata could not withstand the weight involved.

The first attempt to find oil or gas in the area surrounding Guerrero was at an end, to the great disappointment of the landowners, who had had great hopes for a source of income that would buffer the insecurities of cattle raising, as well as the general hope of providing employment for the poor, as Lorenzo remarked in a letter of March 18, 1931, to Harper. After seeing Humble's failure, the Watchorn Oil and Gas Company decided to pull out of Guerrero and severed its connection with Lorenzo as well. In a letter of May 2, 1931, addressed to Lorenzo at his post office box in Zapata, Frank Harper thanked "Dear Senor de la Garza" for his recent correspondence and regretted the outcome of the Humble well: "It would have meant so much for all concerned, and particularly for the landowners and those who were interested in the royalty." Harper also thanked Lorenzo for "the good work you did for us from time to time." This work "from time to time" had nonetheless yielded a regular income for Lorenzo. For approximately three years (since July of 1928), he had received a monthly stipend of one hundred dollars (no laughable sum in Mexico of the 1920s), plus expenses from the Watchorn company, and this was now at an end. Frank Harper's parting words were gracious, telling Lorenzo: "We feel that you did everything that was possible, and that you always worked for our best interests." But, he added in no uncertain terms and in his own handwriting, "we do not wish to do anything more."

Since its beginning, the decade of the 1920s proved to be eventful for Lorenzo de la Garza and his family in both the public and the personal spheres. Perhaps with renewed hope in the political process after the election of Alvaro Obregón as president in 1920, Lorenzo participated again in local elections, as he had done in 1912. In the 1923 municipal elections in Guerrero, he was chosen for a place on the *cabildo*, or city council, as a *síndico* for the period of 1924–1925. In La antigua Revilla, de la Garza describes the cabildo in Guerrero as consisting of a *presidente municipal* (mayor), three *regidores* (aldermen), and a "síndico, en funciones de Ministerio Público" (23). This last office would translate as "prosecutor" or "municipal attorney," although it clearly did not call for a law degree. The vote canvassing by the Junta General de Escrutinio, or canvassing board, declared Lorenzo elected síndico with 415 votes on December 3, 1923. At home he had a full house with five children, ranging from his firstborn and namesake, already in his twenties and employed in the customs service, to the youngest, Rafael, who attended elementary school at the Escuela de

Varones "Miguel Hidalgo," the boys' school located next to the church, and three daughters who came between the sons. His second son, Fabio, was the only one out of the nest, trying to establish himself in business in the fast-growing "Magic" Rio Grande Valley of Texas.

In the summer of 1925, fourteen-year-old Nela compiled a school graduation album that she titled "Recuerdos de mi infancia" (Childhood Memories), with poems and essays related to her school days. Barely out of school, Nela was already filled with nostalgia for the friends and the teachers that she had left behind. In this notebook she also included a genealogy of her family, giving the birthdates of her parents and siblings. She noted that her mother, Esther Peña, had been born on December 26, 1876, and at the bottom of the page she added: "Mamá murió el 19 de Sep. de 1924—a las 6 de la tarde" (Mamá died on September 19, 1924—at six in the afternoon). What Nela did not mention, although it could be garnered from the list of her siblings' birthdates, was that September 19 was also the birthday of her sister Esther, the middle daughter and her mother's namesake. Esther Peña de la Garza was not yet forty-eight when she died, leaving six children orphaned, the oldest twenty-six years of age and the youngest a ten-year-old.

Excavating family history often carries the risk of discovering unsettling facts (although usually nothing so dramatic as finding out that an ancestor was hanged as a horse thief, which was not the case here). Perhaps because my paternal grandmother died some twenty years before I was born, she was always a shadowy figure to me. The distance in time, though, did not fully explain why her daughters (the aunts who raised me) seldom spoke about her, and this silence may have also inhibited me from inquiring about her. Still, I must have asked at some point about the cause of her death, because I was left with the impression that she had contracted typhoid fever and died of it. This explanation seemed plausible because the disease was common at the time, often caused by drinking contaminated water, which could happen when the water supply was an *aljibe*, or cistern, as it was in my grandparents' house. I did not give further thought to my grandmother's death until, wanting to verify facts for this work, I obtained a copy of her death certificate. I was shocked to learn from this document that the official cause of death was listed as *consunción* (consumption). The time of her death was just as Nela had written it down: six o'clock in the afternoon of September 19, 1924.

It is difficult to believe that Mamá Esther died of tuberculosis in the late summer of 1924, when only two years earlier she had written to Fabio in Texas that she was well and planning to spend the summer at the ranch.

However, an article in the *Journal of the American Medical Association* that was published in June of 1905 (and reprinted one hundred years later) stated that many of the early symptoms of the disease were difficult to recognize, although "it is in individuals of special physical constitution that tuberculosis is most likely to occur." These individuals were "underweight and lacking in normal thoracic development and respiratory power" ("Early Diagnosis" 2804). The latter symptom is impossible to determine from a passport photo taken around 1920, but the same photo shows Esther, although only in her mid-forties, looking thin and what can only be described as careworn.

The recent (2005) article in JAMA states that "[a]t the turn of the [twentieth] century tuberculosis was the leading cause of death in the United States" (Barclay 2696). Among Mexicans in the United States the disease reached epidemic proportions, and in the 1920s San Antonio, the city with the second-largest number of Mexican residents, had the highest rate of tuberculosis among cities with a population of more than 100,000 (Balderrama and Rodríguez 48). Obviously, there was also a high incidence of tuberculosis in Guerrero and the other Villas del Norte (Great-uncle Lucio García had lost his twenty-one-year-old bride to consumption in 1911), in spite of the hot and dry climate and the uncrowded living conditions, which would seem unpropitious for the development of the disease. Nonetheless, tuberculosis, although common, still carried a stigma, which may explain Esther's family's reticence to discuss her death. It also explains why thinness, now fashionable, was viewed with suspicion one hundred years ago, since weight loss was one of the most visible signs of the disease.

That Nela had noted the precise moment of her mother's death in her journal indicates that Mamá Esther died at home and not in some sanitarium, such as existed in the Southwest of the United States, where patients were sent "more out of fear of contagious disease than out of concern for the patients they housed" (Barclay 2696). However, out of concern for the children, Lorenzo must have isolated his wife's sickroom. The house where they lived (and where she died, according to the death certificate) on Calle Jiménez was certainly large enough to do so and was divided by the *pasillo*, or entryway, into two wings. Perhaps this physical separation prepared the three daughters for their mother's death, and it may have even blunted the loss for ten-year-old Rafael. Esther seems to have faded away from their lives, leaving behind more of a vague sadness than deep grief in her survivors. Perhaps in that household there was room for only one forceful personality, and that was Lorenzo, the father.

After his wife's death, it may have come as a shock to the widower to realize that he did not even have a likeness of her to remember her by (except for a passport photo with her youngest child). To remedy this glaring lack, he wrote a letter on December 25, 1924, to N. W. Clarkhoff Photo Finishing in Chicago, Illinois, stating that he had enclosed "a small photography" (literal translation of *fotografía*), which he desired "amplified" to sixteen by twenty inches, "made in cloth." He wanted "a good work . . . [an] exact similar face," in crayon, sepia, or oil. If it was to be in oil, he gave "herewith particulars as following: Color of eyes—Dark Brown. . . . Face [meaning skin tone]—Pearl [*aperlado*, meaning neither fair nor dark] Hair—Gray (black and white)." He added that he enclosed $5.00, presumably as a deposit, and asked to be informed when the work would be ready and what the total price would be.

The letter to the photography studio in Chicago was notated at the bottom left of the page as having been typed by "f. g.," undoubtedly Fabio de la Garza, who was probably home for the Christmas holidays. When she died, Esther may not have known whether her second son was finally "established in commerce" in Texas, as Lorenzo had told his correspondent in Oklahoma City in early 1927. The only indication that I have found as to when he opened his store in Raymondville, Texas, is a holiday card from that city to his sister Ofelia, dated January 1, 1925, wishing her "un feliz y próspero año nuevo" (a happy and prosperous new year).

After several years of considering the various young communities in the Lower Rio Grande Valley, Fabio had cast his lot with Raymondville, which, like many of the neighboring settlements, owed its origins to the arrival of the railroad in 1904. It was named after E. B. Raymond, a foreman on the King Ranch who, representing the Raymond Town and Improvement Company and the Kleberg Town and Improvement Company, laid out town lots in several Spanish land grants in what was then Cameron and Hidalgo counties. After several changes of boundaries, the present-day Willacy County was organized in 1921, with Raymondville as the county seat.

Raymondville is physically isolated from the population clusters that run from Mission to Brownsville. It is closer, as the crow flies, to the Gulf of Mexico than to the Rio Grande, and its development lagged behind that of the rest of the Valley by several years. In 1915, for example, Donna had a population of 1,500, whereas Raymondville did not reach 1,800 until 1929, according to *The New Handbook of Texas* (Addington 5:460). However, just as in the rest of the Valley, farming and ranching were the principal "industries" in Willacy County, according to a county history prepared in 1937 under the auspices of the Works Progress Administration (*Willacy County Scrapbook* 2). The same source noted that orange seeds were first planted in the area around 1885 by "a Mexican ranchman named Cantu" who had brought the seed oranges from Montemorelos, Nuevo León (Montemorelos is famous for its oranges throughout Mexico).

Commercial farming began with the arrival of the railroad, which also brought the Anglo immigrants from the north. Soon, cucumbers, watermelons, and, particularly, Bermuda onions were being shipped out of the Raymondville area to supply the demand for produce in the rest of the country. With commendable humor, Raymondville adopted the lowly onion as its emblem, and soon after there followed the Onion Festival with an Onion Queen and a royal court presiding over carnivals and parades. When the Onion Festival was in full swing—in early April—its events took up most of the space in the *Willacy County News*, along with references to anyone even remotely involved with the festivities. However, a reader would have been hard-pressed to find a single Spanish surname mentioned in the newspaper unless the item related to crime. This was so, even though "Texas Mexicans" constituted about 40 percent of the county's population in the mid-1930s (*Willacy County Scrapbook* 4).

Raymondville, like its sister communities in the Valley, maintained a system of apartheid in regard to Mexicans, with Mexicans restricted to living only in designated areas, as a story in an unidentified newspaper clipping included in the *Willacy County Scrapbook* made clear. According to the news item, which was dated July 27, 1931, three Willacy County officers (W. F. Haywood, Precinct 2 constable; his deputy, Francisco Cisneros; and José Guzmán, the county jailer) had been patrolling the Raymondville *Mexican section* (emphasis added) when they encountered a man who had been arrested earlier for bootlegging (and presumably set free). The bootlegger had opened fire on them, killing Haywood and Cisneros and wounding Guzmán.

Perhaps because of its isolation, Willacy County had a particularly dark history, and the *Scrapbook* could not avoid including snippets about the "Raymondville Peonage Cases," which revealed the shocking employment practices in that corner of the state. A clipping from another unidentified newspaper, with the dateline of Corpus Christi, Texas, February 5, 1927, reported briefly that Sheriff Raymond Teller, a former deputy sheriff, a justice of the peace, and two other men had been convicted in federal court of peonage, or as the paper explained: "These men were charged in connection with the alleged working of boys arrested on vagrancy charges by the Willacy County peace officers." David Montejano provides greater detail about the particular incident that gave rise to the federal charges, pointing out that the boys in question were Anglos who had stumbled into a well-established forced labor system whereby the Willacy County authorities furnished the area farmers with Mexican field labor during harvest time. Workers who refused to work for the Anglo farmers under the conditions and the pay offered were arrested and convicted of vagrancy charges and put on the fields as convict labor until they had worked off their fines. In addition, laborers could not leave the county as long as they were needed unless they had passes signed by a local farmer, allowing them to travel. Montejano adds that "generally only Mexicans ended up being 'hired' through the Willacy County system" (203). It was only when two Anglos fell into the labor trap that a local attorney "who was 'politically hostile' to the sheriff" brought the situation to the attention of the federal authorities, who then prosecuted and convicted the county officials (Montejano 204).

This was the environment in which Fabio de la Garza decided to "establish himself in commerce." If, by 1925, he had already settled in Raymondville, he must have been aware of the labor practices to which his compatriots were subjected, but perhaps he felt that they at least deserved to have an alternative to the Anglo-owned shops for purchasing their staples. It must be noted, though, that the peonage system involved mostly seasonal workers brought from Mexico (like the braceros some twenty years later), which did not make the system less evil but deprived the workers of local support. The majority of the "Texas Mexicans" in the Valley probably did not identify closely with the unfortunates brought from the interior of Mexico because the former, although displaced by the Anglos, retained the pride of having descended from the Original Grantees and of having a sense of place. Among this group, Fabio was well known and apparently popular, as surviving correspondence indicates. For example, in a postcard to his sister Ofelia, dated November 4, 1927, he relates that he had attended a Halloween costume "ball" ("un gran baile de disfraces") in Weslaco, dressed as a Spaniard ("vestido de español") and masked. He added that there had been hundreds of guests ("había cientos de concurrentes") at the party, all in costume.

Fabio's postcard may have been in response to a gentle chiding from Ofelia (his twenty-one-year-old sister, who at eighteen had been forced into the role of housekeeper after her mother's death), reminding him that he had overlooked sending flowers for November 2, the Day of the Dead. This supposition is credible because his note opened with an apology for not having sent the floral wreaths that he had prepared, due to having been ill. He negated the apology by speculating that his illness had been caused by too much partying on Halloween ("Yo creo que de esa desvelada me enfermé"). These comments and descriptions of festive excesses were, at the very least, insensitive because since his mother's death three years before, his family had added another grave to the cemetery.

Rafael, the youngest de la Garza child, had died the previous year, drowned in the Río Salado. On the first day of July of 1926, the twelve-year-old had left his house to go swimming in the river with his friends. As he walked away, he was singing (according to his father) a song that was also a prayer in that scorching, arid land: "Agua le pido a mi Dios" (Water/Rain Is What I Beg from God). A man on horseback saw the struggling boy from the riverbank, but he was too stupid or too cowardly to even throw him a rope to rescue him.

Whereas the wife and mother had slipped away sadly but not unexpectedly, the boy's death was a wrenching blow to all in the family, especially to his father. Rafael had been a lively and mischievous boy, if his fourth-grade report card from 1924 is any indication. In the weekly school report, his teacher, Ernesto Zenteno, gave him a grade of 8 (out of a possible 10) for work and study habits and only a 7 for conduct. His father may not have been able to curb the boy's high spirits, but he did insist that Rafael have perfect school attendance, as the report card, signed by Lorenzo de la Garza as parent, attests to.

Lorenzo's household now consisted only of himself and his three daughters, aged fifteen through twenty. Lorenzo Jr. had married Juana Flores in the summer of 1925, and on August 10, 1926, on the feast of San Lorenzo and the birthdays of Lorenzo Sr. and Fabio, the first grandchild, Elvia Lorenza, was born. Her arrival may have brought a ray of cheer to the grieving family, but the house remained a place of mourning. Photographs of that sad period show Ofelia in mourning black, an apprehensive expression in her eyes, as if bracing herself for the next blow. Her young shoulders were clearly too frail to carry the weight of running the household for her father and her siblings. This weight was not merely metaphorical. Although people like my grandparents were described as having *una situación desahogada* (a comfortable position), which translated to owning land, living in solid stone houses, and not worrying about a paycheck, little thought was given to physical comforts, probably because the lack of these comforts affected mostly the women of the household. On the ranches, it was expected that the owners had one or more hired hands to help with the ranch work, but in town very few households employed servants, the housewives relying mainly on their unmarried daughters for help and perhaps bringing in someone to do the laundry. However, when the wives followed their husbands to the ranch, as Esther wrote of doing in the summer of 1922, even the occasional help they had in town was missing.

Lorenzo was not entirely blind to his young daughters' need for relief from the gloom of prolonged mourning, and he frequently dispatched one or more of them to stay in Raymondville with Fabio. There is a postcard, for example, conveying birthday wishes (April 1, 1927) from a friend in Guerrero to Nela in Raymondville. In Raymondville "the girls" (*las muchachas*), as they were always referred to, fortunately made new friends who wrote to them when they returned to Guerrero. In September of 1927, for example, Ofelia received a postcard sent from a friend in Raymondville to the post office box the family kept in Zapata. It shows a photograph of the Willacy County courthouse, a severe rectangular brick structure with two stories and a basement, sitting in the middle of a desolate square. The friend, who identified the photograph as *la casa corte*, wrote that she was sending the postcard so that Ofelia would have a reminder of Raymondville. The courthouse was obviously an object of civic pride in Raymondville, having been constructed only some five years earlier, and most likely was the only distinctive building in town.

Lorenzo may have had a secondary motive for sending his girls to stay with their brother, in addition to providing distraction for them. They would not only keep house for Fabio but also keep an eye on him. He may have been too much of the young man-about-town for his father's peace of mind. A postcard (clearly the preferred medium of communication at the time) showing a photograph of the Cortez Hotel in Weslaco, Texas, an imposing five-story building, contained a message addressed to "Dear Fabio," dated June 4, 1929. After the salutation in English, the writer—a female—switched to Spanish, hoping that he was doing well, as she was. She informed him that she was "now in Weslaco," implying that such was not always the case, and that she planned to remain there for two weeks. She therefore expected a visit from him and asked him to reply to Box 441. Although she informed him that she expected his visit, she did not specify where she would be. Instead, she proceeded to ask him: "¿Qué te parece de este Hotel? ¿Verdad que está bonito?" (What do you think of this hotel? Isn't it pretty?) The questions could have well been instructions directing Fabio where to find her. Writing in code—so to speak—would have been necessary because anyone could read the message, and any woman wishing to preserve a shred of her reputation would not openly make an assignation with a man in a hotel, even if this was the Roaring Twenties. After all, they lived in provincial South Texas and were part of the Hispanic culture. Fabio's correspondent closed by reiterating that she hoped to see him soon and signed herself "'Tuya' [Yours], Carlota." I did not discover who Carlota was, but she must have meant something to Fabio, or why would he have saved her postcard otherwise?

It appears that the three sisters spent a great part of 1930 in Raymondville, for that year they began keeping an album of snapshots of themselves and their friends in South Texas. Sometimes they would alternate staying with their brother and visiting their relatives in Laredo — on the paternal side the family of Cándido de la Garza (his widow and her children) and their maternal aunt, Francisca Peña, and her children. On September 16, 1930, for example, Ofelia mailed a postcard from Laredo to Nela in Raymondville, reporting that she and Fabio had arrived well, but that she hoped that he had arrived safely in the Valley because heavy storms had developed in Laredo after his departure.

Their father also spent periods of time away from Guerrero in 1930. In mid-March he was in San Antonio with his friend Don Gilberto Pérez, and from there he sent a postcard to Fabio in Raymondville. In his message he remarks that he and Don Gilberto had expected to find Fabio in San Antonio and had inquired about him "por todas partes" (everywhere), without success. It seems probable, then, that they had arranged to meet at some designated place, but Fabio had not shown up. An interesting aside related to this trip, from a social historian's perspective, is the caption on the postcard, which shows the multistory Milam Building in downtown San Antonio. On the back of the photograph, the caption reads: "Milam Bldg., San Antonio, Texas. 21 story commercial office building. Largest reinforced concrete building in the world. First skyscraper completely equipped with air conditioning system."

In August of the same year, Lorenzo took a trip that must have been the culmination of a long-held desire: he went to New York City, and in so doing, he was able to visit the places where his hero Col. Bernardo Gutiérrez de Lara had endeavored to find support for Mexico's independence movement. In a postcard to Nela in Raymondville, dated August 26, 1930, Lorenzo references her letter of the twenty-second and informs her that he might leave New York on the following day, visiting Baltimore, Washington, and Little Rock, Arkansas, on the return trip, the same spots Gutiérrez de Lara visited during his arduous journey from Revilla to Washington to present his credentials before President James Madison in 1811.

It is clear that Lorenzo admired the United States and enjoyed traveling in this country. His visits to Oklahoma City two years earlier had obviously piqued his desire to travel farther inland, but his forays north of the border had begun much earlier. A photograph dated 1906 shows a clean-shaven Lorenzo (he had been fully mustachioed before) and another man (apparently an American) in bathing costumes, sitting on a beach identified as Galveston, Texas. From that visit to the seashore—probably his first—there still survives a magnificent seashell that fascinated me as a child when I was told that if you held it up to your ear, you could hear the roar of the sea within its labyrinth of nacre.

All this family travel back and forth across the border was remarkable for the time, if we recall that the construction of the suspension bridge connecting Guerrero and Zapata across the Rio Grande did not begin until 1928. The bridge was built by private investors—a Lon P. Piper and two partners from San Antonio—at the cost of $80,000 and was not completed until 1931, according to Ted Treviño's recollections (20). Another suspension bridge was constructed in 1929, linking Roma, downriver from Zapata, with its Mexican counterpart, San Pedro (now Ciudad Miguel Alemán, Tamaulipas). Before these structures were built, there were only two bridges across the Rio Grande between Laredo and Brownsville, at these two cities. Crossing the river at any other point was done by chalán, which could accommodate up to ten persons, or "six persons, plus a car," according to old-timers in Zapata (Izaguirre 46).

However, neither the physical barrier of the river nor the immigration restrictions imposed by the United States in 1917 kept the members of the de la Garza family from traveling back and forth across the border, although always legally. With the overdeveloped regard for rules and regulations that seemed a heritable trait in them, they had their photographs taken and obtained border crossing cards as soon as these were required. Their trips across the border were thus duly recorded, as a surviving identity card for Lorenzo Jr. attests. Border manifests from Laredo and Brownsville also show Fabio's multiple entries into Texas in the 1920s and early 1930s. In these he describes himself as a "merchant" and lists his destination as Raymondville, Texas.

These border crossings also required, according to the U.S. immigration regulations of the time, payment of an eight-dollar head tax and a literacy test. According to El Paso writer Leon C. Metz, the tax and the test were meant primarily to keep out riffraff from Europe (coming through Ellis Island and other seaports), but since they were eventually also implemented along the southern border, "they inadvertently slowed legal crossings by Mexicans except for the wealthy" (374). Metz also generalizes that "Mexico had no educated middle class" and that only the very poor and the very rich crossed into the United States, the former illegally to seek work, the latter presumably as tourists (374). However, the statement about the lack of an educated (or at least literate) middle class does not square with the situation along the Rio Grande, particularly the Villas del Norte. Photographs of school groups in Guerrero during the first decades of the twentieth century portray large groups of students with their teachers, evidence that literacy was valued in the region.

As late as the 1920s, though, the U.S. government was less concerned with keeping out people at its borders (unless they might carry disease, and then they were doused with gasoline to forestall this) than it was with keeping out goods or merchandise. According to Lott and Martínez, in *The Kingdom of Zapata*, the Southwest Customs Patrol was created in 1853, only five years after the Treaty of Guadalupe Hidalgo had made the Rio Grande the border between Mexico and the United States. This group consisted of mounted guards who patrolled the banks along the Rio Grande to prevent smuggling. At first the men sent to the Zapata area came from other parts of the country, but they did not last long on the border unless they assimilated into their new culture: "Some [newcomers] came here as mounted customs men, married here, and, having tired of the stringent, dangerous vocation . . . dismounted and never saddled up for another scout" (181). One example of such men who came and stayed was Johnnie Rathmell, who arrived in Zapata County in 1922 and, after serving as a supervisor with the Sanitary Livestock Commission of Texas and as a mounted customs inspector, "unsaddled, married Miss Celia Cuéllar, and just settled down for the rest of his life" (Lott and Martínez 187–188). Rathmell did not actually unsaddle, since he was a rancher, as were most of the population of Zapata County and as his descendants still are.

In the 1920s, after the United States had amended its constitution to ban demon rum from its territory, the main job of the customs patrol was keeping alcohol out of the country. In trying to intercept the importation of alcohol, the customs patrol had to deal, not only with Americans' thirst, but also with the border people's relaxed attitude toward smuggling. This attitude did not mean that the border population was inherently lawless; rather, it meant that the government rules impeded the normal flow of their lives, and like a river that is obstructed, they had to find a way around the obstruction. Américo Paredes explains this situation in *A Texas-Mexican Cancionero*: "When the river became a dividing line instead of a focus for normal activity, it broke apart an area that had once been a unified homeland" (42). And nowhere else was this more true than with trade. As Paredes summarizes it: "One side of the river always had something that was lacking on the other side, and ways were found to get things across without going through the red tape of customs" (41). The smuggler, therefore, not only served a useful function in expediting trade but also became a folk hero who supplied items that were in demand on one side of the river—namely, alcohol and, specifically, tequila. These folk heroes came to be known as *tequileros*, and like the heroes of olden times, they had ballads, or *corridos*, written to commemorate their exploits. One of them, aptly titled "Los tequileros," was reproduced by Paredes in his *Cancionero*. The ballad tells the story of three men from Guerrero who were shot near Zapata, on their way to deliver *tequila anisado* in San Diego, Texas (100–101).

However, Fabio, in Raymondville, was dealing not in tequila but in other, more basic stuff—food and clothing—trying to lure customers by offering them a 10 percent discount on shoes and clothing and selling a twenty-four-pound sack of flour for eighty-three cents. His customers were, as was to be expected, the Mexican laborers who picked crops for the Anglo growers, and he would make his pitch to his compatriots in flyers distributed throughout the community, an advertising method that implied that his customers were literate in Spanish and capable of rational economic behavior. Taking into account that his *marchantes* (customers) were paid only after the harvest and that in the off-season they were very short of cash and needed to economize ("Hemos visto que en estas semanas que faltan para los grandes trabajos, la gente necesita hacer economías"), Fabio announced (in surviving flyers) a two-day sale for a Friday and Saturday, offering not only flour but also shortening ("Manteca—3 lbs.—.40"), sugar, corn, potatoes, coffee, rice, and *chorizo mexicano* at less than a dollar a pound, and customers responded favorably.

He celebrated his success in Raymondville by issuing—undoubtedly to his best customers—commemorative plates painted with colorful fruits or Norman Rockwell–like scenes and a message in gilt lettering: "Un Recuerdo de Fabio de la Garza, Comerciante en Mercancías Generales [A Memento from Fabio de la Garza, General Merchant], Raymondville, Texas, 1929." Even today, the year 1929 is indelibly etched in people's consciousness as the year of the stock market crash and the beginning of the Great Depression. However, we forget that the crisis that devastated Wall Street occurred toward the end of the year and that the market where most people traded was not the stock market but the meat and grocery markets, and these were not immediately affected by the faraway events.

Fabio, not being clairvoyant, did not foresee economic ruin in the near future and expanded his business to a second location. By 1929, when San

Perlita's post office was first established, he was already in the new community, focusing on providing shoes and clothing to his clientele (men's dress shoes, $3.49; ladies' dresses, 99 cents). San Perlita was one of the latecomer instant communities of South Texas, having been created in 1926 by a developer named C. R. Johnson, who named it after his wife, Pyrle Johnson, by bastardizing Spanish ("Perla," being a feminine name should have been preceded by "Santa") and by inventing a saint that did not exist. Although San Perlita was only thirteen miles east of Raymondville and its population did not reach two hundred, Fabio must have felt that it had a bright future apart from Raymondville, since both a highway and the Missouri Pacific Railroad had reached it by 1930. Fabio opened his second store on Saturday, April 6, 1929, according to a surviving flyer in which he announced that the new establishment was located in a brick building made available by "el señor Johnson, dueño de estos lugares" (Mr. Johnson, owner of these places), the self-same C. R. Johnson, who, as developer of San Perlita, was clearly lord and master of those domains. Fabio himself did not live in the "simpática población" (pleasant settlement) of San Perlita (as the flyer described it), but he did maintain a post office box there—Box 295—which his sisters shared, as shown by a surviving postcard dated October 24, 1929, from Francisca de la Garza in Laredo to her cousin Nela in San Perlita.

In spite of the distance between New York and South Texas, the shocks from Wall Street eventually reverberated throughout Main Street in the small towns where Fabio de la Garza had staked his future. Canceled checks from Lorenzo's account at the First National Bank of Laredo show various sums paid to his son in 1929 and 1930. The sums are small, from three to fifty dollars, but a letter dated January 26, 1931, from Lorenzo to Rafael San Miguel Jr. in Zapata directs him to forward two hundred dollars to Fabio. This larger check was drawn on the National City Bank of New York. The inescapable inference from these payments is that Fabio needed frequent infusions of cash for his business, a state of affairs that must have concerned his father.

Although Lorenzo engaged in extensive correspondence and presumably maintained an ample supply of writing paper, natural frugality apparently prompted him to utilize any piece of paper at hand to jot down notes. That must explain why he used the blank backs of tear-away calendars for the years 1928 and 1929 to itemize—in pencil—his assets, as well as each of his five children's share of the family property. In addition to listing the small tract out of El Pedernal Grant in Zapata County and the land in Sabino Seco (San Juan Ranch) in the municipality of Guerrero, both constituting the separate property of Esther Peña at the time of her death, Lorenzo set down for himself a share of seven-twelfths in the Raymondville house ("1 Derecho de 7/12 partes en la casa de Ray"), which was valued at $2,515. His interest in the house amounted to $1,467.06, according to his calculations. Each of his five children also owned one-twelfth of the house in Raymondville. These penciled notations put Fabio's business in a different context: it was a family business and not his alone—or, at least, the house in Raymondville was held in joint ownership with his father and his siblings. The timing of the opening of the business—probably in late 1924 or early 1925—also suggests that the funds for the venture may have come from money inherited by the children after their mother's death in 1924. Therefore, if the capital for the business in Raymondville came from their mother's inheritance, any losses suffered there would be family losses and not Fabio's alone.

By 1932, individuals and businesses were going bankrupt at an alarming rate throughout the country, with no letup in sight, although the *McAllen Monitor* told its readers on February 12, 1932, that "the Valley has every indication of being the first section of the country to recover from the depression." The recovery did not come soon enough for the Valley merchants, though, as the *Monitor*'s advertisements showed: "This Bankrupt Stock Must Be Liquidated," announced Westerman's on Main Street in the May 20 issue of the same year, which was also the same year that Fabio's business venture in Texas came to an end.

Just as they kept silent about their mother's death from consumption, Fabio's business failure was something else that his sisters did not talk about (at least to me), perhaps because they resented him for losing their inheritance. The nature and the time of the event must therefore be inferred from extraneous sources. It may have unraveled suddenly in 1932, for in 1931 there seemed to be little cause for concern. On February 12, 1931, for example, Nela was in Raymondville with her brother, taking part in an amateur theatrical performance of *Doña Clarines*, by the Spanish playwrights Serafín and Joaquín Alvarez Quintero. According to a notation in Nela's handwriting, the play was directed by Señora Paquita P. de Lozano, and Nela played the leading role. The rest of the cast were Sofía Cantú, Ofelia Garza (a friend of Ofelia de la Garza), Julia Cavazos, Mikey Lozano, Carmen Garza, Domingo García, Gonzalo Cantú, and Emilia Cavazos, all descendants, most likely, of the Original Grantees of the lands out of which Raymondville and San Perlita had been carved. This was particularly true for the Cavazos women, since San Perlita had been founded on part of the Cavazos grant, San Juan de Carricitos, after Richard King and Mifflin

Kenedy had persuaded the State of Texas to nullify the grant, which was later sold to the King Ranch (Garza, "San Perlita," 5:876).

The percentage of Mexicans in the Lower Rio Grande Valley who took part in staging Spanish plays was undoubtedly small and probably held itself apart from the untutored farmworkers, but in the 1930s they all suffered, both from the economic hardships brought by the Great Depression and from the xenophobia that targeted even the native-born, as long as they had Spanish surnames.

Anti-Mexican sentiment was endemic in Texas and periodically erupted in violence, as was the case in 1915 and 1916, when vigilantes and Texas Rangers lynched or expelled Mexicans from their homes as a result of the Bandit War. However, beginning in the late 1920s, it became official U.S. policy to exclude Mexicans from entering the United States *legally*, by denying visas to most of those who applied for them. In *Unwanted Mexican Americans in the Great Depression*, Abraham Hoffman states that between 1923 and 1929 an average of 62,000 Mexicans entered the United States legally every year, but beginning in 1928, U.S. consular officials denied most visa requests from Mexicans on orders from the State Department. Hoffman adds: "Between 1 July 1930 and 30 June 1931, only 2,457 Mexican immigrants were granted visas" (32). Illegal entry was also combated with the creation of the Border Patrol in 1925.

The purging of Mexicans from the United States was accomplished not only by excluding those who wished to enter but also by expelling those already here. A recent report from the *Christian Science Monitor* compared current record deportations to those in the 1930s: "The only other time deportations came close to existing levels was in the early 1930s, during quasi-official deportation campaigns against Mexicans. Expulsions peaked at 136,000 in 1931 and were done primarily by local officials" (Medrano, August 12, 2010). Hoffman states that, during the Depression, "Mexican workers were among the first to be dismissed from their jobs" (33). Without means of support, these workers turned to welfare agencies for help, thus becoming public charges and therefore deportable. Hoffman adds that the federal government, "viewing the large number of aliens in the United States in a time of depression[,] . . . commenced an active drive on aliens living illegally in the country" (37). But although the government ostensibly aimed its campaign at illegal aliens in general, Hoffman states that Mexicans, "those in the country legally as well as those who were deportable," were the prime targets of the Department of Labor's Bureau of Immigration (37).

Soon after the stock market crash of 1929, carloads of Mexicans began returning to Mexico, many of them after years of living in the United States. Those who did not have access to automobiles were sent to the border by the trainload on trains often chartered by local government entities, such as the County of Los Angeles, California, with support from private charities, including those from established Mexican communities. For example, the Comité Mexicano de Beneficencia in Southern California provided food for the deportees during their journey to the border (Hoffman 87–90). Inevitably, many of those deported, although Mexican-born, were the parents of children born in the United States, and these children could not be repatriated but were nonetheless expelled. The officials putting their parents on the trains would not have dreamed of separating parents from their children (neither would the parents), and, thus, many native-born U.S. citizens were expelled in this manner from the only home they knew.

The arrival of thousands of compatriots at the Mexican border cities naturally caused a stir, not only due to their numbers, but also because of the stories they told of the circumstances surrounding their exodus. Mexican public opinion turned against the United States, something that concerned the chambers of commerce along the Texas border, since their local economies depended heavily on the Mexican trade. The *McAllen Monitor* reported on May 15, 1931, that the South Texas Chamber of Commerce had prepared a press release in Spanish to correct "misleading Mexican press stories that Mexican citizens are being deported on a wholesale basis without proper cause, and that Mexicans in South Texas are being subjected to unnecessary and unlawful abuses." The *Monitor* explained that the Mexicans leaving the United States were *repatriates* and not *deportees*, as the Mexican press referred to them, and that the reason for their repatriation was lack of work, an explanation that tried to give the idea that the exodus was a voluntary act.

Fabio was in the United States legally, and not as an unemployed worker but as an entrepreneur, and yet he, too, was involuntarily repatriated or deported. The only reference that his sister, Nela, ever made to the incident revealed that she, and perhaps one of her sisters, had been in Raymondville when it happened. She recalled bitterly that they had lost all their household belongings, even the *colchas*, or quilts, that covered the beds. Fabio's car, the Model T in which Nela and Ofelia had been photographed during one Christmas season when the car was festooned with garlands and the girls wore fur-collared coats, was also taken. Their brother Lorenzo Jr. had had to take his sisters home, Nela related. This brief recollection of Nela's raises more questions than it answers as to what exactly happened. The thought that she originally left with me was that Fabio's business, like so many others, had been a victim of the Depression and that he had been driven to bankruptcy.

This conclusion is quite plausible if we review the many factors arrayed against his small venture. Even before the debacle of 1929, mom-and-pop stores were beginning to fail, unable to compete with the arrival of chain stores and the early supermarkets, as Jovita González, a contemporary chronicler, points out. In her master's thesis of 1930, which became *Life along the Border*, she wrote: "[T]he introduction of chain stores and Piggly Wigglies has driven the middle class grocers out of business. The same thing has happened with owners of dry goods stores, drugstores, etc." (111). In Raymondville, Fabio had to compete with Jitney Jungle supermarket, which encouraged its customers to "Save a nickel on a quarter" and which undercut him by selling, for example, the twenty-four-pound sack of flour for eighty-one cents to his eighty-three, just enough to steal away the customers that still remained after the deportations.

In addition to the bad economic situation, Fabio had also lost the residual goodwill that had been generated for years by his cousin and mentor, Irineo de la Garza Jr., who died suddenly in the summer of 1928. This was undoubtedly a personal blow to Fabio, who had learned merchandising at his cousin's store in Donna. An added blow to the de la Garza clan in South Texas was the death, in the following April of 1929, of the patriarch Irineo de la Garza at Rancho El Tigre de Arriba in Zapata County. The ranch, owned by his wife, Teresa Ramírez, had been founded by her father, Benito Ramírez, who had "carved it out of the wilderness" of the Spanish porciones (Lott and Martínez 32–33).

Bad business conditions, added to a sense of vulnerability after the deaths of his cousin and his uncle, plus his own mercurial temperament, may have prompted Fabio to making bad business decisions that in turn led to bankruptcy. This premise, however, does not explain the totality of the losses. Texas, in adopting Spanish and Mexican law as it pertained to the protection of the homestead, exempted the family home and household contents, plus a wagon and its modern incarnation—the automobile—plus the tools of a trade, from seizure for debt. Why the house in Raymondville and its contents were seized, when, according to Lorenzo's notes, the structure was owned free of mortgage, is a mystery. There remains only the likely explanation that, with deportations in full force, Fabio was in no position to assert his ownership rights to anything, not even to his own home, and he had to leave it all behind under duress.

In that climate of xenophobia prevailing in the United States, Fabio, like so many of his compatriots, returned home to Mexico. Like the prodigal son in the Bible, he returned poor and defeated, but at least he had a home to return to, although it had changed much since he had left it years before. His mother and his little brother had died in his absence; his older brother had married and established his own household. The house now held only his father and his sisters, and they, too, shared in his loss. It could not have been a happy homecoming, but he had come home at last.

《 SIX 》

"You and I Will Die of Love"

When Fabio and Rogelia died, they left behind a few photographs and a bundle of love letters (mostly from him to her), but hardly any memories for their daughters to cherish. They died so early in their marriage that to their children, orphaned barely out of infancy, they might have always been ghosts. Were it not for those letters, Fabio and Rogelia would have remained strangers to me, their daughter, mere faces that looked out of picture frames. As I read their letters, though, the two came back to life, and when they did, they also resurrected the world they had inhabited, preserving it from oblivion.

Among that bundle of letters there is a small envelope containing two or three dried flowers, already turning to dust, that he, no doubt, gave her during their courtship and that she kept as mementoes. A two-inch heart cut out of red fabric and pasted onto paper shares the envelope with the flowers. On the reverse (the paper side), written in red ink, are the words "Tú y yo de amor nos moriremos" (You and I will die of love), and above the words, in the same ink, is the date "3-17-45," while at the bottom, also in the same ink and hand, the number 47 was added. At first glance, it seems obvious that Fabio must have written those words and dates soon after her death in 1947, but a comparison of the handwriting on the heart with that of his letters to her reveals differences between the two. The numbers, in particular, are different in each instance; specifically, the 7 on the back of the heart is done in the European style, with a bar across the stroke, unlike the 7s that appear elsewhere.

If Fabio did not pen that epitaph on the back of the heart, then only the heart itself is left to elucidate the mystery of the inscription. On close inspection, two pinpricks are visible in the fabric of which it is made, indicating the likelihood that at one time it had been pinned to a lapel, perhaps as an *etiqueta*, or admission badge, to a subscription dance, such as were held in Guerrero. The heart would make one think of a Saint Valentine's Day dance, but the date corresponds instead with Saint Patrick's Day, which is not celebrated in Mexico.

The dance held on March 17, 1945, may have celebrated Carnival, whose date varies according to the liturgical calendar. Usually, though, dances in Guerrero were held at regular times set by the sponsoring organizations, such as the Club Femenil Guerrerense, the local ladies' club, or La Fraternal, a men's club. For whatever reason, the middle of March seems to have been set aside for a dance on more than one occasion, for Fabio refers to another such event in his earliest surviving letter to Rogelia, dated March 16, 1938. In it he mentions a dance recently held, where he had hoped to see her: "Esperaba verte en el baile" (I expected to see you at the dance), he tells her. But what significance that particular dance held seven years later, in 1945, remains a secret between the two.

Still, the author of the caption on the heart must have had a reason for bracketing those two years from 1945 to 1947, which spanned the last two years of Fabio and Rogelia's marriage. The writer—if it was not Fabio himself—must have known the couple, perhaps even read their letters, to have summarized their history in those few words: "Tú y yo de amor nos moriremos." For their history—particularly the unfolding of their troubled courtship—can be found in those letters, primarily those from him to her. Indeed, in one of his early letters, dated December 8, 1938, he writes, as if he wants to leave a record for posterity, "Haré historia" (I will recount our history), and he proceeds to recount the story of how he fell in love with her.

"Te conosí, o te encontré un domingo en la tarde" (I met you, or I encountered you, on a Sunday afternoon)." In Spanish, *conocer* means either to meet or to encounter, and that is, undoubtedly, why he clarified his meaning. He "encountered" her because he most certainly had already met her or at least knew who she was. Guerrero was a small town, and his family knew her family. Her maternal uncle Don Gilberto Pérez, the civilian administrator of the customhouse, was a close friend of his father, although Fabio may not have seen much of her since childhood. Fabio was six when she was born, and when their respective families left Guerrero during the Mexican Revolution—in 1913 or 1914—to flee to Texas, she was five or six and he eleven or twelve. Once in Texas, his family went to stay with relatives in the Lower Rio Grande Valley and hers to the family ranch of Las Escobas in the brush country of Zapata County, a separation of less than one hundred miles but a difficult distance to traverse in those days of poor roads and few automobiles. It is safe to assume, then, that neither saw each other during those years spent in Texas.

When the revolutionary violence finally abated in Mexico, her family returned to Guerrero, as did his, but he did not remain there long. He returned to Texas and apprenticed himself with his merchant cousin Irineo de la Garza Jr., while he sought the opportunity to establish his own business, which he did in the mid-1920s. For her part, after returning home, she undoubtedly completed the primary education that she had begun in the one-room schoolhouse maintained by her Treviño relatives in Las Escobas.

The first school that she attended in Guerrero would have been that run by her mother's aunt Vidala Pérez, who had remained at her post throughout the Revolution, combating ignorance in the midst of violence. Vidalita, as she was known to students and parents alike, had her school in part of the family home, across from the central plaza, for fifty years. In that period of time, she taught the first letters—and more—to several generations of Guerrero residents.

According to José de la Garza—who was a pupil of Vidalita's in 1916, when he was six years old—the school day began at eight in the morning and lasted until five in the afternoon, without recess, except for Saturday, which was a half day. According to José in his interview with Lori McVey, "Vidalita told us about history, geography, even about the human body. She had a whole human skeleton and taught us about every bone, starting with the fingers and continuing to the largest bone in the body" (*Guerrero Viejo* 47). And she did all this for tuition of only one peso a week!

As she grew older, Rogelia probably attended the school for girls founded by the local philanthropist Don José María González Benavides. This school was a solid sandstone construction located at Avenida México and Calle Hidalgo, across from the old Parián, the meat and vegetable market, and had been built in the prosperous years of the late nineteenth century (Treviño Martínez and Treviño de León 50). According to Lorenzo de la Garza, this institution had its origins in the founder's firm belief in the importance of education for girls and women. In a biographical profile of the philanthropist, de la Garza cited the school founder's often expressed maxim that the education of women was of paramount importance because out of it would come good children, good parents, and good citizens: "Educad a la mujer y de ello saldrán buenos hijos, buenos padres, buenos ciudadanos" (*La antigua* 37).

The Escuela González Benavides taught the girls the usual subjects of an elementary education, which, according to Nela de la Garza's second-grade report card, were arithmetic, geometry, elements of natural science, Spanish language, singing, and physical education. It also taught them *trabajos manuales*, or handiwork, especially the exquisite needlework for which the women of Guerrero had been known since early in the nineteenth century. The Swiss naturalist Jean Louis Berlandier, traveling through northern Mexico in 1829 on a government mission, noted in his journal that in Revilla, "recently named Ciudad Guerrero" (in 1827), most of the women "work on making... *jorongos* [blankets] and *colchas* [quilts] that are highly esteemed throughout the country" (*Journey* 2:426).

Building on this needlework tradition, twin sisters, Misses Otila and Elvira González, founded in the 1920s an academy that taught dressmaking and machine embroidery to young women who had already completed their primary education. According to Fernando Garza González, before the sisters opened their academy in Guerrero, they completed a course in Monterrey on the subjects they later taught (13). The sisters practiced a division of labor in their academy, Elvira teaching *corte y confección* (cutting and sewing) and Otila machine embroidery. The dressmaking course was, in reality, a course in tailoring that taught students to cut their own patterns according to a method—*el método Acme*—"invented" by Profesora H. [Hester] A. S. Woolman. Rogelia received her *diploma de honor* after completing the course on June 6, 1928, and by all accounts she was an excellent seamstress.

Another student of the academy was Octavia (Nela) de la Garza, Rogelia's future sister-in-law, who also graduated in 1928 from the Escuela Comercial y de Labores Femeniles José María González Benavides, Departamento de Bordados a Máquina (Academy of Commercial Studies and Ladies' Handiwork, Department of Machine Embroidery). Nela's graduation project was an album containing dozens of samples of exquisite embroidery and even lace. Her classmates, likewise, submitted their individual albums, which became heirlooms passed on to their descendants and proof of the needlework tradition in Guerrero.

According to a surviving handbill, on May 19, 1928, the twenty-plus young ladies who made up the student body of the Escuela Comercial y de Labores Femeniles and the school faculty organized a soirée—*velada conmemorativa*—to commemorate the eighteenth anniversary of the death of the champion of women's education. Admission to the event was free, but those attending were requested to maintain *debida compostura* (proper demeanor). The program opened with the unveiling of a portrait of the founder by the mayor, Presidente Municipal Anastacio García Treviño, and by Lorenzo de la Garza Sr., followed by a speech by Lorenzo de la

Garza Jr., who was identified as "Contador de la Aduana" (accounting officer of the customhouse). The rest of the program included songs, poetry recitations, and more speeches.

While his father and siblings (as well as his future wife) honored the educational benefactor of Guerrero, Fabio appeared well entrenched in the Texas Rio Grande Valley, where he was on the verge of opening a second store. At this point, Fabio and Rogelia's lives could have been as two ships passing in the night, so near and yet unaware of each other, except for the misfortune of the Depression, which brought on his business failure and the xenophobia that drove Mexicans out of their Texas homes (see chapter 5). The precise timing of his return to Guerrero is unknown, but his presence in his hometown was already noted in 1936, when he took part in a musical revue sponsored by the Sociedad de Padres de Familia (the equivalent of the PTA) at the Teatro Salón Anáhuac, located in one of the buildings facing the plaza.

These cultural events were an integral part of the social life of Guerrero, which, according to Treviño Martínez and Treviño de León, included soirées, dances, and promenades around the plaza (65). It was at the central plaza, named in honor of the War of Independence hero Vicente Guerrero, that Fabio likely met or "encountered" Rogelia on a Sunday afternoon. The Sunday promenade around the plaza was probably the most important courtship ritual for the young people of Guerrero, as it was throughout Mexico. Treviño Martínez and Treviño de León relate that the young men would walk along the periphery of the plaza in a clockwise direction while the young ladies promenaded counterclockwise. When a couple's glances met, and both showed interest, each would separate from his or her group and retire to sit on one of the wood (later granite) benches that lined the walks to converse (65).

José de la Garza also recalled the Sunday promenades when he and other children would go to the plaza to hear the orchestra play and to watch the young men and women promenade around the plaza in opposite directions: "When the boys and girls met during the *paseo*, they would say 'hello.' Sometimes the boys made a small envelope with a heart in it like a Valentine and the message would say, 'I love you'" (McVey, *Guerrero Viejo*, 48). Perhaps this was the origin of the small heart among Fabio and Rogelia's letters, but though it may explain the message on the back of the heart, it does not explain the dates.

Courtships began during the *paseo* around the plaza, progressing from meaningful glances to conversations held on the benches lining the square, both stages being conducted in public, in view—and often within hearing—of practically the entire community, a situation that could be inhibiting to suitors. Fabio certainly felt that the presence of his sisters, who also took part in the promenade, hampered his courting and advised Rogelia in his letter of March 16, 1938, to avoid his sisters and their friends when she went to the plaza so that he might converse more freely with her: "Me gustaría que te juntaras en la plaza con algunas amigas que no se junten con mis hermanas, pues así es más fácil platicar contigo." Her reply did not survive, so we do not know if she acquiesced to his wishes.

Courtships begun during the Sunday *paseo*, if they marched satisfactorily, passed from the plaza to the dance floor of the ballroom of the Hotel Flores, where Guerrero society held its celebrations. The Hotel Flores was a landmark in Guerrero, having been built by Don Juan Manuel Flores in the second half of the nineteenth century, and it remained in the family through the first half of the twentieth. The hotel was one of the few two-story structures in Guerrero, and its second-floor balconies overlooked the plaza. A descendant of the original owners recalled that, during the early days of the hotel, "horses were stabled in the interior courtyard . . . and a large kitchen with a gigantic fireplace adjoined the café on the western side of the hotel away from the plaza" (McVey, *Guerrero Viejo*, 40). During the Mexican Revolution, when Guerrero was bombarded and occupied by the various factions, the hotel owners fled to their ranch in Texas. In their absence, soldiers and camp followers were quartered in the hotel, causing much damage to the furnishings and the fixtures. Sometime in the 1920s or early 1930s the hotel was closed down, only to reopen with great fanfare under the ownership of María Eulalia Flores in the summer of 1937. The reopening was celebrated with a formal dance, a *baile de inauguración* held on August 22 at 9 p.m. Admission was strictly by invitation, and payment of one peso allowed the guests to tour the refurbished hotel and restaurant and to dance to the music of the Orquesta Flores, composed of Flores family members, in the grand ballroom upstairs (McVey, *Guerrero Viejo*, 41).

Since Fabio and Rogelia's surviving correspondence dates only from March of 1938, we do not know if he attended the inaugural dance of the Hotel Flores; however, we can deduce that she did not, from a postcard addressed to her by her cousin Teodora Treviño Mendenhall. The postcard—dated August 13, 1937, and sent from Petroleum, Texas, an oil-field village near the Zapata and Jim Hogg county line—reminds Rogelia that Teodora and her husband were to go to Guerrero on Wednesday, August 18, to take her back with them to Texas. Whether Rogelia's parents arranged her trip in order to keep her from attending the dance that surely most of Guerrero would attend (including Fabio), or whether the overlapping dates were coincidental is, of course, a matter of conjecture, but the timing of the visit is suspicious.

Unlike stereotypical Victorian parents, Rogelia's were not so much against their daughter having suitors as they were against a particular one: Fabio de la Garza. Fabio's early youth in South Texas, where he was reputed to have sown more than his fair share of wild oats, appears to have spun a "black legend" around him. In wooing her, Fabio had to struggle against the fear held by her family and friends that he would "trifle with her affections" and against her own natural caution.

In his letter to Rogelia of July 25, 1938, he reproaches her for her coldness to him on the previous evening, anxiously querying her as to how he had offended her, and concluding with his suspicions that certain people, who did not have her best interests at heart, had set her against him: "Sé mas o menos de donde viene esa malquerencia para mí, pero no sabía que tu dieras oído a personas que solo bien no te pueden desear." He surely did not mean her parents when he referred to people who did not wish her well; therefore, the rumors against him must have come from persons who did not wish *him* well. Trying to combat the ill will that he sensed against him, however, he was more defiant than contrite, reminding her that she had been aware of his defects from the beginning of their relationship: "Cuando me diste tu amor sabías de todos mis defectos . . . se había formado una leyenda mala en mi derredor." He closed by assuring her that he had never loved a woman before as he loved her ("Jamás había llegado a querer a una mujer como a tí"), thereby tacitly admitting that he had loved others before. His assurances must not have been sufficiently reassuring, though, and she probably ended their relationship, for the next surviving letter was dated two months later, on September 26. He begins this by telling her that he had decided to write to her again to find out how things were with her: "Por fin he resuelto volver a escribir para saber de tí." He then asks her plaintively: "¿Es que yo no tengo derecho a saber nada de tí?" (Don't I have the right to know anything about you?) Further on, he laments: "Como han sido raros nuestros amores . . . ni un minuto nos hemos amado tranquilos" (Our love has been so strange . . . we have never had a moment to love each other in tranquility).

Her response must have been encouraging, for he wrote again some two weeks later, on October 13, although the letter reveals a relationship that still hangs in the balance. At times he sounds confident, addressing her familiarly as *linda* (lovely), instead of the earlier, more conventional *Querida Rogelia* (Dear Rogelia): "Te seré franco, linda, no quería haberme enamorado porque sabía lo impetuoso que soy" (I will be frank.... I did not want to fall in love because I knew how impetuous I am). At other times, he is filled with anxiety, begging her not to be influenced by persons who no longer remember what it is like to be in love (an unfair allusion to her parents, perhaps), closing with the plea: "Pero, linda, por el amor de Dios, que sepa lo que te pasa" (But, for God's sake, let me know what is troubling you).

The crisis point of their relationship came later that fall and is revealed in his letter of December 8, 1938. He must have learned that Rogelia was on the verge of leaving Guerrero, and he wrote to her, frantically trying to change her mind. His letter is all the more urgent because he wrote it from the isolation of his family's ranch, where, he explains, he did not even have access to pen and paper but had to send a ranch hand to purchase it at the country store in a nearby ranch compound (*ranchería*), where the schoolteacher also furnished pen and ink: "Anoche mandé a un hombre a La Lajilla a comprar papel. El maestro de allí me envió pluma." He added that he was sending the same worker to Guerrero to mail the letter and that he hoped it would reach her in time—in time to dissuade her from leaving, we can infer.

In that letter of December 8, Fabio ran the gamut of emotions from indignation to despair but ended on a hopeful note. He began in a somber tone by explaining that he was breaking his promise not to write again, because he had heard rumors that she planned to leave town to get away from him: "Confieso haber faltado a mi palabra . . . había prometido no escribir más [pero] han llegado hasta mí rumores que quieres o quieren que hullas." He went on in this vein, first reproaching her for yielding to outside pressures, then pleading with her to be strong and fight for their love. In the end, he must have trusted in his persuasive powers because he added a postscript, making plans to return to town by Christmas Eve or before, if it pleased her: "Iré para Nochebuena o antes ¿quieres?"

Fabio's letter apparently succeeded in reuniting him and Rogelia, because he spent Christmas in Guerrero—and so did she, having abandoned any plans for going to visit her relatives in Texas. He sent her a Christmas postcard that showed a couple in a loving embrace with a message of love and peace and his hopes for an end to all disagreements. He added, calling her "Dear honey" (in English), that his gift to her would be forthcoming in the following days as he had promised, coyly asking, "Engagement ring?"

The engagement ring may have led to a more tranquil stage in the relationship between Fabio and Rogelia, clarifying once and for all that his intentions in her regard were completely honorable, but there is no record of exactly when they became engaged. The surviving correspondence for the year 1939 is limited to three exchanges—one letter from him and her reply to it and a Christmas card. His letter, dated May 1, was primarily a note of condolences for the death of her mother's first cousin, licenciado Enrique Medina, Guerrero's eminent son and benefactor, who was illustrious, according to Fabio, both for his intellect and for his kindness to his countrymen: "Una persona ilustre en su inteligencia y por su bondad para todos sus coterráneos."

Enrique Medina was the son of Isabel Pérez, Zoila's paternal aunt, and Lucio Medina, who were married in Guerrero in 1887. Enrique spent his early years in Matamoros, where he studied law, according to *El Cronista del Valle*, a border newspaper (May 4, 1926). During his student days, he met Emilio Portes Gil, who went on to become the preeminent political figure in Tamaulipas from the 1920s to the 1940s, serving first as governor of the state and later as interim president of Mexico from 1928 to 1930. As young men, the two embraced the revolutionary movement of Francisco Madero and organized the Sociedad Democrática Estudiantil (Democratic Student Society) in their native state (Zorrilla 146). After Madero's assassination in 1913, the two friends supported Venustiano Carranza's struggle to restore constitutional government in Mexico, an effort that culminated in the Constitutional Convention called in Querétaro in 1916, which Enrique Medina attended, representing Tamaulipas (*Diccionario de la Revolución* 7:145).

After President Alvaro Obregón's assassination following his second election in 1928, the outgoing president, Plutarco Elías Calles, appointed Emilio Portes Gil as interim president, and he in turn named his friend Enrique as attorney general of the country. Enrique Medina was no neophyte in government service, having been elected previously to the federal congress as a candidate of the Partido Socialista Fronterizo (Border Socialist Party), founded by his friend and mentor, Portes Gil (*Diccionario de la Revolución* 7:145). Before the latter assumed the presidency, both he and his attorney general had enacted progressive legislation in their state ("progressive" being synonymous with "socialist" in those days), such as the first labor code and a new penal code, and—although unsuccessfully—fought the alcohol epidemic that spread along the border as Prohibition drove Americans to drink in Mexico. When Portes Gil completed his interim term as president of Mexico, he was rewarded with an appointment as Mexico's ambassador to France. It is not known whether he took his friend with him there, but since Fabio's letter of condolences to Rogelia makes no mention of a funeral, it is probable that Enrique Medina died abroad (most likely in Spain, since there were family stories of a son who aspired to be a bullfighter and a daughter who favored lace mantillas).

In writing to Rogelia, Fabio also conveyed his condolences to Doña Isabel, Enrique's mother, who, Fabio surmised, must be grieving his death, particularly because he had been "a very affectionate son." His aunt, the schoolmistress Vidalita, must likewise be greatly distressed because she was "very emotional in expressing her sentiments" (*por ser ella muy extremosa para mostrar sus afectos*). Fabio ended the letter by gently chiding Rogelia for being remiss in writing to him: "Termino, pues tú nunca contestas y eso es una falta de educación." His parting shot hit the mark, perhaps because he had described her reticence as *falta de educación* (bad manners). She replied a few days later, on May 6, thanking him for his condolences and promising to convey them to her great-aunts. She admitted her shortcomings as a letter writer, but on this occasion, she said, she did not want to let time pass without replying, because she knew that she would not be able to see him for some time, adding that his letter had brought her solace in those days that seemed so long and sad.

The days were long and sad, not only because of her cousin's death, but also because of the mourning customs that demanded the wearing of black clothing and the seclusion of family members (particularly the women) in their homes, at least during the nine days following the funeral. This time period was the *novenario*, when a rosary was recited by relatives and friends on nine consecutive evenings on behalf of the soul of the departed. In her privately published memoir of life in the Villas del Norte in the nineteenth and early twentieth centuries, Rosalinda Marroquín de Garza describes the custom, which began on the day after the funeral: "El novenario se iniciaba al día siguiente del sepelio, en la misma casa con un rosario cada tarde, hasta completar nueve" (n.p.). Indirectly, the novena period alleviated the seclusion of the mourners by providing them with visitors.

In Rogelia's case the mourning seclusion was probably of short duration, since Enrique Medina was not an immediate family member, but still she could not tell Fabio when she would be able to see him next, remarking wistfully: "Yo quisiera salir, nomas por platicar contigo pero tal vez sea en otra venida que des" (I would like to go out, just to be able to talk with you, but perhaps it will be next time you come to town). She signed her letter "Te quiere siempre" (Love you always), as far as she would go in replying to his constant queries of whether she loved him and thought of him often. Just as she was sparse in her letter writing, she was also reticent to put her feelings down on paper: "Me preguntas en tu carta si había pensado en ti, no puedo contestarte más que lo de siempre" (You ask me in your letter if I had thought about you, and I can only tell you what I always do). Presumably she refers to what she usually told him in person but which she did not find prudent to put in writing, since love letters could be read by unintended eyes.

Her discretion, while admirable, must have driven him to distraction; it was such a contrast to the pages filled with ardent professions of love that he addressed to her. In his Christmas card to her that year, which was dated only "Navidad de 1939," he expressed his wishes that she would spend a happy holiday with her family and that she would think of him once in a while ("y que a ratos pienses en mí un poco"). His Christmas gift to her was a book, and the passionate note that accompanied it made up for the briefness of the Christmas card: "Para ti, domadora de voluntades, sembradora de deseos" (For you, tamer of wills, sower of desires). The book has been lost, but Fabio said of it that in it she would find something that her spirit would gather with love: "[E]n el que encontrarás algo que tu Espíritu sabrá recoger con cariño."

The next surviving letter from Fabio to Rogelia is dated June 11, 1940, and in it he asks her to return to him (in person) a magazine that he had lent her, complaining that she had probably not read it. However, his good humor overrode any disappointment as he wrote to her on that "primorosa mañana" (beautiful morning), imagining that he was conversing with her to make up for the brief conversation they had had the previous evening. He wanted to describe to her the impression she had made on him when he saw her "al pasar a caballo por tu casa" (as I rode on horseback past your house), presumably on his way home from the ranch. She had been feeding some baby chicks in the yard and looked very fetching: "Estabas dándoles de comer a los pollitos y te veías guapísima." He had envied the chicks because they were close to her, and he wished he were one of them—but only if he could always remain small because once chickens grew big, they ended up in the stock pot.

In both this letter and the one from May of the previous year he tells her that he is writing from the office. On May 1, 1939, he asked in a postscript: "¿Sabes dónde estoy escribiendo? Pues en el escritorio del Presidente Municipal" (Do you know where I am writing this? Well, I'm at the Mayor's desk). He elaborated: "Beto está viendo y me dice que si es correspondencia oficial para ponerle el sello" (Beto is watching me and asks if it is official correspondence that needs the official seal). Beto was Gilberto Pérez Muzza, Rogelia's first cousin and the son of Don Gilberto Pérez. Although Beto was some ten years younger than Fabio, the two were close friends, as their fathers had been, and both worked out of the municipal offices where Don Francisco Muzza, Beto's maternal uncle, was the mayor.

Fabio, unlike Beto, though, had to juggle his position in the local government offices with his responsibility for running the family ranch, a responsibility he had assumed after his return home from Texas. Fabio's letters often contain references to his dual role, frequently dwelling on the ranchman's constant preoccupation with the weather, even when he is at the office. In that arid climate, rain was always an occasion, and he notes it in his letter of June 11, 1940: "En este momento me quitan la atención en la otra mesa para decirme que está lloviendo" (At this moment they call me from the other desk to tell me that it is raining).

On July 17, 1940, Fabio wrote to Rogelia, again from the office, in a lighthearted vein more reminiscent of a schoolboy sneaking a note past the teacher than a municipal employee at work. When his boss, the judge, asks him to whom he writes, Fabio assures him that it is to the superior court, and then justifies his fib by telling Rogelia that she is, indeed, the supreme tribunal that rules over him: "Te estoy escribiendo en la mesa de trabajo y se me acerca el juez para decirme a quien le escribo y le he dicho que al juzgado superior que es quien nos manda y se ha quedado conforme." If these comments make his municipal position seem like a sinecure, his letter to Rogelia of October 8, 1940, dispels this idea. He opens his letter by explaining to her that he had not planned to come to town until the following week because they were working at the ranch on a project that required his presence, but he had been called back to Guerrero by the judge to take care of an urgent matter. He had left the ranch at daybreak and ridden to town "a todo galope" (at full gallop), before reporting to work at the municipal offices. He felt so tired as he wrote to her that he asked if they could meet at the plaza on the following evening—rather than the same day—because he had to finish reviewing an extensive file before going home to get some sleep.

Even today, it is not unusual for a rancher to supplement an uncertain income with a steady government job or any job in town. However, Fabio may have felt a particular urgency to assure his financial position at this time as he contemplated the next step in his relationship with Rogelia: marriage. Although his situation seemed secure as a member of a landowning family, the ranch that provided a large part of his livelihood was not his alone but belonged also to his siblings and his father. Whatever the specific financial arrangements were within Fabio's family—whether he received a specified salary for running the ranch or simply received his pro rata share of the profits—it was clear that he needed to work hard in order to undertake the support of a separate household, and his letters reveal a more serious mind-set than before.

The realization must have come to Fabio that year of 1940 that he was in his late thirties and that his brother, Lorenzo Jr., although only four years older than he, had already been married fifteen years and had four children. However, Fabio left no definite clue as to precisely when he had determined to marry Rogelia. Among his many letters to her, there is not one containing a formal proposal of marriage, or at least none couched in the passionate phrases he so often utilized in his correspondence with her. His letter of July 23, 1940, contains, instead of a proposal, a rather serious meditation on the incompleteness of the single person. He had apparently escorted her home the previous evening, and after leaving her, he had realized that a single person was not complete ("una persona sola no es completa"). However, he added with an impish sense of humor, it depended on whether the helpmate was industrious ("cuando nuestra compañera es trabajadora"), because if two idlers got together, the result was worse. He added, more seriously, that he had concluded that they should establish their own home as soon as possible: "[P]ensé en lo necesario que es el que cuanto más pronto formemos nuestro hogar sería mejor." By way of justification for this conclusion, he assured her that he had never truly loved a woman before her. Proof of this was that he had never worried about a woman's well-being and that now he worried if she complained of not feeling well, as she had done the previous evening. Furthermore, he argued, his anxiety about her health showed, not only that he truly loved her, but also that he loved her more than she loved him. After these irrefutable proofs, he ended his letter by hoping that, after taking her medication, she now felt better and that when she recovered fully she would be even prettier than before and not so argumentative.

Marriage was in the air that summer, and his letter of July 27 makes reference to a wedding to which they had been invited, asking her if she planned to attend. He added that he was not inclined to do so, but he thought that she should—if she wished to—since it would look bad if neither of them was present. They were now publicly a couple and needed no subterfuge to appear together at social events. On July 2, for example, he had written to her, informing her that a "flock" of actors ("una parvada de cómicos") had arrived in town and were giving a performance that evening and that it would please him if she attended the show. Apparently she did not, because on July 17 the troupe was still in town but preparing to give its final performance, although he questioned if it would really be the last ("¿Será la última?"). He reminded her that he had not seen her in two days since Sunday the fifteenth ("desde el domingo quince") and that he missed her already, a hint that perhaps the play was only an excuse to see her.

However, his love for the theater was long-standing, and not only did he attend performances, but he also took part in amateur theatricals. That year in May he participated in a revue sponsored by the ladies' club, the Club Femenil de Acción Social y Cultural. The club secretary, his sister Nela, thanked him by letter for his participation in that event. Rogelia's reserved nature, on the other hand, precluded her from taking part in any type of performance, and there is no indication that she enjoyed music. Still, like most Guerrero women, she was a member of the Club Femenil, and the club organized an annual dance that was one of the most significant social events of the town. On July 17, 1940, Fabio commented to Rogelia that he had heard that her club would hold its annual dance on the following Saturday: "He sabido que el sábado van a tener Uds. su baile reglamentario." He added: "Con seguridad que va a estar hermoso" (I am sure that it will be beautiful).

If, as according to Fabio's letter of July 17, July 15 was a Sunday, then the Club dance was held on Saturday, July 21, 1940, and clearly both he and Rogelia attended the event, after which he concluded that it was time for them to be married. They must have set the wedding date soon after, although the correspondence makes no specific reference to this. The following August 10 was Fabio's thirty-eighth birthday, and she sent him a card, saying that she had "remembered" that it was his birthday and hoping that he would be happy on this day and for the rest of his life, which she prayed to God would be a long one.

He, in turn, sent her a letter that must have crossed paths in the mail with hers. Since she was a little remiss in the matter of correspondence ("un poquito desobligada"), he wished himself a happy birthday in her name. He reminded her that August 10 was *his* day, almost immediately adding that it was also his father's birthday and his niece Elvia's, as well as the feast day of his brother Lorenzo Jr. Putting it in a nutshell, he told her: "En nuestra familia el que no nació el 10 de agosto se llama Lorenzo, que es lo mismo" (In our family those not born on August 10 are named Lorenzo, which amounts to the same thing). As he continued, the playful tone of the first lines turned somber as he confided to her that he had never before spent such a melancholic birthday, remembering that in the past his family had always gathered on this day "to consume at least a humble chicken." This year, no matter how hard his sister-in-law, Juanita, tried, she could not fill the empty spaces left, he said.

This remark about empty spaces is somewhat puzzling, but it probably related to something alluded to in his letter of July 23 and the comments about the incompleteness of the single person. That letter had begun with Fabio's confession to Rogelia: "Anoche no fui sincero contigo" (Last night I was not truthful with you). She had asked him if he was happy when he was alone, and he had replied that he was quite content with his own company. However, as soon as he had left her and returned home, he had realized that he was not happy on his own.

In Mexico, unmarried sons and daughters continued to live in the family home until they married and left to set up their own households, so, in spite of his age, Fabio would still have lived with his father and sisters. Lorenzo Sr., however, had remarried at some time during the 1930s, and rather than bring a stepmother to live with his grown children, he had moved into his wife's home. Fabio, though, would have stayed in the family home with his sisters, who would have kept house for him. However, "the girls," as they were always called, often traveled to Texas to visit their cousins there, and this may have been one of those occasions, which would have left Fabio alone in the house. Apparently, this time his father must have also been away because Fabio informed Rogelia in his letter that his only birthday co-celebrant would be Elvia, his fourteen-year-old niece, who had baked several cakes in their honor and who had assigned to him the task of contributing lemons and ice to make lemonade for their birthday party. Still feeling sorry for himself, Fabio ended his letter by telling Rogelia that he had just informed her cousin Beto that it was his birthday. Upon hearing this, Beto had promptly wished him a happy day and given him an *abrazo* (hug). Fabio had responded by telling his coworker that he preferred a more "solid" token of affection, especially if it was "liquid."

The remaining letters of that year make no mention of the activity that must have occupied Rogelia all that fall—preparing her trousseau. She undoubtedly sewed her own wedding dress—being the good seamstress that she was—as well as all her wardrobe and filled her hope chest. According to Mrs. Diamantina García Ramírez, formerly of Guerrero, the traditional hope chest of a bride contained two quilts and several sets of embroidered bed sheets and pillowcases, as well as table and kitchen linens, all of them made by the bride, except for the quilts, which also involved the bride's female relatives (McVey, *Guerrero Viejo*, 52–53).

However, Rogelia's wedding preparations that fall were overshadowed by the failing health of Zoila's aunt Vidalita Pérez, the schoolmistress. On November 15, 1940, Fabio wrote to Rogelia, arranging to meet her and expressing his hopes that her great-aunt was better. It was a vain hope, for on December 5 he wrote to his fiancée, expressing his condolences "for the passing of the woman who was a teacher to us all" ("por la desaparición de aquella que fue nuestra maestra"). Fabio himself gave the eulogy at the funeral on December 4, saying that Vidalita had been a teacher to two generations of Guerrero residents and had spent fifty years educating children without benefit of government funds ("sin presupuesto oficial"). He gave Rogelia a copy of the funeral oration, dedicating it to her "con todo cariño" (with all my love).

In addition to Vidalita's death and the mourning restrictions it imposed (particularly since she had been a local icon), Fabio did not see much of Rogelia in December of 1940 because of the cold weather, which kept her indoors. Knowing how keenly she felt the cold, Fabio remarked that she must be spending most of her time next to the stove, especially since she had come down with the flu. Indeed, she had been ill at the time of Vidalita's death, and Fabio chided her that, more than a chill, her illness had been brought on by overexertion. He scolded her, saying that it seemed as if she had wanted to worsen her condition by overwork: "Supe que la causa era que habías trabajado en una forma como que tú misma buscabas empeorarte."

Rogelia must have recovered sufficiently by the date of the wedding, but there is no further correspondence, except for an undated note from Fabio, asking her to furnish him with information required to file the marriage application at the Civil Registry. He needed to know her parents' ages, as well as hers, "without subtraction" ("la tuya—sin quitar"). It was amazing that he had either forgotten or she had avoided telling him that she was thirty-two.

Fabio and Rogelia were married in a civil ceremony (which, by Mexican law, must occur before the religious celebration) on December 26, 1940, and at Mass the following day in the Church of Nuestra Señora del Refugio. Due to Vidalita's recent death, the wedding was probably a quiet affair, perhaps with only a wedding breakfast for the family, very different from the wedding festivities recalled by Mrs. Diamantina García Ramírez, who related that she had danced all night at the Hotel Flores at her wedding in 1937 (McVey, *Guerrero Viejo*, 52). There is no surviving wedding announcement or invitation to provide information about Fabio and Rogelia's wedding, because in Guerrero wedding invitations were delivered orally by designated persons, as Fabio had remarked to Rogelia in his letter of the previous July 27. In referring to the wedding under discussion at the time, he asked her: "¿Te invitaron? A mí fueron tres comisiones, dado que las dos primeras no me encontraron" (Were you invited to the wedding? I was, three different times, since the first two delegations did not find me).

And apparently there was no wedding portrait, either, to capture how they looked on their wedding day, for none survived.

After the wedding there was, obviously, no further correspondence, and from then on Fabio and Rogelia's lives can be traced only from indirect sources, such as public records. During 1941 or 1942 she delivered a stillborn child from her first pregnancy, but in October of 1943 their first daughter, Beatriz Eugenia, was born, followed by another daughter, Alicia Margarita, in August of 1945. Fabio continued to run the family ranch and to work at the municipal offices while Rogelia was undoubtedly busy with housekeeping and child rearing during the first five years of their marriage.

The ranch was still nominally headed by Lorenzo de la Garza Sr., and it was he who signed the yearly inventory of livestock that was required to be filed with the state authorities, although Fabio managed it. In 1945 the Rancho San Juan (located within the Sabino Seco tract) reported a total of 153 head of beef cattle and 125 goats, as well as two workhorses. If the weather was favorable, dryland farming was also attempted on the property. Lorenzo Sr. kept an intermittent journal that he termed "Efemérides" (Ephemera), and in it he noted, for example, that on a Saturday in June of 1944 Fabio had left for the ranch at four in the morning to see if it were possible to plant a late crop, taking selected seed with him. On June 7 Lorenzo reported that it had rained again at the ranch and that the stock pond had probably spilled over the dam. And on October 17, 1946, he noted that Fabio had left for the ranch at five in the morning to check out conditions ("a campear").

Starting in 1943, with the election of Gilberto Pérez Muzza as mayor (*presidente municipal*), a younger generation of leaders began to take over the helm of civic affairs in Guerrero. Thus, when a committee was organized in the early 1940s to promote the reconstruction of the road that linked Guerrero to the national highway that ran from Mexico City to Nuevo Laredo, both Fabio and his father were on the committee. This road was the major artery connecting Guerrero to the rest of the country, and it was unpaved. At this time few people in Guerrero owned automobiles, and the principal means of transport out of town was a bus that ran from Guerrero to the *empalme* (junction with the national highway). From this junction, travelers could continue on the paved highways to either Nuevo Laredo or Monterrey.

However, concerns over road improvements soon paled next to an international event of critical importance to Guerrero. Since the 1920s Mexico and the United States had squabbled over the division of the waters of the lower Río Bravo/Grande as it flowed from El Paso to the Gulf of

Mexico. Finally, in 1944, the two countries settled the issue by providing for the construction of several international reservoirs on the river that would accomplish both flood protection for the Lower Valley and generation of hydroelectric power. Unfortunately for Guerrero, the first of the proposed dam sites was located below the point where the Río Salado emptied into the Bravo, and when filled, this reservoir would cover Guerrero.

This was the situation that confronted Fabio when he assumed the office of mayor in January of 1946. Immediately after organizing his staff (which included reappointing his sister Nela as municipal clerk), he undertook to ensure that the interests of the guerrerenses were taken into account by the federal government, which had condemned the town to die. One of his first actions was the creation of the Comité de Orientación y Defensa Pro-Guerrero, a group charged with seeing that Guerrero property owners were adequately compensated for the losses they would suffer and that the town's inhabitants would receive housing after their displacement. The committee was headed by three honorary presidents: the state governor, the presidente municipal of Guerrero (Fabio), and the parish priest of Nuestra Señora del Refugio Church, Father José Madrigal Barragán, known by all as Padre Madrigal. The active members of the executive committee included Lorenzo de la Garza Jr. (but not his father, which may indicate that he was no longer in good health), Juan Ángel García (Rogelia's brother and the municipal secretary), and Dr. Rubén Flores, son of the old doctor, Dr. Filemón Flores. Out-of-town property owners were represented by Rafael San Miguel Jr. of Zapata, Texas, whose father had been Lorenzo de la Garza's friend and business partner some twenty years before.

During his difficult mayoral term, Fabio could have benefited from the experienced counsel of his father, but Lorenzo Sr. and his siblings had begun to succumb to age and infirmities. On June 15, 1944, Lorenzo had noted in his journal that his sister, Juanita, who, after losing her eyesight, had come to live in his household, had died that day and that the out-of-town family members (nephews and nieces) were expected for the funeral. Although lamented, Juanita's death was not unexpected, due to her age (older than Lorenzo) and her serious respiratory ailments. Lorenzo himself was frail, and his care, as well as Juanita's, had fallen on Lorenzo's daughters, as Lorenzo Jr. remarked in a letter of June 12, 1944, to a cousin who feared being asked to care for the elderly aunt; Lorenzo Jr. disabused him of that concern. When the senior Lorenzo's death came, it would sadden his children, but it, too, would not come as a surprise.

The next loss, however, was both unexpected and untimely. Who could have been prepared for the death of a thirty-eight-year-old wife and mother of two toddlers? According to family sources, Rogelia had never fully recovered her strength after giving birth in 1945, and when she became pregnant again the following year, the pregnancy was a difficult one. She was under the care of the local doctor, but there was no hospital in Guerrero. Therefore, when eclampsia developed late in the pregnancy, there was no way to prevent the seizures that can result in death, because treatment for the condition requires termination of the pregnancy by cesarean section. As a result, both mother and child died in early February of 1947.

Fabio was left with two little girls, one three years old and the other eighteen months. The older of the two he turned over to his three unmarried sisters, and the younger one to his sister-in-law and her husband, who had no children. He remained alone in the matrimonial home to live the incomplete life of a widower. He still had almost two years left of his mayoral term and the ranch to take care of, so he did not lack for work to take the place of love.

One year later, in late January of 1948, his father became seriously ill with pneumonia and died. It must have been difficult for Fabio and his siblings to imagine their lives without the overpowering presence of their father. Not only had Lorenzo de la Garza lived an interesting life, but he had also felt it to be a life of consequence that must be recorded, therefore writing down both the significant and the trivial events as they occurred. On June 14, 1944, for example, he wrote in his diary: "Today I wore the new shoes that I ordered from Mexico City." On the following day he recorded the death of his last surviving sibling, Juanita. Guerrero had been part of his life since he was a young child, and he spent his last decade documenting its history. In 1944 the official press of the State of Tamaulipas published *La antigua Revilla en la leyenda de los tiempos*, which he had subtitled as an "Anecdotic, Historic, and Geographic Review" of the municipality, from its foundation in 1750 to the present, 1944. This edition was soon out of print, and it was reissued by his daughters in 1952.

Six months after Lorenzo's death, before the five siblings had finished sorting out their father's inheritance, another fatal blow struck the family: Lorenzo Jr., who was still active in the customs service, was killed in an automobile accident in Laredo, Texas, leaving behind a widow and four children; the oldest of the children was in her early twenties, and the other three were teenagers. Fabio was now the sole male in the family. Somehow he managed to finish out his mayoral term on December 31, 1948, and turned over the office to his successor, Lorenzo González Vela.

It seemed as if the de la Garza home had always been in mourning, especially to the women, who must have felt that they had always worn black. As a man, Fabio did not wear mourning garb (except a black armband or a black tie in the early days after a death), but his heart certainly mourned, or, rather, his heart itself had already begun to die. In the first months of 1950 he became morose and seldom left the house. As the bicentennial of the founding of Revilla/Guerrero approached that year, the city planned one final celebration before it, too, died. Fabio was still trying to help the residents present their claims for compensation from the federal government, which had now committed to build a new town to house the displaced guerrerenses, and he still had among his papers a number of property deeds when he died of heart failure.

At noon, on June 14, 1950, his niece Elvia Lorenza burst into her aunts' house to tell them that Fabio was still asleep and would not wake up, although people were knocking at his door and calling for him to open it. They could see him through an open window as he lay in bed, but he did not respond. The death certificate listed heart failure as the cause of death. More accurately, it was heartbreak that killed him. He would have been forty-eight years old on the following August 10.

《 SEVEN 》

"Not a Stone upon a Stone"

"No quedará piedra sobre piedra" (Not a stone will be left upon a stone). This was the anathema that the bishop was supposed to have pronounced about Guerrero some one hundred years before, and in 1950 it was coming to pass. To coincide with the bicentennial of its founding, Guerrero was to be destroyed by water, as decreed from above—not heaven but the national capitals of Washington and Mexico City. After twenty years of talks between Mexico and the United States, a treaty had been concluded between the two countries, providing for the construction of several dams on the Rio Grande. The first of these was to be constructed near Guerrero. Those cheering on the project—especially the commercial farmers in the Lower Rio Grande Valley—saw great benefits resulting from the dam, primarily expanded irrigation, flood control, and hydroelectric power. However, collateral damage would also result from the project, such as the flooding of thousands of acres of agricultural land and the destruction of several communities on both sides of the river, the largest and oldest of which was Guerrero. Naturally, those who would lose their property and their way of life saw little benefit in damming the river, but the public debate was couched in terms of progress prevailing over backwardness, and progress won.

In 1950, as the cataclysm approached, the dire prophecy of the bishop reverberated whenever guerrerenses speculated fearfully about their future. No one knew for certain who had uttered the fateful words, and two different versions—perhaps both apocryphal—of the story still survive. One is related by Lott and Martínez in *The Kingdom of Zapata* and makes no mention of a bishop. The authors attribute the prophecy to a newspaper editor in nineteenth-century Guerrero who, "disgusted with the indifference of the people[,] ... suddenly decided that he had had enough" and, locking up his shop, walked out of it and never went back. "Asked why, he replied that one of these days a town like that would just fold up and die" (145). The second version is more dramatic and more memorable. Lilia Treviño Martínez and Eduardo Treviño de León, in their history of the two Guerreros (the old and the new), recount that in 1862 a Catholic bishop visited Guerrero, just as the anticlerical provisions of the Leyes de Reforma (Reform Laws) promulgated by Juárez were causing friction between church and government officials. During this visit, the bishop took offense at the treatment he received from the local authorities, and from the pulpit of the church the prelate fulminated against Guerrero: "In a town such as this, not a stone shall be left upon a stone" (70–71).

Prophecy or curse, the bishop's words found their mark and remained in the collective memory of Guerrero because Guerrero was, indeed, a city made of stone—of the distinctive sandstone that lined the banks of its river, the Salado, which emptied into the Río Bravo/Grande. Its houses were built of blocks quarried from the riverbanks, and its church—Nuestra Señora del Refugio—from a dedicated quarry known as *las piedras de la Virgen*. The settlers who followed Don Vicente Guerra from Coahuila and Nuevo León to found Revilla (Guerrero's original name) clearly did not immediately build stone houses, which was just as well since they had to move three times (each time to higher ground) between 1750 and 1754. Since they had to build quickly, the first shelters they made were *jacales*, huts made of logs and mud with thatched roofs. The humbleness of these early abodes undoubtedly also reflected the absence of government financial aid in the founding of Revilla, the cost being borne solely by Don Vicente Guerra and the settlers.

These first structures were haphazard in location, as well as construction, according to Tienda de Cuervo's inspection of Revilla in 1757 (as cited by Eugene George), and were not arranged around the customary plaza but were scattered over broad areas, "typical of communities devoted to ranching" (George 24). However, once Revilla was located where it remained for two hundred years, the settlers built fortress homes that protected them not only from the elements but also from their enemies, los indios bárbaros, the nomadic tribes that raided as far south as the environs of Monterrey. George describes these permanent constructions as fortified stone structures, windowless and flat-roofed, with "a defensive parapet around the perimeter of the roof," and adds that the "smooth, plastered walls were high enough to deter scaling by a mounted attacker." In addition, the "exposed surface of the roof was covered with a thick layer of lime concrete, rendering all exterior surfaces, other than doors, fire resistant" (George 29–30).

According to Treviño Martínez and Treviño de León (50), the first major structure built in Revilla was the chapel of the Franciscan Mission of San Francisco de Ampuero, whose purpose was to convert the local Carrizo Indians, as well as to minister to the settlers—although it seems to have served more for the latter than the former. This chapel faced the central plaza, which had been laid out in accordance with the urban planning precepts promulgated by the Spanish king Philip II in 1573 (Jones 6–7). The plaque placed before the restored Church of Nuestra Señora del Refugio in Guerrero Viejo states that the first religious act on this site was the baptism of San Silverio Galán in July of 1751 and that the missionary priest who performed it was Fray Buenaventura de Rivera. However, this ceremony took place before the actual construction of the chapel. Building of that structure began in 1755, according to the same plaque, whose text was authored by Carlos Rugerio Cázares, the archivist of the State of Tamaulipas and the architect in charge of the restoration.

San Francisco de Ampuero served the spiritual needs of the revillanos until the latter part of the eighteenth century, at which time the building of the now iconic Church of Nuestra Señora del Refugio commenced. Treviño Martínez and Treviño de León cite Rugerio, who dates the beginning of the construction as 1801, referring to "a document of that period" that indicates that masses were being said in the old church while the new one was under construction (Treviño Martínez and Treviño de León 50). Lorenzo de la Garza, in *La antigua Revilla*, appears to support this date, recounting that from June 27 through 29 in 1801 the Salado flooded Revilla up to the street that flanked the church on the southeast, and that the chalán that normally ferried passengers across the river was moored at the door of the old church (53).

In an article published in 2004, Carlos Rugerio describes the layout of the Church of Nuestra Señora del Refugio as basilica-like, "with three naves separated by columns linked by semi-circular arches, above which rise the walls crowning the central nave." He adds: "The central door is flanked by smooth sandstone columns reaching up to a long frieze.... Atop this is a large belfry with three windows and sandstone voussoirs" (103). Not only its size (fifteen by thirty meters) and its massive construction (sandstone blocks) but also its embellishments (semicircular arches, a triglyph-decorated frieze, and a molded cornice) bespoke a prosperous community that could erect and support such a landmark church. Less impressive—but not by much—were the private homes built in the vicinity of the church and the plaza for the leading citizens of Revilla. Houses such as that belonging to the Gutiérrez de Lara family on what became Juárez Street displayed facades decorated with "lintels, cornices, frames, and carved stone sidewalks" (Rugerio Cázares 103).

However, the beginning of the War of Independence in 1810 marked the end of this first period of prosperity for Revilla. It was fortunate that the church had been completed by 1810 because the eleven years between the declaration and the consummation of independence (1810–1821) were a time of intermittent warfare, not only between royalists and insurgents, but also between the inhabitants of the Villas del Norte and the indios bárbaros who descended from the north, attracted by the power vacuum left when the Spanish troops were redeployed elsewhere. The years following independence were not much better for the pobladores, who were now responsible for their own defense while the central government in Mexico City was primarily occupied with internecine wars, leaving them no resources with which to rebuild their towns. Still, the stone structures survived.

When Swiss naturalist Jean Louis Berlandier traveled through the Villas del Norte in 1829 with a government mission, he observed that Revilla, recently renamed Ciudad Guerrero in honor of Vicente Guerrero, a hero of the War of Independence (and, subconsciously perhaps, also in honor of the founder, Vicente Guerra), was situated "on the slope of a small hill, at the foot of which flows the Rio Salado, close to the top of the delta formed by the confluence of that river with the Rio Bravo" (*Journey* 2:426). In the seventy-two years since José Tienda de Cuervo's official visit to Revilla in 1757 the population of Guerrero had increased almost tenfold, although to Berlandier the town had a population of *only* 3,167 inhabitants. Berlandier added that the "flat-roofed houses, as well as the *jacales*, are built of the same stone that is extracted from the terrain" (426). Jacales, though, are not made of stone but of logs or wattle, so Berlandier may have been contrasting small dwellings with the large houses. In addition, Berlandier seems to have approved of the layout of the now Ciudad (rather than Villa) because he described the streets of Guerrero as "straight, quite well aligned, but laid out on rather uneven ground." He contrasted Guerrero with the neighboring Villa de Mier, which, although proclaiming a "certain ease" with its well-constructed sandstone houses, had streets that were not well aligned (*Journey* 2:426–428).

The conflict between the northern Mexican settlements, accustomed by their isolation to a certain autonomy, and the central government erupted first in the secession (or independence, depending on point of view) movement in Texas in 1836 and then in the unsuccessful Federalist movement of the Republic of the Rio Grande from 1838 to 1840. These two insurrections were followed by sporadic hostilities with the new Republic of Texas, involving incursions by Texas forces into the Villas del Norte. In November of 1842, for example, the Texans sacked Laredo and then marched into Guerrero, where they extorted supplies from the mayor. From Guerrero the marauders continued to Mier, where their luck ran out, and many were captured. The Texans did not get to see much of Mier, but what they had seen of Guerrero impressed them favorably. Jerry Thompson recounts that in Guerrero the invaders had "found a town much larger than Laredo with well-built homes neatly arranged around two plazas," and he observes that "with 2,000 inhabitants [a decrease of 1,167 since Berlandier's visit], the town also had a number of well-kept gardens and several groves of orange trees" ("Historical Survey" 38).

These hostilities were a prelude to the annexation of Texas by the United States and to the invasion and occupation of Mexico by the latter from 1846 to 1848. The conclusion of this war with the defeat of Mexico and the signing of the Treaty of Guadalupe Hidalgo resulted in Mexico's loss of half of its territory, including a large part of Tamaulipas. For the Villas del Norte this meant the severing of the one sister settlement on the eastern bank of the river—Laredo—and the hinterlands of the others, which now lay in a foreign country. The Rio Grande was now the dividing line between two countries, each one calling it by a different name: Rio Grande in the United States and Río Bravo in Mexico. The river settlements became frontier outposts on the new international border.

Eventually prosperity returned to the Mexican settlements along the river, particularly Guerrero, in the last third of the nineteenth century. This prosperity was the result of increased commerce following the abolition of tariffs on the Texas border in what was designated as La Zona Libre, or the Free Trade Zone (F. R. Calderón 2:282–284). The Zona Libre attracted merchants from Europe, such as the Volpe brothers from Italy who settled in Guerrero and built handsome houses for themselves, in addition to contributing to the construction of public buildings, the most important of which was the Palacio Municipal.

According to Lorenzo de la Garza, in *La antigua Revilla*, the *ayuntamiento* (city council) of Guerrero voted, in extraordinary session held on October 11, 1869, to erect a structure on the west side of the plaza to house the municipal offices and the *juzgados locales*, or local courts. Don Sabás Vázquez, a transplant from Agualeguas, Nuevo León, was the mayor at the time and headed the council that decided this matter in ex post facto fashion, for the actual construction work had already begun the previous August. The project was under the supervision of Agapito Martínez, who received a monthly stipend of thirty pesos, an impressive salary, considering that the highest-paid municipal employee was the municipal and court clerk, whose salary was twenty-five pesos a month (25–26). Construction of the Palacio Municipal was complete by the end of 1871, at which time the alcalde was Don Jesús Peña Vela, whose previous role in Guerrero had been as military commander; in that post, he had seen much action, first against the French in the 1866 battle of Santa Gertrudis near Camargo, and later against the indios bárbaros, who raided the area the following year (L. de la Garza, *La antigua*, 44–46).

The Palacio Municipal was one of only a handful of two-story structures in Guerrero. The top floor of the building was crowned by a pediment that housed a clock that had been brought from France with funds provided by the local philanthropist Don José María González Benavides, whose great cause was women's education and who built a school for girls in the 1880s (L. de la Garza, *La antigua*, 37). The second story of the Palacio Municipal opened to the street and the plaza below through four windows that led to balconies, the two interior windows being outlined by carved sandstone pilasters. The building itself was, like the rest of Guerrero, made of quarried sandstone. During patriotic holidays the balconies would be swaddled in tricolor bunting (green, white, and red), and the alcalde and other important functionaries would address the citizenry gathered below on the plaza during these occasions.

Another important structure built during the heyday of the Free Trade Zone was the aduana, or customhouse, which was established by fiat of Gen. Porfirio Díaz on March 2, 1876, according to Lorenzo de la Garza (*La antigua* 22–23). Díaz had launched his rebellion against President Lerdo de Tejada from the border, specifically from Brownsville, Texas (Herrera, *Breve*, 198–199). He therefore knew that the way to the hearts of the *norteños* was through the ports of entry, and promising an aduana to the people of Guerrero was a sure way to gain their support in his quest for the presidency. However, the customhouse—another sandstone structure—was probably not built until the 1880s, according to Lori B. McVey, who describes the ruins of the building as "faint stone outlines of house foundations," adding that "fallen date stones on the southeastern corner of La Aduana show the inscription 188-" (43).

Also important to the economy of Guerrero was the construction, in the years from 1877 to 1881, of the bridge across the Río Salado that connected Guerrero with neighboring Mier, as well as with many of the ranches and *rancherías* (hamlets) that belonged to the Guerrero municipality. It was a solid structure, resting on sandstone arches, and was named in honor of Gen. Servando Canales, the region's strongman at the time, a son of Antonio Canales. The bridge was built mostly with local funds, as was pointed out in 1896 by a petition to President Díaz from the merchants of Guerrero. The petition from the Gremio Mercantil (equivalent to the chamber of commerce), whose president was Luis Volpe, reminded Díaz that the federal government had furnished only three thousand pesos toward the bridge construction, while twenty thousand pesos had been paid out of the surplus of the municipal budget, and additional funds had been donated by private citizens.

A copy of this petition was found among the de la Garza family papers. It was addressed to the firm of Blas María de la Garza e Hijo, the son being Lorenzo, who was in partnership with his father, and both men were requested to use their "valuable influence" with President Díaz to grant the petitioners' request. The request was that the government refrain from increasing tariffs on goods imported into the Free Trade Zone. The Zona Libre had already been under threat of extinction for some years due to pressure from the United States, whose merchants resented the competition from European imports in Mexico, and by 1891 President Díaz had acceded in part to American demands by levying a 10 percent tariff on goods "destined for consumption" along the Free Trade Zone (F. R. Calderón 2:284).

The detrimental effects of this tariff had been quickly felt in Guerrero, according to the petition, which mentioned that, since the tariff, eight mercantile establishments had closed, the local population had declined to five thousand inhabitants, and the municipal government, lacking revenues, had been forced to close three schools. The petition, which was dated October 15, 1896, added that since the previous July, when the tariff had increased to 17 percent, the exodus of people from Guerrero had become alarming, and real estate values had plummeted. Many houses now stood empty, and the rental income that others had fetched previously had also dropped precipitously, in some cases from thirty pesos a month to only two ("llegando a valer la renta de algunas, que en otra época fueron rentadas por $30.00 mensuales, a la insignificante suma de $2.00 cada mes"). Some property owners asked their tenants to pay only the property taxes and demanded no rent.

Another reason for the population loss—and consequent economic decline—of Guerrero in the 1890s was its failure to achieve a connection to a railroad. In *La antigua Revilla*, Lorenzo de la Garza mentions that in

1882 the Compañía Constructora del Ferrocarril Internacional Oriental de México y Nacional had begun to lay a line that departed from Nuevo Laredo toward Los Aldamas, Nuevo León, passing just outside Guerrero and Mier, but the project had been discontinued, depriving Guerrero of modern access to outside markets (19). The railroad did reach Laredo in 1881 and shifted the focus of regional commerce to that city.

The Guerrero merchants alluded to this situation in their petition by describing the high cost of transport that Guerrero traders incurred because the nearest railroad connection, in Villaldama, Nuevo León, was 140 kilometers away, and they had to traverse that distance by oxen cart with their wares. Laredo's situation was the opposite: it was served by two railroads in 1881. The International and Great Northern arrived there from Saint Louis, Missouri, via San Antonio; and the Texas-Mexican Railway, known as the Tex-Mex, came from Corpus Christi on the Gulf coast. The International and Great Northern, or I&GN, connected in Laredo with the Mexican National Railroad (which, despite its name, was owned by Americans) and continued to Mexico City. The Villaldama station mentioned in the Guerrero petition was, presumably, on this line. As a result of these railroad connections, both Laredo and its sister city, Nuevo Laredo, had begun to grow since the 1880s. "The Laredo of the 1880s resembled a Wild West boomtown," according to John A. Adams Jr., who added, in his history of border commerce, that the population had nearly tripled between 1880 and 1890, from 3,811 to 11,319 (114). Guerrero, on the other hand, lost population after 1891, according to the petition to President Díaz, which claimed that since that year, when the Zona Libre began to be dismantled, more than six hundred families had emigrated to Texas.

Among the families leaving Guerrero for Texas were those of my grandfather's two older brothers, Irineo and Cándido de la Garza, both of whom had married women from Guerrero who owned land in South Texas. Irineo, who married Teresa Ramírez, already appeared as a Texas resident in the 1900 census, in which he gave his occupation as a rancher. Cándido, who was married to Prudencia Benavides, a daughter of Manuel Benavides Vela, was already living—at least part of the time—in Laredo by 1886, as a letter from his father-in-law in Guerrero indicates. The letter, reproduced by Stan Green in his history of the Guillermo Benavides family, is dated "C. Guerrero Agosto 9 del 1886" and is addressed to "Sr. Cándido G. de la Garza" in Laredo, Texas. Manuel Benavides addresses his son-in-law as "Querido hijo" (Dear son), which bespeaks a warm family feeling, and makes reference to Cándido working with his brother-in-law, Servando, on the family ranch in Webb County (25–26).

By 1905, when the Díaz government, by action of its finance minister, José Ives Limantour, finally caved in to American pressure and abolished the Zona Libre, the economic downward slide on the Mexican border was irreversible (F. R. Calderón 2:292). The citizens of Guerrero, who had so hopefully petitioned President Díaz in 1896 to restore the previous 3 percent tariff, must have been bitterly disappointed by the turn of events. However, there were worse things to come in a few years. The decade between 1910 and 1920, particularly the three-year period between 1914 and 1917, saw the bloodbath of the Mexican Revolution, which turned many towns, among them Guerrero, into ghost towns. Irineo de la Garza's grandson José spent a year in Guerrero, from 1916 to 1917, when he was six years old and never forgot "the beautiful city of Guerrero[, which] was almost a ghost city," adding that the population had gone from ten thousand (probably an exaggeration) to about eight hundred in that year (McVey, *Guerrero Viejo*, 49). Lilia Treviño Martínez and Eduardo Treviño de León, too, state that by 1914 many families had abandoned their properties in Guerrero and crossed the Río Bravo, seeking safety in Texas, and that the situation was very difficult for those remaining, because the town was under military occupation. Even after the violence had abated, many families did not return to Guerrero, and those who did found there a scene of "destruction and desolation," according to the same authors (56).

Along with destruction and desolation, the returning guerrerenses also found many empty houses whose insides might have been damaged but whose stone walls still stood. Lorenzo de la Garza, who had remained in Guerrero throughout the violence while his wife and children were in South Texas, perhaps found it necessary (or merely advantageous) to move into a different—or even better—house when his family returned. It seems curious that although Lorenzo and his wife, Esther Peña, had been married for some twenty years and had six children, the couple did not own a house in town, but there may have been a number of reasons why they had not felt any urgency to acquire one. For example, when Esther's widowed father, Juan Martín Peña, died in 1909 and his estate was partitioned between his two daughters, the eldest, Francisca, had received her share of the ranch and the house in town while Esther had received ranchland and the ranch house. On Lorenzo's side of the family, his parents (Blas María and Francisca) had built or bought the house at the intersection of Matamoros and San Luis Potosí Streets shortly after moving to Guerrero in 1872. Blas María died in 1910 and Francisca in 1915, but the house continued to be occupied by their daughters, Juanita and Petrita, until the death of the latter in 1939. Irineo, the oldest of the siblings, also owned a house on

Matamoros, two blocks northeast of his parents' house, where, according to José de la Garza, he and his grandparents stayed in 1916. There was, obviously, no shortage of housing at the time, for as José recalled, "I slept at my grandparents' home, and the next day my uncle and aunt moved to another house" (McVey, *Guerrero Viejo*, 47).

I have not learned where Lorenzo and Esther lived when they were first married in 1896, but by 1902, when their second son, Fabio, was born, they resided on Calle Allende (renamed Obregón after the Revolution). However, the births of their three daughters, from 1906 to 1911, took place while the family lived on Calle Morelos, according to the birth certificates of the three. They were probably still living there when Esther and the children left for Texas during the Revolution. Ofelia, the oldest of the girls, was ten or eleven when they returned to Guerrero, but she never forgot finding her broken dolls when they entered their old home, which must have, indeed, been a "scene of destruction and desolation." Perhaps this is what prompted Lorenzo to install his family in the house on Calle Jiménez that became known thereafter as Lorenzo de la Garza's house, although it was carried on the Guerrero tax rolls as being owned by the descendants of Manuel Benavides Vela, among whom was his sister-in-law Prudencia Benavides, widow of Cándido de la Garza.

One puzzling aspect about this house (which I still think of as my childhood home) was the inscription on one of the ceiling *vigas* (beams). It was the custom in Guerrero—and in neighboring settlements—to inscribe the date of the construction of the house, as well as some other significant fact or thought, on a prominent viga. I remember noticing, as a child of five or six (soon after learning to read), the inscription "Servando Benavides 1876" on a center viga of the parlor and growing up believing that Servando Benavides had built the house in that year. Only later did I learn that this was incorrect, for Green gives Servando's birthday as October 13, 1865 (*Benavides* 30), so that he would have been only eleven when it was built. His father, however, was the mayor of Guerrero in 1876, and he may have built the house with his son in mind.

Although I was unable to find the exact year that Lorenzo and his family moved into the Benavides house (old correspondence was no help, since it was simply directed to the addressee at Domicilio Conocido—Known Address), they were already there in 1924, as noted on Esther Peña's death certificate. A surviving receipt from the Laredo National Bank, dated April 9, 1930, states that on that date the bank received $19.94 from Lorenzo de la Garza and credited it to the account of Servando Benavides, who, at his father's death in 1892, had acquired many of Manuel's properties in Guerrero. The payment was almost certainly for rent of the house in Guerrero, which otherwise would have been vacant, since by then the Benavides family lived in Laredo (Green, *Benavides*, 32–34).

Although the rent paid by Lorenzo for the house on Calle Jiménez amounted to more than the proverbial peppercorn, the sum must have still been negligible, which may explain why he took no steps to purchase the property. On the other hand, I recall comments by the grown-ups (my three aunts) to the effect that, when approached by Lorenzo, the Benavides heirs had declined to sell the house, assuring him instead that he could live in it for as long as he wished. In addition, Lorenzo may have felt no urgency to buy a house, since his parents' home would surely pass to his own children when his sisters ceased to occupy it, the other grandchildren being in Monterrey or Texas.

Lorenzo's three daughters grew up in the Benavides house and felt it to be their own. It was a house built for a family with a secure position and therefore with no need for ostentation, suitable for both the family that built it and for the one that occupied it for more than thirty years. In the 1940s Nela, Lorenzo's youngest daughter, acquired a platonic gentleman friend with whom she exchanged letters, a middle-aged bachelor named Federico Ruiz, who was some fifteen years her senior and lived in Mexico City. The friendship did not appear to have troubled Lorenzo, who usually discouraged suitors for his "girls," probably because Nela's friend lived a considerable distance away and was also vouched for by Lorenzo's sister, Juana, who was acquainted with Federico's family. A photograph showing a plumpish Federico in his early forties, wearing a tuxedo (a "smoking," as it was called in Mexico), was dated February 19, 1944, on the back and dedicated by him to both aunt and niece: "Con respetuoso cariño para mi amiga la Sra. Juana G. Vda. de Caso y con gran afecto para Octavia Amelia, mi amiguita muy estimada" (With respectful regard for my friend, Mrs. Juana G., Widow Caso, and with great affection for Octavia Amelia, my esteemed little friend). Don Federico, as Nela always referred to him, was clearly the acme of respectability, with a brother who was a bishop in the Catholic Church and whose photograph in ecclesiastical robes was also preserved with the surviving correspondence.

Other photographs sent by Don Federico did not survive. On one occasion he apparently sent Nela photos of his home (which he shared with his mother). Nela, perhaps lacking access to a camera, replied to him with a written description of her own home. Unlike her father, Nela did not leave carbon copies of her correspondence, but she frequently wrote first drafts, which she kept. An undated, typewritten scrap of paper contains her reply to the letter that had apparently accompanied the photographs. In it she thanks Don Federico for allowing her to see his surroundings but diplomatically excuses herself from commenting specifically on the objects reproduced, assuring him, though, that they revealed an "exquisite, refined taste." She laments that she cannot reciprocate his kindness with photos of her own home, although, she explains, the photos could not have captured the sense of comfort created by its spaciousness, nor its coolness in summer or warmth in winter. A photograph, she adds, would have only shown the severity of a fortress: "No ofrecería a la vista . . . más que severidad, como 'fortaleza.'" However, she attempts a written description of the house, to see "if it comes out prettier" than in a photograph. Nela's description was brief: "Está ubicada en esquina, varias puertas, 2 ventanas grandes de fierro, un portón que da entrada al pasillo. Desde éste se ve un añoso limón al centro del patio, cerca el aljibe, y total" (It is located on a corner, several doors, two large iron-barred windows, a double door leading into the entryway. From there one can see an ancient lemon tree in the middle of the courtyard, nearby [is] the cistern, and that is all).

That was certainly not all. What Nela left out was that the entryway separated the house into two wings. To the left—on entering—were two rooms used for business. The nearest one was Lorenzo's office and library, containing not only his books, stacked several feet high on a large worktable, but also his collections of rocks and fossils, the floor safe, and his mahogany rolltop desk, where he worked for hours every day. This room had a door opening directly to the sidewalk, as did the corner room that adjoined it. This end room had, at one time, been used as a dry goods store, and it still contained a wooden counter that ran the length of the room. Behind the counter, shelving ran up the wall, almost to the ceiling.

To the right of the entryway were the living quarters, first a long *sala*, or parlor, that could accommodate twenty persons comfortably. The sala had been partitioned with a screen at the back to make a bedroom that held two double spool beds and a tall armoire. This front room had a wood floor, although the rest of the house, like most of the houses in Guerrero, had floors made of *chipichil*, a material described by architects as a lime concrete with pea-gravel aggregate, which was also used for roofs (*A Shared Experience* 185). The combined parlor-bedroom opened to the sidewalk and the street through the two floor-length windows mentioned by Nela. In warm weather, the solid wood Dutch doors, which opened inward, remained open to provide light and ventilation, privacy and security being ensured by the ornamental—but strong—iron bars that created an embrasure between doors and sidewalk. Two doors also opened from the sala to the patio. These doors had small windows cut into them that were guarded by light metal rails called *ventiles*, balancing, again, the need for light, ventilation, and security, since none of the windows had glass.

The street frontage of the house ended at the back of the sala (the bedroom part), and the other rooms continued at a right angle to the front, along the common wall with the adjoining house. The remaining rooms were another bedroom, which led into the dining room, and from there to the kitchen, which had an elevated hearth that was used primarily for cooking, along with a small kerosene stove. There were six large rooms in all that formed two sides of the square encompassed by the property, the two remaining sides consisting of high stone walls enclosing the patio. These walls were unbroken, except for a carriage entrance on the side street, Calle Guadalajara.

In the middle of the patio stood the aljibe (cistern) mentioned by Nela that furnished water for the household, as well as for some of the neighbors. Rainwater was channeled from the extensive roof into a metal spout that emptied its contents through a fine mesh screen that filtered out leaves and debris. Water was drawn with a bucket attached to a heavy rope, and a domestic crisis would arise whenever the bucket came loose and had to be retrieved with a three-pronged hook. Our aljibe was remarkable for not having ever gone dry, even in times of drought, undoubtedly because it was unusually deep.

The household storage of sufficient water was crucial for survival, but not every house had an aljibe. Those that did not had to rely on the unreliable flow of the Río Salado. By the 1940s, as Lorenzo de la Garza reported in *La antigua Revilla*, Guerrero had both an electric plant and a water plant (18). However, many houses were not wired for electricity or piped for water, and even those that were did not always receive electricity and water, because both depended on the flow of the Salado. When the river was too low, there was not enough pressure for water or for turning the electric turbine, nor could water turn the turbine when it was flooding. Improving the utilities was difficult because the plants were privately owned by local investors (among whom was Don Isidro Gutiérrez Escamilla, who also operated the bus service between Guerrero and Laredo) with limited financial resources. Those who had neither piped water nor aljibes obtained their water from *barrileros*, men who hauled water directly from the river and delivered it in barrels, door to door. Barrileros, like *chalaneros* (ferrymen), were a fixture in the Villas del Norte throughout the nineteenth century and into the early part of the twentieth.

According to Lorenzo de la Garza, the 1940 census showed that Guerrero had a population of 3,387 persons (*La antigua* 17). At the same time, Laredo, Texas, had slightly over 39,000 inhabitants, a number that constituted approximately half of the total population of *los dos Laredos*. The choice was obvious when it came to determining which community would be sacrificed for the construction of the dam on the lower Rio Grande. Not that the Laredo communities had ever been considered for destruction, since the dam site was originally described as below Laredo and close to Roma, Texas. Ultimately, because of topographical and engineering considerations, the site chosen was such that it would result in the flooding of Guerrero by the Río Salado, which would no longer empty into the Bravo. Additionally, the Texas communities of Zapata, Ramireño, Uribeño, Lopeño, and Falcón, plus much farmland and ranchland lying close to the Rio Grande, would be covered by the dammed river (J. G. Quezada 148).

Fabio de la Garza's mayoral administration, from 1946 to 1948, was largely taken up with making provisions for the Guerrero residents who would be displaced when the dam was completed. To safeguard property rights, local citizens formed the Comité de Orientación y Defensa Pro-Guerrero under his leadership. Equally important, according to Treviño Martínez and Treviño de León, was safeguarding the autonomy of the municipality of Guerrero, since it stood to lose much land to the dam construction (58). A municipality consists of the *cabecera*, equivalent to the county seat in the United States, and lesser settlements and ranches, hinterlands that are part of the municipality's jurisdiction and tax base. Guerrero's jurisdiction, according to Lorenzo de la Garza, included more than seventy-nine ranches and ranching communities (rancherías), some of which had sizable populations that supported their own schools (*La antigua* 18–19). The Guerrero Defense Committee sought compensation from the federal government for both the municipal and the private losses that would be incurred by the construction of the dam.

Undoubtedly because of the work done by the committee, the Mexican government determined to compensate the guerrerenses for the loss of their town by constructing a new Guerrero. The fly in this ointment turned out to be that, in order to accomplish this, the government would have to take land from the municipality of Mier, which would place Nuevo Guerrero within that municipality. Both communities fought this outcome, and, adding insult to injury, Mier lost some of its jurisdiction in 1950, when part of it was severed to create the new municipality of Ciudad Miguel Alemán, whose seat of the same name was formerly known as San Pedro de Roma and was located across the river from Roma, Texas (Zorrilla 199–200). Eventually Guerrero reclaimed its autonomy as a *municipio libre* (free municipality) by an act of the Mexican Congress (Treviño Martínez and Treviño de León 58).

Compensating urban property owners by giving them new houses in a new town was no simple matter, though. Houses in Guerrero may have been of similar construction and style, but they were of different sizes. The housing project, administered by the Department of Water Resources and built by private contractors, could not duplicate individual dwellings; therefore, an inventory of houses was taken, and each house was then classified according to size and placed in one of five categories. Roughly, the owners of the largest houses in Guerrero would receive the largest houses in the new town. However, this rule applied only to single owners/residents. Absentee owners, owners of multiple properties, and cotenants would be compensated in cash. Renters were eventually given lots in the new town and allowed to salvage building materials from the vacant houses in what became Guerrero Viejo for use in constructing new shelters. During those last months before Guerrero was vacated, people who did not own the houses in which they lived scurried to clear their titles by paying delinquent taxes, buying out cotenants, or instituting neglected probate proceedings, not always successfully.

Meanwhile, in Zapata County, on the Texas side, the situation of the property owners was not any better — and perhaps even worse — than that of their counterparts in Guerrero. In 1949 the U.S. government had begun condemnation proceedings against more than eighty-five thousand acres in Zapata County that would be affected by the dam (Byfield 14). However, in determining compensation for the resulting losses, the International Boundary and Water Commission (IBWC), the agency in charge of the project, did not take into account the special circumstances that prevailed in the county. According to J. Gilberto Quezada (in his biography of Zapata County judge Manuel Bravo), the government appraisers "established a market value on each house and then subtracted 20 percent for obsolescence," which, as Quezada points out, yielded a meaningless price (153). First of all, market value was difficult to establish because there were few sales in the county, and, second, a number of the houses slated for destruction were over a hundred years old, clearly obsolete from the government's view. The government's proposal not only displaced the Zapata County residents but also impoverished them and left them unable to replace their losses. Not surprisingly, the residents rejected the government compensation plan.

Another way in which the situation in Zapata County differed from that across the river was that the dam affected several communities in the county. According to the IBWC, the affected Texas communities—Zapata, Falcón, Ramireño, Lopeño, Uribeño, and San Ygnacio—would be aggregated into one new location—called New Zapata—where the government would have built a courthouse, schools, and infrastructure but no individual homes. The residents of the individual communities opposed this plan and insisted on each keeping its separate identity since each had its own distinct history (Byfield 16–17). San Ygnacio, located farthest upstream from the dam, was able to argue successfully to the IBWC that it would not be affected by the construction of Falcon Dam, and it was allowed to remain undisturbed (Lott and Martínez 125).

It was perhaps a small consolation to the inhabitants on both sides of the river that the instrument of their destruction was to be known by a name famous in the area: Falcón. The surname "Falcón" was specifically associated with the community of Falcón, Texas, which had been named after a grandchild of Capt. Blas María de la Garza Falcón, the founder of Camargo, one of Escandón's Villas. María Rita de la Garza Falcón married Don José Eugenio Ramírez, who acquired Revilla Porción 15 from Don Clemente Ramírez. After the marriage, the couple moved to this land, where they constructed their residence, circa 1781. This settlement was known at first as Ramireño de Abajo (Lower), to differentiate it from Upper Ramireño, located upstream, five miles southeast of San Ygnacio. In 1915, when a post office was established in Ramireño de Abajo, the name was changed to Falcón to avoid confusion with the other Ramireño and to honor Doña María Margarita (Rita) de la Garza Falcón (Lott and Martínez 6–7).

Meanwhile, across the river, the guerrerenses undoubtedly reflected on the irony of the death sentence having been passed on their city almost exactly two hundred years after its founding. On October 10, 1950, Guerrero would celebrate its bicentennial, in the midst of preparing for its end. Defying their fate, guerrerenses decided to forget the impending end and concentrated, instead, on celebrating their beginning. To organize the celebration, a Bicentennial Committee was formed, presided by Dr. Rubén Flores, the town physician (like his father before him). The doctor was aided in this by a number of civic leaders, all of whom "displayed admirable dedication to the various tasks necessary to carrying out the memorable event" (L. de la Garza, *La antigua*, 74–75).

Because of my father's death in June of 1950 (see chapter 6), my aunts and I, being in mourning, did not participate in the bicentennial celebrations, which we followed only at second hand. The contest to elect the Queen of the Bicentennial and her court had aroused in the town greater interest than any political campaign. Civic pride had never been greater. Everyone wanted to give the expected visitors a glimpse of the glory that had once been Guerrero. Many people aired out their houses and even whitewashed them, making them ready for out-of-town friends and relatives. Sidewalks were swept and water sprinkled on the streets to calm down the dust raised by the influx of automobiles. Paper garlands and strings of lights were festooned across the main streets and the central plaza. The city had not seen celebrations on such a scale since 1906, when the Benito Juárez centennial had been commemorated throughout the country, and Guerrero had unveiled the statue of the hero that still presided over the plaza.

To facilitate the attendance of out-of-town visitors, the festivities were held on the weekend of October 14 and 15, although the date of the founding was October 10. I felt a special affinity with the celebration because my birthday was October 13, which that year fell on a Friday. Although there was no question of having a birthday party for me, and although my aunts stayed home while the entire town celebrated, they sent me to the festivities on Saturday afternoon under the care of four women friends from Nuevo Laredo who were staying with us. The occasion was memorialized with a snapshot taken in front of the church that shows four well-dressed women in dark dresses and high heels and a thin little girl, right hand at her hip, the better to display a small handbag (green, if I recall correctly) that was probably a birthday gift.

Things did not go well for me after that photo, for somehow I wandered away from my minders and turned up alone at the Gutiérrez residence, next to the church, where I found two of my classmates in long, billowy dresses. They were to carry the train for the Queen of the Bicentennial and had no time for onlookers like me. When my friends were called to assume their ceremonial positions, I wandered off to the plaza, apparently enjoying myself until darkness fell. I became anxious then. I had never been in such a large crowd before nor out alone after dark.

I seemed to be lost in a forest of legs that hemmed me in toward the middle of the plaza and cut me off from any familiar sights. Above me were the dazzling lights crisscrossing the darkening sky, and all around me reverberated voices and music, amplified by microphones, as entertainers brought from Mexico City performed on the platform erected in front of the Palacio Municipal. The queen and her court and, above all, my friends, the train bearers, were up on that platform, listening to speeches and recitations and watching dancers pirouetting and spinning around, but I could see nothing but the trousered legs of strangers. Finally, someone must have realized that I was lost, for I was eventually delivered to the familiar—and familial—care of my maternal grandmother and aunt. Both of them were also, technically, at least in "half-mourning" for the recent death of their son-in-law and brother-in-law, respectively; however, they were able to follow the festivities from the front door of the old Pérez house across from the plaza without actually taking part in them. Eventually, one of my maternal relatives—probably my uncle—returned me to my aunts' house later that evening.

The following day, Sunday, churchgoers filled the three naves of Nuestra Señora del Refugio Church and spilled out into the *atrio* (forecourt) in attendance at the solemn Mass commemorating the founding of Revilla. Afterwards, the people retired to the favorite picnic spot by the river known as Las Brisas, where, under the ancient *sabinos* (white cypress trees) they consumed *barbacoa* (the original barbecue) and drank cold beer. That evening a public dance was held on the plaza, and rich and poor, locals and out-of-towners, all danced late into the night (L. de la Garza, *La antigua*, 71–73).

And then the fiesta was over. The visitors departed, and the residents returned to contemplating the end of Guerrero. The venerable Hotel Flores, which during the festivities had briefly shone in a blaze of lights, as in its glory days, sank again into darkness. Other buildings that had been an important part of daily life in Guerrero stood empty, as well, except for a few flickers of intermittent activity. The old school for girls, constructed in the heyday of the Free Trade Zone, had been replaced by a new coeducational facility and now opened its doors only infrequently, usually when the town had to quarter the occasional detachment of soldiers sent by the federal government. During those times, the townspeople would wake up in the morning to the sound of reveille, joined by the crowing of the roosters. Across the street from the girls' school, and surrounded by an open area known as the *plazuela*, stood the old marketplace, the Parián, no longer in use, except on those occasions when a butcher would set up shop there early in the morning until he sold out, usually by noon. Beef was scarce because of drought, and, lacking refrigeration, people consumed what had been slaughtered on the same day. The dam would remedy that—they were reminded—by providing reliable hydroelectric power for electrical appliances.

These assurances, though, did not stop the exodus of guerrerenses who had begun to depart for Monterrey, Laredo, or the Rio Grande Valley, among whom were my aunts and I. By the summer of 1952 we had completed immigration procedures and were ready to move to Laredo, Texas. My aunts had packed up the belongings that we would be able to take—

including some of my grandfather's books—and sold many of his other things, such as his rolltop desk and the floor safe, as well as his collection of fossils. Still, there were large pieces like two beds and an armoire that, because of their size, had to be left behind.

After we left for Laredo, the people of Guerrero and the affected Texas communities continued to cope in different ways with the impending change, especially as the time grew near for the completion of the dam and the closing of the Rio Grande. There had been plans in Guerrero for making a gradual move to the new town, as the houses and facilities were completed. Because of the prevailing drought, the reservoir was expected to take several years to fill, but nature surprised everybody. Lilia Treviño Martínez and Eduardo Treviño de León recount that, beginning in August of 1953, the long-delayed rains fell along the watershed of the Río Bravo. Overfull, the Bravo rejected its tributary, the Salado, which overflowed its banks and spilled into Guerrero (23).

One of the first places affected by the flooding was the new school that had been built by the state government at a distance of only one hundred meters from the bridge on the Salado. Treviño Martínez, who was a teacher there, relates that the school personnel relocated the desks, chairs, and supplies in great haste to the old girls' school on higher ground. This move, though, was only a stopover on the way to Nuevo Guerrero, as children and equipment were forwarded there before the floodwaters cut off evacuation routes. The Guerrero historian describes turning the key in the lock of the old doors on the last day of school in the old town on October 7, 1953: "El día 7 de octubre giré por última vez la gran llave de hierro en la cerradura del vetusto portón de madera." And on October 11, in the presence of civil and military authorities, the official archives of Guerrero were removed from the Palacio Municipal, as was the clock from its frontispiece, and, together with the statue of Benito Juárez and the iron cross from the church, were taken to the new town (Treviño Martínez and Treviño de León 24).

In Zapata County the August rains first affected the areas closest to the dam—Lopeño, Falcón, and the surrounding ranches: "Emergency evacuation plans forced the residents to flee, many of them leaving behind their personal possessions, furniture, livestock, and, of course, their homes" (J. G. Quezada 176). The county seat, Zapata, was not affected at this point and provided shelter in its public buildings and in tents to the refugees from the flooded communities. However, even as refugees from downriver were arriving, Zapata residents were hurrying to move to the new settlement, which was not ready for them, for the elementary school and the courthouse were still under construction, and the new water plant was not yet functional (J. G. Quezada 177).

While the living were being resettled—badly or adequately—on both sides of the river, behind the scenes the dead, too, were accommodated in new resting places. In Zapata County twenty-one separate cemeteries were affected by the dam, and the IBWC proposed consolidating them all into one location. The residents disagreed, and the IBWC eventually carried out their wishes, since it "did not cost the government additional funds" (Fish, *Zapata Roots*, 95). In Guerrero the cemeteries were located at the highest point and were not affected by the floodwaters, but many survivors chose to remove the remains of their ancestors to the new town or elsewhere. At the time of the inauguration of the dam, a Mexican periodical, *Revista de Revistas*, devoted almost an entire issue to Guerrero Viejo, including its cemeteries. In "También los muertos emigran" ("The Dead Also Emigrate"), the author, Heriberto García Rivas, described the bizarre scene of hastily recruited gravediggers busily digging up bodies and placing them in small coffins, which in turn were sealed inside metal boxes. This was the only way in which American customs officials allowed Texas residents to bring the remains of their ancestors for burial in Texas.

The initial onslaught of the floodwaters in 1953 was followed by a second wave in the summer of 1954. In Guerrero the water, at its highest, reached the top of the arches of the church and covered the bandstand in the middle of the plaza. "When the water was high in Lake Falcon," writes Eugene George in his book on borderland architecture, "fishermen in boats were able to inscribe their names above the springing of the arches in the [Guerrero] church interior" (88). When the water recedes during the periodic droughts, such as those in 1983 and 1994, goats and cattle graze in the lush pastures left behind and take shelter in the standing structures, even inside the church.

Since 1953 Guerrero Viejo, periodically submerging and emerging from the lake waters, has captured the imagination of photographers and writers. In 1997, for example, the renowned Mexican writer Elena Poniatowska wrote the text that accompanied the haunting photographs of Guerrero Viejo taken by architect Richard Payne in the 1990s, which were published in a book. In *Guerrero Viejo* Poniatowska writes a paean and an elegy to the deserted city. Recalling the bishop's curse that not a stone would be left upon a stone of the town, she refutes the prophecy by affirming that the ruined houses of Guerrero Viejo proudly remain "stone on top of stone" (*permanecen alzadas piedra sobre piedra*; 89). As long as one stone of the old town remains, Guerrero Viejo endures.

《 EIGHT 》

The Streets of Laredo

One of the first things I learned after arriving in Laredo was that the streets of Laredo ran east to west and the avenues from north to south. It was my aunt Nela who imparted this bit of knowledge in order to prepare me to live in a place that was some twenty times larger than that we had left behind. This was in the summer of 1952, and the direction the streets ran was just one of the many things I had to learn as I began the first grade in English after having completed the third grade in Spanish.

Of course, I was not surprised that the streets of Laredo were laid out in a grid. Ciudad Guerrero, Tamaulipas, our former home, had been laid out in a similar fashion, as were most of the settlements founded by the Spanish in the New World. The Spanish had been town builders, and they strived for order and planning in their settlements. The towns were compact, with streets running (whenever possible) in parallel and perpendicular lines to each other, radiating out from the main square, or plaza, which was flanked by the church and government buildings, as well as by the houses of the principal citizens. These precepts had been formalized as far back as 1573 by the Spanish monarch Philip II in his "Royal Ordinances Concerning the Layout of Towns" and were adhered to in the colonies as far as it was possible.

In laying out Laredo the founder, Don Tomás Sánchez de la Barrera, had followed the royal directives. According to Gilbert R. Cruz in *Let There Be Towns*, when the royal commissioners visited the Villas del Norte in 1767 to assign lands to the settlers, these officials marked the spot where the plaza would be with "visible and durable stakes." The north and south sides of the plaza were laid out with four lots for "the leading families of the community," while the west side of the square was set aside for government buildings, and the east was reserved for the church (98). This procedure was followed in the five Villas del Norte, including Laredo, which retained its Mexican "air" into the next two centuries. As late as 1881, more than thirty years after Laredo had become part of the United States, the *Laredo Times* felt it necessary to advise the newly arrived Anglo-Americans: "Laredo is a Mexican town. The streets [are] at right angles" (Green, *Laredo in 1881*, 5).

The specific reason for my aunt's describing the layout of the streets of Laredo was to help me find my way to the school where she had enrolled me, San Agustín, situated next to the church of the same name, on the east side of the plaza where the Villa de San Agustín de Laredo had been founded in 1755. Not that the church dated back to that year (much less the school), since for the first five years of its existence Laredo did not even have a priest but shared one with Revilla. However, by 1760, a priest had arrived from Boca de Leones (Villaldama), Nuevo León, after Don Tomás Sánchez had committed to building a chapel and to contributing 150 pesos a year toward his maintenance, the amount to be matched by an equal sum from the bishop of Guadalajara's personal funds (Green, *San Agustín*, 1).

The first proper church building (its predecessor had been a jacal, or hut) in Laredo was erected in 1778, according to Kathleen Da Camara in *Laredo on the Rio Grande* (55). That church served Laredo for almost one hundred years. In that time, Laredo went from being a Villa of New Spain to a Mexican settlement and, after 1848, to a border town of the United States (with a detour, before that, as capital of the Republic of the Rio Grande and later part of the Confederacy).

In 1848, when the United States severed Laredo's ties to Mexico and to the rest of the Villas del Norte, the city's connection to the Catholic church in Mexico was also broken, but more gradually. According to Stan Green, San Agustín Church technically came under the bishop of Galveston after 1850, but, in disregard of national boundaries, a single parish register was kept until 1854 for both Laredo and Nuevo Laredo, and Laredo priests ministered to parishioners in Nuevo Laredo until 1867 (*San Agustín* 7–8). Green also remarks that since the bishop of Galveston was French, San Agustín had "a French tone" during the second half of the nineteenth century that also stemmed from the presence of the French parish priests assigned to the church, among them Louis Marie Planchet, Louis Claude Dumas, and Alphonse Martin Souchon, who soon became Padre Alfonso. It was the latter who rallied his parishioners to building the current church structure, beginning the project in 1866 and blessing the finished church in 1872 (Green, *San Agustín*, 9–10).

With its elongated steeple and Gothic arches, San Agustín owed its style after 1872 more to French architecture than to its Spanish origins. This may have been due not only to the bishop of Galveston's appointees but also to another compatriot, an Oblate priest who spent most of his religious life traveling from ranch to ranch in South Texas. Father Pierre Yves Keralum was born in Brittany in 1817, and before being ordained a priest, he had been a cabinetmaker and an architect. His former occupations came in very useful in South Texas, for he designed and built churches in Roma and Brownsville and may have also been instrumental in building the new church of San Agustín in Laredo (Green, *San Agustín*, 10–11).

In the early years of the twentieth century, the wood altars of the church were replaced by marble, and stained glass windows were put in, and in the 1920s the clock was added, but only after the church tower was raised some twenty feet to accommodate it (Da Camara 55). Clearly, San Agustín was a work in progress, and the next step in its progression was to build a school adjacent to it. The school opened in 1927, five years after the Oblate priests had taken over the parish, and it was placed under the direction of the Sisters of Divine Providence from Our Lady of the Lake Convent in San Antonio.

San Agustín parochial school began with the first five grades, and within two years it included a four-year high school. The school building was constructed immediately north of the church, within the same property allotted to the church by the Spanish Royal Commission. It was a three-story brown brick building housing fourteen classrooms, a library, and laboratory facilities. It also had an auditorium with a fully equipped stage where plays and musical programs were performed. At first the nuns lived on the third floor, but in 1947 they moved across Zaragoza Street to the García-Martin residence, overlooking the river (Shanks 75). At about the same time that the nuns moved out of the school building, San Agustín Church began another improvement project, completed in 1952, which not only enlarged it but also modernized it with air conditioning and fluorescent lights (Green, *San Agustín*, 17).

San Agustín Church and its school were my destination almost every weekday for the next decade, although in order to reach them, I had to walk past a public school located less than three blocks from our house. In Guerrero, I had attended the newly built state school where all the children were educated; it was the only school in town, and the community was proud of it. But in Laredo things were different, as the husband of one of our relatives reminded us when Nela boasted that I had always received top grades, the implication being that I would not do as well in English as I had in Spanish. After that warning, the relatives' next piece of advice was that we should avoid the neighborhood school because it was so overcrowded that students attended classes in two shifts—morning and afternoon. This was a sad commentary on the state of the school that had been founded by Mayor Refugio Benavides in the 1870s and had been Laredo's largest elementary school. In the early years of its existence, the building had been painted yellow and therefore had been known as La Escuela Amarilla. In the first decade of the twentieth century the Yellow School had been replaced by a three-story structure of pale yellow brick and officially renamed Central School, but most people continued to call it by its original name.

Since attending La Escuela Amarilla was not advisable, my aunts enrolled me at San Agustín (or St. Augustine, depending on the speaker), which, being a parochial school, charged very modest tuition, since the parish partially subsidized it. San Agustín was therefore both financially and physically accessible to us, the latter also important since we did not own a car. It was for the second reason that Nela taught me the names and directions of the streets that I would have to traverse on my way to school.

However, in the early days I was not left to find my way alone. During the first weeks of classes, Ofelia, the oldest of my aunts and the one who appeared on the school records as my legal guardian, would take me to school in the morning and would be waiting for me in the afternoon when classes let out. On our way to school we would walk past the Escuela Amarilla, whose playground swarmed with noisy children over whom a few adults unsuccessfully tried to exert control. One morning, as we waited to cross the street in front of the school while the traffic light was red (we paid serious attention to traffic lights, these having been unknown in Guerrero), a man who stood next to us asked Ofelia why she walked a child of my age to school, thinking her, no doubt, excessively protective or me unusually slow. She explained that we were new in town and that my school was some distance away, which appeared to satisfy him. That evening at supper Ofelia repeated the man's question to her sisters, and they all found the incident quite amusing. I did not.

Perhaps the man's comment prompted my aunts to finally allow me to walk to school by myself, and after that, as I progressed from childhood to adolescence, I devised three or four different routes to cover the distance. Avoiding monotony was perhaps the main reason for varying the itinerary, but occasionally it was also to avoid the territory of an unfriendly dog. The first route that I followed, though, had been set by Ofelia when she was still walking me to school, and it was one that took us near the houses of two sets of cousins on the paternal side. My aunts still clung to the small-town custom of dropping by briefly to visit friends and relatives if they were in the neighborhood, and this we did with the cousins in the afternoons after school.

Sometimes we would stop at a house on Grant Street (the street that flanked San Agustín on the north) to visit a male cousin who was tall and thin and had a luxuriant handlebar mustache and who looked very much like Grandfather Lorenzo in photographs taken when he was in his thirties or forties. The other house that we visited was on Iturbide Street (one street north of Grant). Two unmarried daughters of Cándido de la Garza and Prudencia Benavides lived there, in their late parents' house. Here we would sit in the deep-shaded veranda that wrapped around the spacious cream-colored brick house and drink tall glasses of ice water presented on lace doilies.

This house was built in the "American" style, set back from the sidewalk behind a wrought-iron fence and in the midst of a lawn and shrubbery. Laredo was like New Orleans in that the construction of the old quarter had been dictated by the Spanish, but as the Anglo-Americans arrived, they had built their houses out of brick (not stone) and laid them in the midst of gardens, rather than enclosed in courtyards or patios. In Laredo the earliest "Garden District" had extended west from the center of town, toward the bend of the river, where the U.S. Army had built Fort McIntosh in 1849 to hold the city that had only reluctantly become part of the United States. After the Civil War, and particularly after the railroads arrived in Laredo in 1881, the number of Anglo immigrants increased, and they laid out the Heights District to the east of downtown according to their urban ideal. Iturbide Street, for example, became Market Street after crossing Zacate Creek, the dividing line between downtown Laredo and the Heights, otherwise known as Las Lomas.

The relatives' houses provided the landmarks for this first route to school, while I still recited the names of the streets I traversed until they became part of my memory map. We lived on Victoria Street, between San Francisco and San Eduardo Avenues. To go to school, I turned left (south) on San Eduardo, in the direction of the river. From San Eduardo on, all the streets and avenues were paved. It may now seem surprising that Victoria, east of San Eduardo, was still unpaved in the 1950s, but it was not an unusual case. In 1949 Kathleen Da Camara had written proudly that, at that time, there were 150 miles of streets in Laredo and that "seventy-five of these are paved" (30). This meant, therefore, that half of the population of Laredo (approximately) lived on unpaved streets, so we did not feel particularly deprived by living on such a street, even if, as Da Camara accurately described, "when there was a heavy wind, the atmosphere was filled with dust; and when a heavy downpour of rain came, the streets were transformed into lakes of water and mud" (29).

The next street that I came to after Victoria was Houston, where the white two-story building of the telephone company stood out among the modest dwellings that surrounded it, dominating the intersection. After Houston came Matamoros, and that intersection was marked by a furniture store whose front was covered with cobalt blue tiles that I found very attractive and by the Escuela Amarilla on the southwest corner. It was at this intersection of Matamoros and San Eduardo that one afternoon in October of 1953 Ofelia and I stood in a small crowd to wave at a smiling President Dwight D. Eisenhower as he passed us in a motorcade of one. He stood up in the backseat of a convertible, flashing his famous grin and waving in response to the friendly but restrained welcome from Laredoans. He was returning from Nuevo Guerrero, where with his Mexican counterpart, President Adolfo Ruiz Cortines, he had inaugurated Falcon International Dam, the mammoth project that had flooded Guerrero and several Zapata County communities and impelled our move to Laredo.

The other street that bordered Central School—on the south—was Farragut; then came Hidalgo, then Lincoln, then Iturbide. The block of San Eduardo between Lincoln and Iturbide contained a business that I found intriguing. It was a gray, inscrutable building, but its stone walls were decorated with murals depicting proud Aztec warriors and beautiful maidens in stylized poses, such as you would find in the colorful Mexican calendars, or *cromos*. The name of the business was—appropriately—Productos La India, and it sold herbs and spices and what are now termed nutritional supplements but were then called tonics. I never saw anyone going in or out of the building, and I did not even know if any business was still actively carried on in that location, but the name and the murals conjured in my imagination exotic aromas that I may or may not have actually inhaled.

The next street after Iturbide was Grant, and here I turned right and began to traverse the avenues in a westerly direction. After San Eduardo, I came to San Darío, then to Santa Ursula, then San Bernardo, and, finally, San Agustín—the avenue, the school, the church, and the plaza: my destination. My aunt had been correct in her instructions for finding my way to school. It was all a question of intersections at right angles and remembering that streets ran from east to west and avenues from south (beginning at the river) to north. What she did not tell me, because I could deduce it for myself, was that the street names alternately honored a Mexican hero and an American hero and that the avenues I was concerned with were named after saints of the Catholic calendar. Someone had planned this nomenclature very well, and that person seemed, at first blush, to have been a most unlikely source. It had been the first Reconstruction mayor of Laredo and the father of the Republican Party in Webb County: Samuel M. Jarvis.

Samuel Jarvis was an outsider, and like many of the men who became the business and political leaders of Laredo, he arrived on the border, not from the United States (or, at least, not directly), but from Europe or Mexico. Jarvis was born in New York City in 1822 to a wealthy family and received an exclusive education in that city. He clearly had an adventurous nature, for, as a young man, he joined a filibustering expedition to Nicaragua. He was captured and imprisoned there but was released in time for him to join Gen. Zachary Taylor's army in northeastern Mexico in 1846. Jarvis later served with Gen. Winfield Scott's army and participated in the capture of Mexico City. Perhaps as a reward for his military activities, after the war he was given an appointment in the quartermaster's office at Fort Brown, the site of the present Brownsville, Texas, across from Matamoros.

Jarvis must have been smitten with Mexico, though, because after two years at Fort Brown he took a management post with a silver mining company in Vallecillo, Nuevo León, where he met Inocencia Flores, married her, and had eight children with her. He is reported to have arrived in Laredo from Mexico after the Civil War (Meza 3:912–913). As a Unionist, Jarvis might be forgiven for having sat out the conflict in Mexico (where another conflict—the French Intervention—was going on), rather than being caught in Confederate Texas. This absence was fortunate for Jarvis, for his arrival in Laredo provided the military authorities with a viable civilian officeholder who had not served the Confederacy. In the summer of 1866 the military commander at Laredo had lamented that "there are so few people on this frontier that can speak and write both the English and Spanish languages intelligently that it is hard to find candidates" (Wilkinson 313). Samuel Jarvis, a northerner who had a Mexican wife and children and was fluent in Spanish, must have seemed like the answer to the commander's prayer. Jarvis was appointed mayor of Laredo in 1868, as well as county judge, collector of customs, and county surveyor. His was, indeed, a case of absolute power.

Jarvis, however, demonstrated that absolute power does not always corrupt, for, by most accounts, he proved to be a most enlightened officeholder, undertaking the physical improvement of the city. Under his direction, the streets were widened, and the city council adopted a new map of the city developed by Jarvis in 1869. Roberto R. Calderón points out that "being a surveyor was one of Jarvis's many talents" and that he "induced the council to widen the streets running east to west" (392). The streets must have, indeed, been narrow, since a *Laredo Times* article published in 1881 described them as being only ten *varas* (twenty-eight feet) wide; however, at the time of the article, an addition to the north of the city had already been laid out with streets that were twenty varas wide (Green, *Laredo in 1881*, 5–6).

Under Jarvis's direction, the Laredo city council also resolved that the streets should be "given Names according to the said Map and henceforth recognized by these names" (R. R. Calderón 392–393). How Laredo had managed without street names since its founding is not known. Calderón asks in a footnote: "Did Jarvis rename old streets? Did he include new streets and in doing so give these new streets their names?" (393). Perhaps old street names were simply subsumed in the new street scheme put forth by Jarvis. This scheme reflected a pragmatic biculturalism, although political partisanship also played a part in honoring Union heroes. General and President Ulysses S. Grant has perhaps not been sufficiently recognized in place-names; Admiral David Farragut certainly has not. Mayor Jarvis did his part to remedy the oversight. Not surprisingly, Abraham Lincoln was also honored with a street named after him, as was Washington, although his street was too far from downtown to command much attention. Houston was the only Texan commemorated in the street nomenclature devised by Jarvis, and this may have been because Houston had opposed secession.

Alternating with the streets named for American heroes were those commemorating important figures of Mexican history. The street north of Washington and the farthest from the river included in Jarvis's map was Moctezuma (with the Mexican spelling), named after the Aztec emperor who made the fatal error of welcoming Hernán Cortés to Mexico. It ran parallel to the railroad tracks that marked the city limits in the 1880s, as mentioned in an article in the *Laredo Times* in 1881 describing the city to newcomers. Laredo, according to the writer, "as laid out and incorporated embraced an area of about one mile in front of the river and extending back about half a mile. The present corporate limits are about one mile from on the river and about the same depth" (Green, *Laredo in 1881*, 6).

At the southern extreme, running parallel to the river, was a street that honored Gen. Ignacio Zaragoza, a hero of the battle of Puebla on Cinco de Mayo who had the added merit of having been born in Goliad, Texas. Agustín de Iturbide may not have been unanimously described as a Mexican hero, but he had been instrumental in concluding Mexican independence in 1821, although he later spoiled this accomplishment by declaring himself emperor of Mexico. He was soon deposed and exiled, and, upon his unauthorized return to the coast of Tamaulipas, had been sentenced to death and executed by orders of the state's first governor, Col. Bernardo Gutiérrez de Lara. Our street, Victoria, honored a hero of Mexican independence, Gen. Guadalupe Victoria, the nom de guerre of Miguel Fernández Félix, who took his name from the patron saint of Mexico. Hidalgo and Matamoros Streets honored two priests who were leaders of Mexican independence, particularly Hidalgo, who is revered for issuing the first call for independence in 1810. Hidalgo is sometimes compared to George Washington, although Hidalgo was much less fortunate, since he was captured and executed by the royalist army in 1811.

When it came to naming the avenues for Catholic saints, Jarvis had thousands to choose from. The custom at the time among Hispanic Catholics was to christen a child with the name of the saint on whose feast day the child was born, which sometimes saddled an infant with an unappealing name. We do not know if Jarvis and his wife, Inocencia (meaning "Innocence"), followed this custom (her birthday would have been December 28, the Feast of the Holy Innocents, the Mexican equivalent of April Fool's Day), but it has been suggested that the mayor named some of the avenues after the saints who were his children's namesakes. It is also possible that the mayor, obviously a good politician, chose this manner to flatter important local political figures. One of the avenues that I traversed was San Darío. The saint was not the king of Persia of ancient times, nor was the avenue named after the great Latin American poet Rubén Darío (the nom de plume of Rubén García Sarmiento). Interestingly, though, two of the most prominent political figures in Laredo at the time were named Darío: Darío Sánchez, who was twice mayor in the 1880s, and Darío González, who was several times elected alderman.

San Agustín was, of course, the obvious choice for naming the avenue where the church and the plaza of the same name were located. Once past San Agustín Avenue, in a westerly direction, Jarvis deviated from using saints' names and began using family names. After San Agustín came Flores Avenue, named, most likely, after Jarvis's in-laws, and after Flores came Convent Avenue, the most important thoroughfare in Laredo because it led to the International Bridge. Convent Avenue was named after the Ursuline Convent and School for Girls that once stood off Zaragoza Street, overlooking the river.

The Ursuline nuns had arrived in Laredo at about the same time that Samuel Jarvis began his tenure as mayor. They had been asked by the bishop of Galveston to establish a school for girls in Laredo, and after their arrival they found lodging in "a small house east of St. Augustine

Church and, within months, had established a day and boarding school" (Thompson, *Laredo*, 284). During the Mexican Revolution, especially during its furor between 1913 and 1916, the Ursuline boarding students were reported to have followed the progress of battles in Nuevo Laredo from the second-story dormitory windows. According to Thompson, the Ursuline convent and school was a three-story building made of native stone. The original structure was expanded in 1896, but by 1939 the school and convent were gone, relocated to a campus in the Heights area, to make room for the United States Customs and Immigration station on the International Bridge (Thompson, *Laredo*, 284).

The construction of the new port facilities on Convent Avenue was confirmation of the importance of the International Bridge to Laredo. The facility that allowed people and goods to cross the Rio Grande was the lifeline on which the twin cities of Laredo and Nuevo Laredo depended for their existence. The first bridge had been constructed in 1889, an outgrowth of the arrival of the railroads to the border. Before the construction of this first bridge, "ferrymen, called chalaneros, did a brisk business in their flatboats poling people across to the other bank and back," writes Laredo historian Ann Shanks, who adds that the first international bridge rested on twin piers across the river and that "wood was interspersed on steel supports creating the floor of the bridge" (37).

Since automobiles were almost unknown in Laredo in 1889, this first bridge was constructed to accommodate wagon traffic and pedestrians. Modernization of the bridge was forced on Laredo by an act of God—the tornado of 1905—at about the same time that automobiles began to appear. The second bridge had concrete piers with steel reinforcements, but it, too, had a wood floor that proved to be its undoing. On April 26, 1920, the second bridge caught fire and its wooden floor went up in smoke, leaving behind only the twisted metal girders. The fire was ascribed both to negligently discarded cigarettes and to Mexican revolutionary activity. During the two years it took to construct and open the third International Bridge, people and goods moved across the river on the Tex-Mex railroad bridge. The old-time chalanes also briefly made a comeback while the third bridge was under construction (Thompson, *Laredo*, 262–263).

The third International Bridge was officially opened in 1922, during a major Laredo festival, the Washington's Birthday Celebration in February. The structure was, according to Shanks, "a beautiful, four-laned, paved bridge with graceful concrete steel reinforced arches under the roadbed... [and] carried pedestrians, automobile and truck traffic" (39). This third bridge remained in place through the following three decades, during which time, Shanks tells us, Laredo became the "Number One Inland Port of Entry into the United States" (39).

Fire no longer imperiled the modern International Bridge, but floods, although infrequent, did. In 1932 the Rio Grande crested at fifty-two feet in Laredo and covered the bridge, inflicting damage to it that was quickly repaired. The flood of 1954, however, was of a greater magnitude. It was, Shanks relates, the worst flood in Laredo's history (41). The river began rising in the last days of June and backed up Chacón and Zacate Creeks in the north and east parts of the city, cutting off the roads to San Antonio, Corpus Christi, and Zapata. The river crested at over sixty-two feet on July 1 and covered the International Bridge. Damage was so extensive that "several spans were literally wiped out" (Shanks 40). The U.S. Army Corps of Engineers came to the rescue, putting up a pontoon bridge downriver from the wreckage.

From 1954 to 1957, when the current structure was completed, Nuevo Laredo residents crossed on the pontoon bridge to go to work and to shop for clothes and cars, toys and toasters in Laredo, as they had done before the flood. My aunts and I, along with countless other Laredoans, crossed the river in the opposite direction, clinging nervously to the hand cable, especially after passing automobiles would set the underlying cylinders rolling and the bridge shaking under our feet, as we made our weekly shopping trip to Nuevo Laredo.

Avenida Guerrero was the continuation of the International Bridge, the main thoroughfare in Nuevo Laredo, and it was here that our destination, the central marketplace, was located. However, our goal here was not the market's periphery, where the piñatas and the trinkets for the tourist trade beckoned the unwary, but its core, where all the foodstuffs were. We came to buy beef, which cost less than in Texas (both in absolute terms and in terms of the currency exchange rate), and staples such as rice, sugar, and coffee, which were also less expensive. The shopping experience here was completely different from the antiseptic American supermarkets, where everything was cellophane wrapped. In the *mercado* the butchers hung the carcasses from hooks and cut the meat as you requested, on the spot. A few aisles away, pyramids of oranges, mangoes, and avocadoes and strings of drying chiles tickled the nose and the taste buds, enticing you to take the produce home, but the U.S. Department of Agriculture prohibited the importation of most of it. It did allow tomatoes and bananas, however, and these we bought and took back with us. We made the return trip laden with shopping bags, along a route similar to that I took to go to school.

After following the original route for the first few years, by the time I was in high school I had devised a diagonal approach to reach San Agustín. From Central School, I would cut across Central Plaza, which lay directly west of the school. The old quarter of Laredo was dotted with several squares, brief shaded oases in that landscape of heat. This attractive feature, while undoubtedly dating back to colonial days, was refined by Mayor Samuel Jarvis. A decade after he left office in 1872, the Laredo newspaper pointed out proudly that "in the old town there are four plazas, of one block each" (Green, *Laredo in 1881*, 6). Jarvis himself was commemorated in the most attractive of the squares—Jarvis Plaza. The federal courthouse and the post office faced Jarvis Plaza, which also contained probably the single largest concentration of trees in town. A sprinkling of benches scattered throughout Jarvis Plaza also provided the weary walker a welcome shady rest, an amenity missing from Central Plaza. Central Plaza, however, was planted with *huizache* (huisache), a hardy tree whose tiny, aromatic yellow blooms are the harbingers of spring in the brush country.

Morning and afternoon I would traverse Central Plaza on my way to and from school. In the mornings I would almost sprint across it, since I was usually late for Mass, which began at eight o'clock and was compulsory. In those harried mornings, as I emerged from Central Plaza, I would make a split-second decision as to whether to approach school from San Bernardo or San Agustín Avenue. It was a case of the proverbial six of one and half a dozen of the other, both routes being equidistant. Sometimes I would choose the San Agustín way, just so I could walk past the Plaza Hotel on Hidalgo Street. The Hotel Plaza (in Spanish, as everyone called it) had been founded in the 1920s as the Robert E. Lee Hotel and was the second-tallest building in town, with its eight stories of dark red brick. In spite of its original name, the hotel décor was California Mission, at least at ground level, where the restaurant was located. The Spanish Grill had bow windows of amber-colored pebble glass, so that all that the passersby, like me, could observe of the diners inside were their silhouettes as they raised their cups or glasses to their lips. Shanks relates that the Spanish Grill was a popular meeting place where many business deals originated and that "Spanish arches, Mexican tile, and French furniture added charm to the lobby" (63).

Once I was past the Plaza Hotel, it was only half a block to the intersection of Hidalgo and San Agustín, where I turned south, in the direction of the river. The municipal building occupied the entire block south and west of the intersection. City Hall was the modern incarnation of the old Market Hall, and dingy grocery stores still lined the block facing the police station, on the east side of San Agustín. A mixture of smells—mostly overripe fruit and meat—emanated from the dark interiors behind the sagging screen doors and discouraged lingering in the area. At this point I usually had only three minutes to cover the remaining three blocks to the church.

When the Gothic-style doors of San Agustín Church had closed behind me, I could slip into a pew with my classmates at the back of the church. The seating was arranged in order of seniority, with the youngest children sitting at the front and the juniors and seniors at the back. Longevity had its privileges: juniors and seniors did not have to march all the way to the front, announcing that they were late. Once inside the church, I could allow myself, for the duration of the Mass, to be swept up in contemplation of the remote purity of the marble altars and statuary (Saint Augustine of Hippo in the place of honor, to the right of Christ). After a long walk in the spring sun that already burned bright at eight in the morning, the white coldness of the marble altars was infinitely more conducive to spirituality than any polychromatic depiction of heaven could have been.

One morning in late May, I chose the San Bernardo route and, instead of gazing into the Plaza Hotel, I found myself contemplating the house of one of my classmates, on the corner of Lincoln and San Bernardo, but still three blocks away from church. It was one of the old houses, built in the Spanish or Mexican period, one story in height and made of stone, "very substantial," as the Laredo newspaper described others like it in 1881, adding that the walls, being two and three feet in thickness were, "consequently cool in the hot summer days and warm in the winter" (Green, *Laredo in 1881*, 6). My classmate was a good student and, no doubt, was already lining up for church while I dawdled in front of his house. There would be no repercussions, though, if I was late this morning, for it was the last day of school, and in the evening I would accept my diploma and my valedictorian award from the parish priest during a High Mass composed by our own Father Janssen.

While the Mass started without me, I stood still, wanting to fix in my retina and in my memory the dazzling sunlight striking the white-washed walls of the house, the black wrought-iron grillwork at the windows, and the purple and fuchsia extravaganza of the bougainvillea spilling over the arbors inside the low wall that surrounded the property. "I shall never walk this way again on my way to school," I told myself, with a sense of finality. "I must always remember this moment." And I was right: I never did, and I still do.

《 NINE 》

Voyages in English

The first word that I learned in English was "umbrella." When I first heard it, I had no idea what it meant, but I was enchanted by its soft sound as it rolled off the tongue. An umbrella figured prominently on a page in the first-grade reader that showed a blonde, curly-headed little girl (Dick and Jane's little sister) marching under the sheltering black canopy that deflected the raindrops. It was one of the first days of school for me in Laredo, and the teacher had assigned us to describe scenes from the book on the following day. I asked one of my English-speaking relatives to tell me what to say in class, and she rattled off a sentence or two, out of which I retained only the word "umbrella." I repeated the sound to myself that day, and on the following day, when the teacher called for a description of the scene, I raised my hand and pronounced, "umbrella." Nothing else. When I realized my gaffe, I was mortified. I had made a fool of myself, not only before the bemused nun, but also before a roomful of six-year-olds, for whom an eight-year-old who towered over them by a head went from being merely odd to being ridiculous. And yet, some six months later, it seemed to me that I was speaking English.

I do not know which language teaching method the nuns at St. Augustine School (otherwise known as Escuela San Agustín) used, if any. I suppose it could be called limited total immersion because only English was used in the classroom, but Spanish was available in case of emergency. The nuns took into account that many—or even most—of the children in the first grade spoke no English, and a Spanish-speaking teacher was usually assigned to that group. Our teacher was Sister Mary Nora, and she was the only Hispanic nun at St. Augustine at the time, the others being Irish, German, or Anglo-American. Sister Mary Nora always spoke to us in English, but we knew that if someone like me got seriously stuck, she could understand and communicate with us in Spanish. The majority of the children in the elementary grades at St. Augustine were Mexican, whether born in Laredo or Nuevo Laredo, and they usually spoke Spanish at home and carried the same language into the playground. Their parents, though, were conscious that they were paying tuition for their children's education and conveyed to the nuns their expectation that the children learn English. We were, therefore, forbidden to speak Spanish in the classroom. However, I do not recall feeling humiliated or otherwise oppressed by this rule, nor did my classmates, since we understood that it was a question of getting your (or your family's) money's worth and not an unfavorable reflection on the language or culture of home.

At St. Augustine, if anyone could have been called a minority in that first grade, it was a little boy named Alvin and a little girl named Mary Ann, both of whom had beautiful blue eyes and rosy cheeks and did not speak Spanish. Although this deficiency did not elicit any unkindness from their classmates, they did not remain long at St. Augustine. It was a reference to Mary Ann, though, that prompted my realization that I was actually speaking English. Sister Mary Nora had directed me to collect the class workbooks or some other papers and later asked me if I had done so. I replied that I had, "all except Mary Ann's." The moment I said it I realized that I had mastered the possessive form in English — not "the book of Mary Ann," as in Spanish, but "Mary Ann's book."

I do not know if Sister Mary Nora noticed what a breakthrough my response had been, but she must have been aware that I was catching on and might be ready to start catching up with my age cohorts. At the end of the school year, therefore, she arranged for me to go to the third grade, skipping the second. This did not mean that I was a prodigy, for I had already done the second (as well as the third) grade in my previous school in Guerrero. In Laredo I had been put in the first grade again because I had to learn English. If I had not had this challenge, I would have been completely miserable because learning had been more accelerated in Mexico than in Texas. In addition, it seemed to me that much of my first grade in English involved unlearning what I had learned before or repeating it in reverse order. For example, in Guerrero I had learned cursive writing but not printing; now I had to learn block printing before advancing to cursive. And yet, I cannot say that the revisited first grade was an unalloyed penance, for not only did I acquire the basic elements of English, but I also absorbed the essence of what I came to view as the cycle of American life.

In my first first-grade, in Guerrero, we had learned that the calendar year was divided into four seasons: *primavera, verano, otoño, invierno.*

Since Guerrero was an agricultural community, the teachers reminded us that the twenty-first of March marked the first day of spring (primavera), the time when farmers began to plant their fields for summer crops. And, indeed, at about that time my grandfather Benito would leave for the ranch to plant melons, squash, corn, and beans. Once in Laredo, though, the year seemed to start in the fall, undoubtedly because that was when the school year started, and with it, a sequence of holidays by which the year was measured. Our yearly cycle now began, not when the farmers planted their fields, but when they harvested enormous orange pumpkins and when witches flew on broomsticks by the light of an equally large orange harvest moon.

Each classroom at St. Augustine (and probably all the American elementary schools to this day) marked the passage of the year by decorating the official bulletin board with icons cut out of construction paper to represent particular holidays: pumpkins and turkeys in the fall, red hearts in February, and so forth. These holidays were either secular or religious; it made no difference to the nuns, since they were American holidays. Christmas and Easter, of course, transcended national boundaries and, being religious holy days, received more attention, but we still marked their arrival with construction paper evergreens and multicolored eggs delivered by rabbits (except for one Spanish priest who thundered from the pulpit that rabbits did not lay eggs).

By the end of the first grade at St. Augustine, I had both extended my ability to communicate by acquiring another language — English — and realized the limits of language. I realized that there were words in English that had no counterpart in Spanish and vice versa. The most obvious example was the English word "fun," as in *Fun with Dick and Jane* (the title of our first-grade reader). Fun seemed to be a prerogative of American children. In Spanish, although you might enjoy playing with Dick and Jane or enjoy their company (*divertirse* or *disfrutar*), it was not the same as "having fun" with them. Fun, I concluded, was the quintessential American word, connoting playfulness, as in "fun and games," and laughter, as in "funny." In the Hispanic world there might be humor and gusto (a Spanish word) but not necessarily fun.

I do not think that my first-grade teacher, although fluent in English and Spanish, shared these linguistic insights; but she felt that I was ready to move to the third grade, and I did, although it meant having to adjust to another set of classmates. The third-grade teacher was not a nun but what was termed a "lay teacher." She was a cheerful and energetic young married woman who, besides teaching us the required skills, inspired the class to good behavior by promising us an end-of-the-school-year picnic at her father's ranch. Her father was a longtime Webb County politician, and as befitted his position, he had a fine ranch that we all longed to visit. We must have been well behaved that year, because we received our reward, and we all had "a lot of fun" at the picnic, although I do not remember any specific activities from it.

In the fourth grade it was back to a religious teacher, a no-nonsense older German nun named Sister Emmanuel, who was more concerned with the serious side of teaching than the fun side of it. Nevertheless, I enjoyed the fourth grade because it was not a repetition of anything I had had before and because I enjoyed our reading book. It was called *Voyages in English* and contained both prose and poetry. It seemed to me, looking at the cover of the book (it was blue, with the outline of a sailing ship), that embarking on a new language was, indeed, embarking on a voyage of discovery. However, *Voyages in English* was only preparation for the journey; the voyage of discovery began at the public library.

The Laredo Public Library was conveniently located some three blocks from school. It took up a large part of the second floor of the City Hall building, which had originally been known as Market Hall. In the year 1881 the railroad had arrived in Laredo to connect the border with the rest of the United States, and in its wake had followed thousands of American immigrants. These newcomers soon set out to erect the edifices of civic life, such as they had known back home but which Laredo lacked. The first structure was the courthouse and jail, built in 1882 for a cost of $58,000, followed by the Market Hall, the finest in the state, according to E. R. Tarver in a pamphlet printed and distributed by the Laredo Immigration Society in 1889, *Laredo, the Gateway between the United States and Mexico*. In this publication Tarver reported that the Market Hall had cost $43,000 and included a "cool and well ventilated market house, elegant rooms for the different city officers in the lower story, whilst the whole of the large upper story is fitted up for an opera house" (3–4). The new Laredo city fathers—the Anglo immigrants—were clearly of a capitalist inclination, for, after setting aside quarters for the mayor, chief of police, city surveyor, city engineer, market master, and city attorney, the remaining space in the market hall was rented out for $8,000 a year (Tarver 5).

Before the construction of these public buildings, the Laredo government functions had been consolidated in one place: the Casa Consistorial, or Council House, located on the south side of San Agustín Plaza, which had been in use since Spanish days. Regardless of political changes, Laredo had continued to be a "Mexican" town, as the editor of the *Laredo*

Times advised prospective American immigrants in 1881 (Green, *Laredo in 1881*, 5). The Laredo civil authorities conducted city business and recorded their actions in the official minutes "entirely in Spanish," according to Roberto Calderón, until the appointment of Samuel Jarvis as mayor in 1868, after which time the minutes were "intermittently written in English or Spanish, depending upon who the city secretary and mayor happened to be" (322–323). And Jarvis's tolerance in matters of language extended to the monetary field; at his arrival, the Laredo city budget was calculated in pesos and reales. In his study, Roberto Calderón notes that in August of 1868 the municipal budget had a surplus of 120 pesos, that fruit vendors at the market square paid a rent "equal to two *reales*" per day, that vendors of alcoholic spirits were assessed a monthly tax of "three silver pesos," and billiard tables were taxed at the rate of two silver pesos per month (386–388).

However, if Samuel Jarvis was willing to work within this "Mexican" framework of municipal government, his compatriots, when they arrived later en masse, were not. Beginning in 1886, the Laredo mayors were no longer Mexican (even by marriage, as Jarvis had been); the language of government business became English, and the coin of the realm was the dollar. In 1881 James Saunders Penn, an "immigrant" from the state capital, began publishing the *Laredo Weekly Times* to chronicle—in English—the doings of the new city leaders in what had become a boomtown.

With the construction of the courthouse, the jail, and the city/market hall, the Casa Consistorial on San Agustín Plaza retained only one public function from the old days, that of a school. In 1889, when Tarver published his booklet touting Laredo, he wrote that the city had assumed charge of the public schools in 1882 and that the schools numbered seven—one high school that went up to the tenth grade and "six schools of intermediate grades." He added that the city owned "two large two story school buildings" (5). One of these large buildings was, undoubtedly, the high school housed in the Casa Consistorial; the other was the Escuela Amarilla, built in the early 1870s, during the mayoral term of Refugio Benavides. The two schools survived in their original form until the early twentieth century, when both were torn down and rebuilt, each on its own site. The Casa Consistorial came down in 1916, and during construction of the new school its students were housed on the second floor of the Market Hall, which apparently had not become the opera house that its builders had envisaged.

The early commercial establishments located in Market Hall eventually moved out, and the building became City Hall. Municipal functions came to absorb all the available space, including the second floor, which finally found permanent use as the Laredo Public Library. I do not recall how I discovered the public library or exactly when I found my way to it, but it was probably in the fourth grade, when I was still reading children's literature. It must have taken some courage for me to enter the imposing arches of City Hall and then to climb one of the twin tiled staircases that led to the second floor. I can almost see myself clinging nervously to the wrought iron balustrade until I reached the double glass doors that admitted me to the churchlike hush of the vast interior. Yards and yards of shelving filled with books lined the walls and jutted out every so often to create alcoves that held large reading tables.

On that first visit it was unlikely that I knew the arrangement and layout of the books, but I soon found my way to the children's biography section. Here I found a collection—easily recognizable volumes in bright orange bindings with black silhouettes on the cover—of juvenile biographies of famous women from American history: the young Martha Washington, Abigail Adams, and other lesser-known but still admirable figures, such as Amelia Earhart, Jane Addams, and Clara Barton, founder of the American Red Cross. My earliest knowledge of American history came from those juvenile biographies, which (perhaps unintentionally) also encouraged girls to develop and utilize their talents.

Toward the end of the fourth grade I took an achievement test that showed that I was reading at tenth-grade level (the result of frequenting the public library), and the nuns decided that I could safely skip the fifth grade. Still, to make up for whatever one learned in the fifth grade, I was directed to attend summer school. My summer school assignment was to read a long list of books that American children were presumed to have read by that level, such as *Tom Sawyer* and *Rebecca of Sunnybrook Farm* (or was it *Anne of Green Gables*?). That summer I was in heaven, spending my days with the March sisters as I read *Little Women*, sharing Jo's dreams of becoming a writer and weeping buckets at Beth's death. Reading was my favorite activity, much to my aunts' concern, who claimed that I did it to excess. My aunts would often recall that before I started school in Guerrero, I would demand to be read to on a daily basis from several books of stories. They must have been relieved when I learned to do it by myself, although their concern then became what I should or should not read.

There had been no public library in Guerrero, but my grandfather's library had been close at hand. His reading tastes were eclectic and ranged from Nietzsche's philosophy (*The Antichrist*, in Spanish) to the Spanish classics (Tirso de Molina's legend of Don Juan, *El burlador de Sevilla*), with a preponderance of historical novels by Alexandre Dumas and Sir

Walter Scott, in translation of course. My preference was for the latter, but my aunts were doubtful of their appropriateness for a seven-year-old. Once I began reading in English, though, my aunts lost the ability to judge the quality of my reading choices and concentrated on the quantity. Nela (the "intelligent one," who had been my grandfather's and my father's secretary) would remind me of the fate that had befallen Don Quijote. Cervantes's hero had gone mad, according to his creator, from too much reading (actually it was due to *what* he read rather than how much, but Nela glossed over that distinction). My brain was not yet fully developed, according to Nela, and I might overload it with too much reading. That summer between the fourth and the sixth grade, though, my aunts had to admit defeat and allowed me to read to my heart's content in order to accelerate my schooling.

My classmates in summer school were older than me, teenage girls for the most part, who had already finished elementary school in Nuevo Laredo or even secondary school (ninth grade) and were now in a "special English" class to study the language, after which they would be tested and placed in the appropriate grade. They would end up placed anywhere from the sixth to the ninth grade and go from there to receive a high school diploma that demonstrated they were proficient in English as well as in Spanish and therefore qualified to be bilingual secretaries or sales clerks in a department store. For those students, learning English had a specific economic purpose, and they probably saw me not only as childish but also as a hopeless dreamer, always with my face in a book.

Although the summer students viewed learning English as a passport only to a job rather than to a journey, as I did, they were correct. Bilingualism was valued in our marketplace, but perhaps not enough; it was so prevalent. I observed an example of the market's expectation of—and the lack of remuneration for—bilingual skills in our neighborhood when I saw the operators picketing the office of the telephone company. In those days before direct long-distance dialing, all calls to Mexico (including the numerous daily calls to Nuevo Laredo) were handled by the Laredo operators in Spanish, but these operators were not compensated for their language skills. It was taken for granted that they understood and spoke Spanish, although they worked for an American company in the United States. Strictly speaking, most people in Laredo were not only bilingual but actually trilingual. The young, especially, also spoke "Spanglish," "Tex-Mex," or "Pocho," as the mixing of English and Spanish was called (derogatively) in Mexico. Each language had its own separate sphere: schoolchildren spoke

Spanish at home with their parents and elders, English in the classroom with their teachers, and "Tex-Mex" among themselves in the playground.

That summer I fulfilled the reading requirements needed to skip the fifth grade, and the following September I began the sixth grade with yet another group of classmates. The sixth grade was difficult both for our teacher, a gangly, middle-aged nun named Sister Rosalia, and for me, the new gangly girl, the two of us having to cope, for different reasons, with an unruly mob of sixth graders affected by unpredictable hormones. By keeping my head down, I was eventually able to blend in and be ignored, but Sister Rosalia had no such escape, having to face us every morning from her desk. Mornings, though, were not so bad; the class seemed to save its mutinous energy for the period immediately after lunch. That was when Sister Rosalia would try to lead us in song, producing a harmonica from within the voluminous folds of her black habit. She would announce the song of the day—"America the Beautiful," "Oh! Susannah," or some other selection from the American Songbook that was part of our course of study—and blow into the harmonica to signal the key. That was our signal to belt out the latest Elvis Presley song or whichever number from the hit parade the class ringleaders had previously chosen. Sister Rosalia would pound on the desk with her ruler until order was restored, but on occasion she would admit defeat and sit quietly until the pandemonium had subsided.

Sister Rosalia should have realized that, in embracing American pop music, we had already embraced a significant part of American culture, but it obviously pained her that we were happily ignorant of the greater American traditions and history. Our teachers must have felt as frustrated by our reluctance to be wholly Americanized as the Anglo immigrants who had followed the railroads had been perplexed by a city council that kept its minutes in Spanish and calculated its budget in silver pesos. Those Anglo newcomers had cast about for a way to convert a Mexican town to the "American way" and decided to showcase American history by celebrating the birthday of the "Father of the Country," George Washington, in late February.

The timing of the celebration coincided with the usual dates for Carnival in Catholic countries, so the Laredo population was likely in a receptive mood for the fiesta when it made its debut in 1898. The sponsoring group was the "Improved Order of Red Men," a fraternal organization transplanted to the border from the East. The Washington's Birthday Celebration soon became the most important festival in Laredo and remains so to this day. Its success was the result of a brilliant fusion of elements from both cultures. Historian Elliot Young explains the phenomenon of the Washington's Birthday Celebration in Laredo thus: "The historic, geographic, and demographic significance of Mexico and Mexicans on the border had to be incorporated into the very concept of America" (50). For example, the Washington pageant featured the appearance of Princess Pocahontas and Capt. John Smith (the pageant was guilty of some anachronisms); this feature could be viewed as an allusion to *mestizaje*, which was quite familiar in Spanish America but not in the United States, where its counterpart, miscegenation, was discouraged.

These two characters from early American colonial history were part of the pageant that centered on George and Martha Washington, who, dressed in lavish eighteenth-century costumes, had been transplanted to the Mexican border in the twentieth century and set atop decorated floats, from where they waved at the spectators that lined the parade route. From early on, the bicultural flavor of the event trumped any claim to historical authenticity. For example, the program for the 1913 celebration included bullfights in Nuevo Laredo scheduled for Sunday, February 23, at four in the afternoon. That year, however, the outbreak of violence in Nuevo Laredo that followed the assassination of President Francisco Madero caused the bullfights to be canceled, as was the ceremony at the boundary marker on the International Bridge at which local, state, and federal officials were to embrace their Mexican counterparts, according to the report in the *Laredo Daily Times* on February 25, 1913. What George Washington would have made of bullfights in his honor, we cannot even imagine, but the people of *los dos Laredos* saw nothing incongruous in this manner of celebrating his birthday, nor in the Noche Mexicana, another popular feature of the event that showcased Mexican entertainers.

If historical accuracy was not of paramount concern to Laredoans in the Washington's Birthday festivities (except for the costumes), it may have been because history—as taught in school—did not seem particularly accurate. Where were we, for example, in the Texas history books? The State of Texas requires the teaching of Texas history at some point in the sixth, seventh, or eighth grade, and St. Augustine followed the state mandate. As a class, our knowledge of Texas probably extended only as far north as San Antonio, and San Antonio was the Alamo, where Davy Crockett, "King of the Wild Frontier," died defending Texas freedom against the wicked Mexicans under the command of Gen. Antonio López de Santa Anna, who managed to combine evil and buffoonery in one. Hearing this, my classmates and I may have looked at each other nervously, wondering if we, too, were evil Mexicans, but since there was nobody to tell us that we were (not even Sister Rosalia, in spite of what we did to her), we mentally shrugged it off, and for our eighth-grade class trip we chartered a bus to go to San Antonio. Once there, we visited the Alamo, where we bought souvenirs, just like the other tourists.

Going from the eighth grade to high school was literally a rite of passage at St. Augustine, in that we passed from the second floor to the third. Once on the third floor, we felt very grown-up, changing classrooms every time a bell rang to signal the end of a class period and with different teachers for different subjects. For English we had Sister Vivian, an Irish nun who was nearing retirement age but was still as sharp as a tack, as the saying goes, and was one of the few teachers who could make diagramming sentences comprehensible. For foreign languages, St. Augustine could stretch only to providing Spanish (which was not really a foreign language to us), and Sister Aquilina, one of our own (a Texas Mexican) and a great favorite with the students for her vivaciousness, managed to inject "fun" into obscure grammatical tenses, such as the past subjunctive.

I continued frequenting the public library, but no longer were these solitary excursions. Now I would appear there accompanied by three or four friends, all of us seeking among the bookshelves the experiences that our sheltered existences did not provide. Impelled by these dubious motives, we discovered some good and some great literature. One friend, for example, recommended *Justine*—one of the four novels from the *Alexandria Quartet*, by the English writer Lawrence Durrell—because she had heard that it was a "dirty" book, and we hastened to check it out, ignoring the disapproving looks from the two elderly librarians. But we undoubtedly committed our greatest sacrilege when we memorized a poem by Federico García Lorca, "Romance de la casada infiel" (Ballad of the Unfaithful Wife), for the sole purpose of reciting the erotic parts, which, considering the topic, were numerous.

The suggestive volumes that we discovered at the public library at least had a good pedigree; not so the reading materials that were to be found in a veritable Aladdin's cave of used paperbacks located only a couple of blocks from school. I don't think the place even had a name, but it occupied the ground floor of the "B-29 Pool Hall," indicating, perhaps, from where the owner expected to draw his clientele. The place was large, dusty, and so dimly lit that it was difficult to make out the titles on the spines of the books that rose in stacks to fill the cavernous space, although not their lurid covers that depicted bosomy blondes and square-jawed heroes in compromising positions. The paperbacks were only five or ten cents each, so from time to time I could afford to buy a few of these forgettable tomes, of which I only remember one titled *Chocolates for Breakfast*, a story of decadent youth among wealthy New Yorkers. After consuming *Chocolates for Breakfast* and other, equally unwholesome fare, I would dispose of them among my friends, since, even without knowing English, my aunts would have realized that they were not school-related materials.

The few paperbacks for which I paid full price came from a newsstand on Jarvis Plaza that carried mostly newspapers and magazines and sold a few books as an afterthought. There I found *The Pocket Book of Verse: Great English and American Poems*, which became the constant companion to which I turned in moments of adolescent angst, when I would find myself "in disgrace with Fortune and men's eyes." I recognized that poetry was language at its most sublime, but though I loved language to the extent of finding enjoyment in reading the dictionary, I knew that rhythm and rhyme were beyond my powers. Prose I could handle, in either an imaginative or a factual mode, and I derived great satisfaction from creating fictional characters who acted out their conflicts within the confines of a short story. However, neither the characters nor their conflicts came from anything I had observed around me. Instead, I patterned my creations after those that appeared in the bible for young women in all things social and cultural, *Seventeen* magazine, which every year sponsored a short-story contest.

I entered the *Seventeen* story contest at least twice during high school, and in two consecutive years I received letters from the fiction editor, congratulating me for having been awarded one of ten Honorable Mention prizes, but, alas, not one of the top three selections that received cash and publication. Still, Honorable Mention awards did carry a $10 prize, a sum not altogether laughable, considering that major magazines paid $250 for a story, and I used my winnings one year for partial payment of a portable typewriter. Encouraged by this modest success, I began telling people—when they inquired what I planned to do in the future—that I wanted to be a writer. My aunts were dismayed when they heard this and hastened to point out that there were few—if any—jobs that paid a living wage for writing stories and that I should acquire marketable skills when I went to college.

My going to college had never been in question; the question had been where to find the least expensive place to do it. Fortunately, Laredo had a junior college where students could take the first two years of a four-year degree while living at home. In addition, as class valedictorian, I received a tuition scholarship to Laredo Junior College, so that, except for books—

and another expense related to attending a public institution — college was free for those two years. The related expense was the need to buy a new wardrobe, for after years of wearing a utilitarian school uniform (navy gabardine skirt, white cotton blouse, brown penny loafers and socks), I now had to shop the sales to outfit myself for looking like a college girl.

Laredo Junior College had come into existence in 1947, in response to the increased demand for higher education created by the GI Bill and the returning World War II veterans. Creating the college had not involved any cost for acquisition of the site or construction of facilities, for both were already available in the old mothballed military post, Fort McIntosh. After Mexico capitulated in 1848 and signed the Treaty of Guadalupe Hidalgo, ceding half of its territory to the United States, including Laredo, the American military authorities established a post on the western edge of Laredo, on a bluff overlooking the Rio Grande. Throughout the next ninety-plus years, the U.S. Army occupied the post in times of unrest on either side of the river and vacated it when the situation calmed down or when it became untenable, as during the Civil War. In 1913, for example, during the Mexican Revolution, Nuevo Laredo became a battlefield of opposing factions, and the *Laredo Daily Times* reported that the commander of Fort McIntosh had stationed soldiers on the U.S. side of the International Bridge to prevent the violence from spilling over (February 17, 1913). Its final use as a military installation came during World War II, when it was a training post for mechanized cavalry. After the end of the war, it was permanently vacated and turned over to the City of Laredo, which put it to use as a college.

Having spent ten years attending school in the same three-story building nestled next to the oldest church in Laredo (whose parking lot was also our playground), I was overwhelmed by the acres of open space in the old army post. Our classrooms at LJC were in the nineteenth-century brick and frame structures that had been the soldiers' barracks, the mess hall, and even the chapel (converted to a library), scattered throughout the campus. And after years of sharing my school days with basically the same forty-odd classmates (some odder than others), only a few of whom were also at Laredo Junior College, it was intimidating to make new friends from among the thousand or so students at LJC. I spent the first few months trying to find my niche in this new environment, and I finally did — in the student newspaper. I began writing opinion pieces, ranging in topics from the need to build an overpass over the railroad crossing in front of the campus entrance (it was built, years after I left) to the benefits of a bilingual society, and ended, in the second year, coediting the paper with another St. Augustine alum, though not a former classmate. Then the two junior college years were almost over, and it was time to decide where to go next.

The majority of college-bound Laredo students usually preferred to stay in South Texas, seldom venturing north of San Antonio, where there were several Catholic colleges. The St. Augustine nuns certainly encouraged their girls to attend their alma mater, Our Lady of the Lake College, located there, but the cost put it out of reach for me. I do not recall how the possibility of attending the University of Texas at Austin came up, but I was hesitant to do so because it was so large and reputed to be difficult, both socially and academically. However, I had some women cousins who had graduated from it, one of them from its law school, which was even more unusual. When I queried her as to whether she had felt lost at UT among so many strangers, she responded by asking me if, when I went to the movies, I knew everybody in the theater. I replied that of course I did not. "It's no different being at the university from being at the movies; you just concentrate on what's happening on the screen."

Based on my cousin's assurance, I made my decision to attend the University of Texas and began the application process, which also included applying for scholarships. My newspaper work at LJC had prompted me to choose journalism for my major and earned me a $200 scholarship (more than a year's tuition) from the Corpus Christi Press Club, which, with a similar award from the UT Laredo Club, paid for tuition, fees, and books. The only amount left to be covered by my family was room and board at Newman Hall, the Catholic girls' dormitory where my cousins had also lived. The amount came to $75 a month, plus incidentals, which, by necessity, had to remain very incidental. I was ready to leave home behind and move to the citadel of learning, only vaguely aware that from now on English would be my principal means of communication.

One Saturday in early September, another brave soul (a girl I had met at LJC) and I boarded a Greyhound bus in Laredo and traveled north, on our way to Austin and the future. I had with me a metal foot locker filled, not only with my frugal wardrobe, but also with the new bed linens that my aunt Ofelia had monogrammed for me on her sewing machine. I also took with me a large carton of books containing all my favorite volumes of poetry and prose. It was this carton that made the taxi driver balk when we arrived in Austin. He objected to loading it into his taxi, and he protested even more vehemently when he had to unload it and carry it inside the dormitory. But he finally did, because it was already dark and he couldn't very well leave us standing on the sidewalk surrounded by our impedimenta. My travel companion (also my roommate) soon went off on some errand of her own, and I was left alone in the room, with the foot locker and the carton of books waiting to be unpacked. I had arrived at the capital of Texas from the Republic of the Rio Grande.

Works Cited

BOOKS AND ARTICLES

Adams, John A., Jr. *Conflicted Commerce on the Rio Grande: Laredo, 1755–1955*. College Station: Texas A&M University Press, 2008.
Addington, Stanley. "Raymondville, Texas." In *The New Handbook of Texas*. 6 vols. Austin: Texas State Historical Association, 1996.
Alessio Robles, Vito. *Coahuila y Texas desde la consumación de la independencia hasta el tratado de Guadalupe Hidalgo*. 2 vols. Mexico City: Editorial Porrúa, 1945.
Alonzo, Armando C. *Tejano Legacy: Rancheros and Settlers in South Texas, 1734–1900*. Albuquerque: University of New Mexico Press, 1998.
Balderrama, Francisco E., and Raymond Rodríguez. *Decade of Betrayal: Mexican Repatriation in the 1930s*. Albuquerque: University of New Mexico Press, 2006.
Barclay, William. "The Cover: Earlier Treatment of Tuberculosis Patients." *JAMA* 293 (2005): 2696.
Benavides et al. v. State. No. 6101. Court of Civil Appeals of Texas. October 8, 1919.
Benavides Hinojosa, Artemio. *El general Bernardo Reyes: Vida de un liberal porfirista*. Monterrey, Nuevo León: Ediciones Castillo, 1998.
Berlandier, Jean Louis. *The Indians of Texas in 1830*. Edited and introduced by John C. Ewers. Washington, DC: Smithsonian Institution Press, 1969.
———. *Journey to Mexico during the Years 1826 to 1834*. 2 vols. Translated by Sheila M. Ohlendorf et al. Austin: Texas State Historical Association, 1980.
Black's Law Dictionary. Rev. 4th ed. St. Paul, MN: West Publishing Co., 1968.
Brenner, Anita. *The Wind That Swept Mexico: The History of the Mexican Revolution of 1910–1942*. Austin: University of Texas Press, 1996.
Byfield, Patsy Jeanne. *Falcon Dam and the Lost Towns of Zapata*. Austin: Texas Memorial Museum, 1971.
Calderón, Francisco R. "La vida económica." In *Historia moderna de México: La república restaurada*. 3 vols. Edited by Daniel Cosío Villegas. Mexico City: Editorial Hermes, 1955.

Calderón, Roberto R. "Mexican Politics in the American Era, 1846–1900: Laredo, Texas." Diss., UCLA, 1993.
Cavazos Garza, Israel. *Nuevo León y la colonización del Nuevo Santander*. Monterrey, Nuevo León, 1999.
Cockcroft, James D. *Intellectual Precursors of the Mexican Revolution, 1900–1913*. Austin: University of Texas Press, 1968.
Cruz, Gilbert R. *Let There Be Towns: Spanish Municipal Origins in the American Southwest, 1610–1810*. College Station: Texas A&M University Press, 1988.
Cumberland, Charles C. "Border Raids in the Lower Rio Grande Valley, 1915." *Southwestern Historical Quarterly* 57.3 (January 1954): 285–311.
———. *Mexican Revolution: The Constitutionalist Years*. Austin: University of Texas Press, 1974.
———. *Mexican Revolution: Genesis under Madero*. Austin: University of Texas Press, 1952.
Da Camara, Kathleen. *Laredo on the Rio Grande*. San Antonio: Naylor Co., 1949.
de la Garza, Beatriz. *A Law for the Lion: A Tale of Crime and Injustice in the Borderlands*. Austin: University of Texas Press, 2003.
de la Garza, Lorenzo. *La antigua Revilla en la leyenda de los tiempos*. 3rd ed. Monterrey, Nuevo León, 1996. (All references are to this edition, unless noted otherwise.)
———. *La antigua Revilla en la leyenda de los tiempos*. 2nd ed. San Antonio, TX: Editorial Quiroga, 1952.
———. *Dos hermanos héroes*. Mexico City: Editorial Cultura, 1939.
del Castillo, Richard Griswold. *The Treaty of Guadalupe Hidalgo: A Legacy of Conflict*. Norman: University of Oklahoma Press, 1990.
Diccionario histórico y biográfico de la Revolución Mexicana. 7 vols. Mexico City: Secretaría de Gobernación, Instituto Nacional de Estudios Históricos de la Revolución Mexicana, 1992.
"Early Diagnosis of Tuberculosis." *JAMA* 293 (2005): 2804.
Etcharren, Adela F. Interview. July 27, 2011.
"Farías, Juan Francisco." In *Sons of the Republic of Texas*. Paducah, KY: Turner Publishing Co., 2001.
Fish, Jean Y. *José Antonio Zapata: A Borderland Hero*. San Antonio, TX, 1993.
———. *Zapata County Roots Revisited*. 2nd ed. San Antonio, TX: Borderlands Press, 2004.
Flores, Esperanza. "A Religious and Benevolent Custom." In *Zapata County Folklore, 1983*, 47–51. N.p.: Zapata County Historical Society, 1983.
Gallegos, Juan José. "'Last Drop of My Blood.' Col. Antonio Zapata: A Life and Times on Mexico's Rio Grande Frontier, 1797–1840." MA thesis, University of Houston, 2005.
García Rivas, Heriberto. "También los muertos emigran." *Revista de Revistas*, October 25, 1953, 46–49.
Garrett, Julia Kathryn. *Green Flag over Texas: The Last Years of Spain in Texas*. Austin, TX: Pemberton Press, 1969.

Garza, Alicia A. "Donna, Texas." In *The New Handbook of Texas*. 6 vols. Austin: Texas State Historical Association, 1996.

———. "San Perlita, Texas." In *The New Handbook of Texas*. 6 vols. Austin: Texas State Historical Association, 1996.

Garza González, Fernando. *Ciudad Guerrero: Sus fundadores, sus hombres*. Nuevo Laredo, Tamaulipas, 1995.

General Directory of the City of Laredo, 1900. Laredo, TX: Arguindegui and McDonell, 1900.

George, W. Eugene. *Lost Architecture of the Rio Grande Borderlands*. College Station: Texas A&M University Press, 2008.

Gilly, Adolfo. *The Mexican Revolution*. Translated by Patrick Camiller. New York: New Press, 2005.

Godoy, José F. *Porfirio Díaz: The Master Builder of a Great Commonwealth*. New York: G. P. Putnam's Sons, 1910.

González, Jovita. *Life along the Border*. Edited and introduced by María Eugenia Cotera. College Station: Texas A&M University Press, 2006.

Greaser, Galen D., and Jesús F. de la Teja. "Quieting Title to Spanish and Mexican Land Grants in the Trans-Nueces: The Bourland and Miller Commission, 1850–1852." *Southwestern Historical Quarterly* 95.4 (April 1992): 445–464.

Green, Stan. *The Guillermo Benavides Family: A History*. Laredo, TX: Border Studies Center, 1993.

———. *A History of San Agustín Church of Laredo*. Laredo, TX: Webb County Heritage Foundation, 1991.

———. *Laredo in 1881*. The Story of Laredo, no. 3. Laredo: Texas A&M University Border Studies, 1990.

Guide to Spanish and Mexican Land Grants. Austin: Texas General Land Office, 1988.

Hall, Linda B. *Oil, Banks and Politics: The United States and Postrevolutionary Mexico, 1917–1924*. Austin: University of Texas Press, 1995.

Harris, Charles H., and Louis R. Sadler. *The Texas Rangers and the Mexican Revolution*. Albuquerque: University of New Mexico Press, 2004.

Hart, John Mason. *Revolutionary Mexico: The Coming and Process of the Mexican Revolution*. Berkeley: University of California Press, 1987.

Haynes v. State. Court of Civil Appeals of Texas. January 25, 1905.

———. Supreme Court of Texas. March 27, 1907.

Herrera, Octavio. *Breve historia de Tamaulipas*. Mexico City: Fondo de Cultura Económica, 1999.

———. *Visión histórica de Reynosa*. Reynosa, Tamaulipas: Ayuntamiento de Reynosa, 1998.

Hoffman, Abraham. *Unwanted Mexican Americans in the Great Depression: Repatriation Pressures, 1929–1939*. Tucson: University of Arizona Press, 1974.

Huston, Hobart. "Iron Men: A History of the Republic of the Rio Grande and the Federalist War in Northern Mexico." Manuscript, 1940. Texas State Library, Austin.

Izaguirre, Beatriz C. "A Memorable Outing." In *Zapata County Folklore, 1983*, 46. Zapata, TX: Zapata County Historical Society, 1983.

Jones, Oakah L., Jr. *Los Paisanos: Spanish Settlers on the Northern Frontier of New Spain*. Norman: University of Oklahoma Press, 1979.

Krause, Enrique. *Mexico: A Biography of Power; A History of Modern Mexico, 1810–1996*. Translated by Hank Heifetz. New York: Harper Collins, 1997.

———. *Venustiano Carranza: Puente entre siglos*. Ser. Biografía del Poder, no. 5. Mexico City: Fondo de Cultura Económica, 1987.

Kurlansky, Mark. *The Basque History of the World*. New York: Walker and Co., 1999.

Lafaye, Jacques. *La pintura de castas*. Ser. Artes de México, no. 8. Mexico City, 1990.

Lehmann, V. W. *Forgotten Legions: Sheep in the Rio Grande Plain of Texas*. El Paso: Texas Western Press, 1969.

Lott, Virgil N., and Mercurio Martínez. *The Kingdom of Zapata*. Austin: Eakin Press, 1983.

Machado, Manuel A., Jr. *The North Mexican Cattle Industry, 1910–1975: Ideology, Conflict, and Change*. College Station: Texas A&M University Press, 1981.

Marroquín de Garza, Rosalinda. *Nostalgia de antaño y algo más*. Reynosa, Tamaulipas, n.d.

McVey, Lori B. *Ciudad Guerrero: Old Guerrero*. Map. Austin, TX: Accelerated Drafting Service, 1993.

———. *Guerrero Viejo: A Photographic Essay*. Nuevo Santander Museum Complex Occasional Papers 3:1. Edited by Kenneth Wolfe. Laredo, TX, 1988.

Metz, Leon C. *Border: The U.S.-Mexico Line*. El Paso, TX: Mangan Books, 1990.

Meyer, Michael C., William L. Sherman, and Susan M. Deeds. *The Course of Mexican History*. 6th ed. Oxford: Oxford University Press, 1999.

Meza, Rene Raymond. "Jarvis, Samuel Mathias." In *The New Handbook of Texas*. 6 vols. Austin: Texas State Historical Association, 1996.

Miller, Thomas Lloyd. *The Public Lands of Texas, 1519–1970*. Norman: University of Oklahoma Press, 1972.

Montejano, David. *Anglos and Mexicans in the Making of Texas, 1836–1986*. Austin: University of Texas Press, 1987.

Nance, Joseph Milton. *After San Jacinto: The Texas-Mexican Frontier, 1836–1841*. Austin: University of Texas Press, 1963.

Narrett, David E. "José Bernardo Gutiérrez de Lara: *Caudillo* of the Mexican Republic in Texas." *Southwestern Historical Quarterly* 106.2 (October 2002): 194–228.

New Guide to Spanish and Mexican Land Grants in South Texas. Introduction by Galen D. Greaser. Austin: General Land Office, 2009.

Olivera, Ruth R., and Liliane Crété. *Life in Mexico under Santa Anna, 1822–1855*. Norman: University of Oklahoma Press, 1991.

Paredes, Américo. *A Texas-Mexican Cancionero: Folksongs of Border Conflict*. Austin: University of Texas Press, 1995.

Pazos, Luis. *Historia sinóptica de México*. Mexico City: Editorial Diana, 1993.

Poniatowska, Elena, and Richard Payne, FAIA. *Guerrero Viejo*. Houston: Anchorage Press, 1997.
Quezada, J. Gilberto. *Border Boss: Manuel B. Bravo and Zapata County*. College Station: Texas A&M University Press, 1999.
Quezada, Jo Emma Bravo. *The Ranching Communities of Las Comitas, Escobas, Randado*. San Antonio, TX, 2006.
Rugerio Cázares, Carlos. "Guerrero Viejo: History Suspended in Time." *Voices of Mexico* 68 (July–September 2004): 100–103.
Samponaro, Frank N., and Paul J. Vanderwood, eds. *War Scare on the Rio Grande: Robert Runyon's Photographs of the Border Conflict, 1913–1916*. Austin: Texas State Historical Association, 1992.
Saragoza, Alex M. *The Monterrey Elite and the Mexican State, 1880–1940*. Austin: University of Texas Press, 1988.
Sayles, John, and Henry Sayles. *Early Laws of Texas*. 2nd ed. 3 vols. St. Louis, MO: Gilbert Book Co., 1891.
Schwartz, Ted. *Forgotten Battlefield of the First Texas Revolution: The Battle of Medina, August 18, 1813*. Edited by Robert H. Thornhoff. Austin, TX: Eakin Press, 1985.
Scott, Florence Johnson. *Historical Heritage of the Lower Rio Grande*. Waco, TX: Texian Press, 1970.
Shanks, Ann. *Laredo: Reflections*. Laredo, TX: Texas Sesquicentennial, 1986.
A Shared Experience. 2nd ed. Edited by Mario L. Sánchez. Austin: Los Caminos del Río Heritage Project and the Texas Historical Commission, 1994.
Tarver, E. R. *Laredo, the Gateway between the United States and Mexico: An Illustrated Description of the Future City of the Great Southwest*. Laredo, TX: Laredo Immigration Society, 1889.
Tello Díaz, Carlos. *El exilio: Un relato de familia*. Mexico City: Cal y Arena, 1994.
Texas Family Land Heritage Registry. Vol. 6. Austin: Texas Department of Agriculture, (1980).
Thompson, Jerry D. "Historical Survey." In *A Shared Experience*, 2nd ed., edited by Mario L. Sánchez. Austin: Los Caminos del Río Heritage Project and the Texas Historical Commission, 1994.
———. *Laredo: A Pictorial History*. Norfolk, VA: Donning Co., 1986.
———. *Vaqueros in Blue and Gray*. Austin, TX: Presidial Press, 1976.
Treviño, Rosalinda. "Treviño Family History." In *Zapata County Folklore, 1984*, 44–47. Zapata, TX: Zapata County Historical Society, 1984.
Treviño, Ted. "Reminiscing with Ted Treviño." In *Zapata County Folklore, 1983*, 19–20. Zapata, TX: Zapata County Historical Society, 1983.
Treviño Martínez, Lilia, and Eduardo Treviño de León. *Guerrero: Hoy desde ayer*. Monterrey, Nuevo León, 2003.
Turner, John Kenneth. *Barbarous Mexico*. 3rd ed. Chicago: Charles H. Kerr and Co., 1911.
Vázquez, Josefina Z. *La supuesta República del Río Grande*. Ciudad Victoria: Universidad Autónoma de Tamaulipas, Instituto de Investigaciones Históricas, 1995.

Vigness, David M. "Relations of the Republic of Texas and the Republic of the Rio Grande." *Southwestern Historical Quarterly* 57.3 (January 1954): 312–321.
Weber, David J. *The Mexican Frontier 1821–1846: The American Southwest under Mexico.* Albuquerque: University of New Mexico Press, 1982.
Wilcox, Seb S. "Laredo during the Texas Republic." *Southwestern Historical Quarterly* 42.2 (October 1938): 83–107.
Wilkinson, J. B. *Laredo on the Rio Grande Frontier.* Austin, TX: Jenkins Publishing Co., 1975.
Willacy County Scrapbook. Vertical Files, Dolph Briscoe Center for American History, University of Texas at Austin.
Worley, Alicia Consuelo. "The Life of John Anthony Valls." MA thesis, Texas College of Arts and Industries, 1954.
Young, Elliot. "Red Men, Princess Pocahontas, and George Washington: Harmonizing Race Relations in Laredo at the Turn of the Century." *Western Historical Quarterly* 29.1 (1998): 49–85.
Zapata: Journalistic Overview of Refugees in Their Own Land. Zapata, TX: Zapata County Public Library, n.d.
Zorrilla, Juan Fidel. *Tamaulipas: Fértil planicie entre sierra y laguna.* Mexico City: Secretaría de Educación Pública, 1982.
Zorrilla, Juan Fidel, and Carlos González Salas, eds. *Diccionario biográfico de Tamaulipas.* Ciudad Victoria: Universidad Autónoma de Tamaulipas, 1984.

NEWSPAPERS

Brownsville (TX) Daily Herald, March 18 and 20, 1916.
La Crónica, Laredo, TX, November 12, 1910.
El Cronista del Valle, Brownsville, TX, May 4, 1926.
El Demócrata Fronterizo, Laredo, TX, December 4, 1912; December 2, 1916; December 1, 1917.
"Estas ruinas que ves." *El Mañana*, Reynosa, Tamaulipas, April 24–27, 2008.
Laredo (TX) Times, February, March, and April 1913.
McAllen (TX) Monitor, May 15, 1931; February 12, May 20, and December 9, 1932.
Medrano, Lourdes. "Obama as Border Cop: He's Deported Record Numbers of Illegal Immigrants." August 12, 2010. *Christian Science Monitor*, http://www.csmonitor.com/USA/Justice/2010/0812/Obama-as-border-cop-He-s-deported-record-numbers-of-illegal-immigrants.
La Prensa, Monterrey, Nuevo León, March 5, 1911.
La Unión Fronteriza, Ciudad Guerrero, Tamaulipas, November 30, 1906.

ARCHIVAL COLLECTIONS

Archivo Municipal. Nueva Ciudad Guerrero, Tamaulipas.
De la Garza-Benavides Family Papers.
De la Garza-García Family Papers.
De la Garza-Peña Family Papers.
Dolph Briscoe Center for American History. University of Texas at Austin.
García-Pérez Family Papers.
Gutiérrez de Lara Letters.
Gutiérrez de Lara Papers. Texas State Library and Archives, Austin.
Luciano Guajardo Historical Collection. Laredo Public Library, Laredo, TX.
Nettie Lee Benson Latin American Library. University of Texas at Austin.
Nuestra Señora del Refugio Parish. Nueva Ciudad Guerrero, Tamaulipas.
Spanish Archives, Texas General Land Office (GLO), Austin.
Texas State Library and Archives. Austin, TX.
Webb County Heritage Foundation, Laredo, TX.

Index

Acta de Posesión (Act of Possession), 36–37, 43
adopted children (S. Tex.), 60, 62
aduana fronteriza (Guerrero, Tamps.), 49–50, 52, 72, 110, 162
Agualeguas, N.L., 24, 75, 110, 161
Alameda Ranch, 107
Alamo River, 3, 36
aljibes (cisterns), 120, 168–169
Allee, Alonzo W., 91
Allende, Ignacio, 4–5, 7
Alvarez de Toledo, José, 8
American Civil War, 41, 56, 107, 181, 183, 201
Ampudia, Pedro de, 20, 35
Anaconda Copper Company, 78
Anaya, Juan Pablo, 16
Anglo-American immigrants (arrival in S. Tex.), 70, 107–108, 181, 193, 197
annexation of Texas (by U.S.), 20, 40, 161
Anson (steamship), 40. *See also* land titles
Anti-Reelectionist Party (Mexico), 79, 86
Apaches, Lipan (in Zapata County and Villas del Norte), 11, 26–28
Arista, Mariano, 14, 16–17, 19–20, 30–35
Armstrong, Joshua, 59
Arredondo, Joaquín, 8
Arreola, Leandro, 18

Article 27 (of the Mexican Constitution), 114–115
Austin, Tex., 16–18, 41, 202
Avenida Guerrero (Nuevo Laredo, Tamps.), 187

Banco de Coahuila, 113
Banco de Londres y México, 111–112
Banco de México, 111–113
"Bandit War," 66, 68–69, 106, 133
barrileros (water haulers), 169
Béjar, Junta de Gobierno, 8
Benavides, Basilio, 11, 22
Benavides, Cristóbal, 32
Benavides, Juan Báez, 32
Benavides, Jesús, 39–40, 43, 45–47
Benavides, Prudencia, 83, 164, 166, 181
Benavides, Refugio, 180, 194
Benavides, Santos, 11–12, 33–34, 56
Benavides, Servando, 164, 166
Benavides–de la Garza house, Guerrero, Tamps., 167–169
Benavides et al. v. State, 46
Benavides Vela, Manuel, 164, 166
Berlandier, Jean Louis, 28, 140, 160
bilimbiques (worthless paper currency), 113
bilingualism (in Laredo), 183, 196–197
Blanco, Lucio, 53, 95

"Blood Title," 38
Boca de Leones, N. L., 178
Border Patrol, 133
Botello (Joaquín) Tract (Guerrero, Tamps.), 118
Bourland-Miller Commission (1850), 40–41
Bravo, Manuel, 171
Brownsville, Tex., 68, 76, 100, 106, 122, 128, 162, 179, 183
Bruni, Tex., 83
Buena Vista, Battle of, 20
Bullard, Henry, 8
Bustamante, Pedro, 39–40, 42–44, 47
Bustamante, Tex., 47

cabildo (municipal council, Mexico), 119
Calderón, Ignacio, 25
Calderón, María Ignacia, 25
Calero y Sierra, Manuel, 85, 87
Calles, Plutarco Elías, 113, 117, 145
Camargo, Tamps., 2–3, 11, 20–21, 31, 36, 39, 172. See also Republic of the Rio Grande; Villas del Norte
Cameron County, Tex., 40, 59, 68
Canales, Antonio, 11, 13–20, 29–34, 39, 44, 46, 163
Canales Molano, Antonio, 21
Canales Molano, Servando, 21, 163
Canales Treviño, Antonio, 11
Cananea, Son., 77–78, 81
Candela, Coah., 20
Cantú, Carlos, 3
Cantú, Gonzalo, 132
Cantú, Sofía, 132
Capitol of the Republic of the Rio Grande, 16–17
Carbajal, José María, 15, 18, 21
Cárdenas, Jesús, 15–18, 21, 31, 33
Carlos IV, King of Spain, 4, 37–38
carrancistas, 52, 98. See also Carranza, Venustiano; constitucionalistas
Carranza, Jesús, 95

Carranza, Venustiano: and currency issue, 113; and the Mexican Revolution, 52, 64, 93, 97, 145; and mineral ownership, 114; and municipal elections, 99; and taxation, 48, 98; and U.S. government, 63
Carrizo, Tex., 13, 23, 57, 76
Carrizo Indians, 23, 159
Casa Blanca, 15, 17, 31
Casa Consistorial (Laredo, Tex.), 193–194
casa fuerte (blockhouse), 44, 54
Casas Grandes, Chih., Battle of, 82, 85
Casasús, Joaquín, 89
Casino Monterrey, 88
castas, 24–25
Cavazos, Emilia, 132
Cavazos, Julia, 132
cemeteries (Guerrero, Tamps.; Zapata County), 176
centennial celebrations (Mexican independence), 80
centralism in Mexico, 10. See also Federalist Wars; Republic of the Rio Grande
centralists in Federalist wars, 14, 17, 19–20, 30, 33
Central Plaza (Laredo, Tex.), 188
Central School (Laredo, Tex.), 180, 182, 188. See also Escuela Amarilla
Cerralvo, N.L., 24
Cerrito Blanco (land grant), 37–39, 47, 55, 57–58
Cervecería Cuauhtémoc of Monterrey, N.L., 110
Chacón Creek (Laredo, Tex.), 187
chain stores, arrival of in S. Tex., 135
chalaneros (on the Rio Grande), 169, 186
chalanes (ferries on the Rio Grande), 54, 71, 128, 186
Chapa, José Florencio, 3
Charco de la India (land grant), 37, 39, 47
Charco Redondo (land grant), 46
Chihuahua (state), 82–84, 89

China, N.L., 31
chipichil, 168
Church of Nuestra Señora del Refugio (Revilla/Guerrero), 24, 31, 49, 96, 99, 152, 154, 158–159, 174
científicos, 81
city budgets, early Laredo, 194
Ciudad Camargo, Chih., 84
Ciudad Miguel Alemán, Tamps., 128, 170
Club Femenil Guerrerense (ladies' club), 138, 150
Coahuila (state), 2–3, 5, 12, 15–16, 22, 93
Coahuila y Texas (state), 13, 15
Coahuiltecans (tribe), 2
colchas (quilts), 134, 140
Comanches, 11, 27–29, 32–33. See also *indios bárbaros*
Comité de Orientación y Defensa Pro Guerrero, 154, 170
Comité Mexicano de Beneficiencia, 134
commercial farming in S. Tex., 106–107
Compañía Carbonífera y Petrolera de Ciudad Guerrero, 114
compensation plans, 170–172
Confederacy (American), 55–57, 178, 183
Congress of Chilpancingo, 1813, 26
constitucionalistas, 52, 64, 94–96, 99
Constitution (Mexican) of 1824, 10–12
Constitutional convention at Querétaro, 145
contre-guérilla, 102
Convent Avenue (Laredo, Tex.), 185–186
Convention at Aguascalientes, 97
Coronado, José María, 41
Corral, Ramón, 79–80
Correo del Río Bravo del Norte (newspaper), 15, 21
Cortes (Spanish parliament), 8, 11
Cortez Hotel (Weslaco, Tex.), 126
Cortina, Juan ("Cheno"), 56–57, 66
Cortina War (S. Tex), 56, 68
courtship rituals (Guerrero, Tamps.), 141–142

Creelman, James, 78–79
criollos, 4
cromos (Mexican calendars), 182
Cuéllar, Celia, 129
Cuéllar, Fernando, 60
Cuéllar, Miguel de, 26, 37

decena trágica, 91–92. See also Mexican Revolution
Decreto 24 (1833, State of Tamps.), 39
de la Barra, Francisco León, 85–87, 92
de la Garza, Blas María, 75, 84, 105, 163, 165
de la Garza, Cándido, 83–84, 111, 127, 164, 166, 181
de la Garza, Elvia Lorenza, 125, 151, 156
de la Garza, Esther, 120
de la Garza, Fabio: business activities of, 105, 122, 124, 128, 130–131, 134–135; courtship and marriage of, 137–138, 141–145, 147, 149–152; political activities of, 153–155; and ranching, 148, 153; social life of, 124, 126, 149–150
de la Garza, Francisca, 131
de la Garza, Irineo, 96, 99, 103, 134, 164–165
de la Garza, Irineo, Jr., 103, 105, 108, 135, 139
de la Garza, José Guadalupe, 111
de la Garza, José M., 99, 107, 139, 141, 165–166
de la Garza, Juana, Viuda de Caso, 97, 100, 154–155, 165, 167
de la Garza, Lorenzo: business activities of, 75, 97–98, 109–119, 131–132, 163; civic activities of, 75–77, 140; correspondence of, 74, 85–88, 90, 104–105; political activities of, 89, 119; and ranching, 104, 109, 153; residence of, 165–167; writing of, 90, 101–102, 155
de la Garza, Lorenzo Jr., 85, 100–101, 110, 125, 134, 149, 154–155
de la Garza, Lorenzo Manuel, 82–84

de la Garza, Nela, 85, 120–127, 132, 139–140, 167, 177, 196
de la Garza, Octavia Amelia, 85, 140, 167
de la Garza, Ofelia, 92, 105, 122–127, 166, 180
de la Garza, Petra, 97, 100, 165
de la Garza, Rafael, 96, 100–101, 104, 119, 121, 125
de la Garza, Vidal, 110
de la Garza Falcón, Blas María, 172
de la Garza Falcón, José María, 3
de la Garza Falcón, María Rita, 172
de la Garza Falcón, Miguel, 3
de la Garza Tamez, José Carlos, 83–84
de la Huerta, Adolfo, 93, 110, 112
de la Peña Berástegui, Father José Antonio, 35
deportation of Mexicans by U.S., 133–134
deuda bancaria (Mexican foreign debt), 111–112
Díaz, Félix, 52, 90–93
Díaz, Porfirio: and *aduana fronteriza* (customhouse), 50, 162; and centennial celebrations, 75, 80–81; deposed, 52, 74, 85; opposition to, 76, 78–82; rebellion by, 50, 76, 162
Dios, libertad y convención, 15, 22
División Auxiliar del Norte, 17
Doña Beatriz, 107
Donna, Tex., 103, 105, 107, 122, 135
Don Porfirio. *See* Díaz, Porfirio
Dos hermanos héroes (book), 90, 101–102
Dumas, Father Louis Claude, 178
Dupin, Charles, 45, 102

Eagle Pass, Tex., 81
East Donna, Tex., 107
El Alazán, Battle of, 8
El Ancla (newspaper), 19
El Cántaro, Battle of, 14
El Encinar de Medina, Battle of, 8
El Grullo (land grant), 46
El Paso, Tex., 82

El Pedernal (land grant), 39, 45–47, 131
Emmex Oil Company, 118
entradas, 3
equitable title (legal doctrine), 44–45
Escandón, Don José de, 2–3, 36, 77
Escandón, P. José, 77
Escuela Amarilla, 180, 182, 194. *See also* Central School
Escuela González Benavides (Guerrero, Tamps.), 139–140, 175
Esparza, Alberta, 25
Eustis, William, 6
Expropiación Petrolera of 1938 (nationalization of petroleum industry), 115

Falcon, Tex., 54, 170, 172, 175
Falcon International Dam and Reservoir, 47, 157, 170–172, 175–176, 182
Farías, Juan Francisco, 15
Farragut, David, 184
Farragut Street (Laredo, Tex.), 182
Federalism (Mexico), 11, 14, 30, 33–34
Federalists (Mexico), 12–21, 30–33
Federalist Wars (Mexico), 20–21, 24, 161. *See also* Republic of the Rio Grande
Fernando VII, King of Spain, 4, 8, 37–38
Ferrocarril Internacional Oriental de México y Nacional, 164
Fisher, George, 21, 31
Flag, Republic of the Rio Grande, 22, 31
Fletcher, Donna Hooks, 107
Flores, Emeterio, 101
Flores, Inocencia, 183
Flores, Juan Manuel, 142
Flores, María Eulalia, 142
Flores, Régulo, 99
Flores, Rubén, 154, 172
Flores Avenue (Laredo, Tex.), 185
Flores Magón brothers, 78, 81
Fort Brown (Brownsville, Tex.), 183
Fort McIntosh (Laredo, Tex.), 95, 181, 201
Fort Ringgold (Starr County, Tex.), 43
Free Trade Zone, 161–163, 174

French intervention (Mexico), 21, 45, 56, 162, 183
Frontera del Norte, government of, 2, 10, 14–16, 21. *See also* Republic of the Rio Grande
Fuentes, Alberto, 88

Galán, San Silverio, 159
García, Andrés, 44
García, Bartolomé, 17
García, Benito, 48, 50, 52–54, 70, 72–73, 192
García, Domingo, 132
García, Guadalupe, 50, 64
García, José Demetrio, 50, 64
García, Juana, 50, 62–63, 70–71
García, Juan Angel, 49
García, Juan Angel II, 49–52
García, Juan Angel III, 48, 59, 70, 154
García, Lucio, 50–52, 64, 70, 72, 121
García, Rogelia, 137–139, 141–153, 155
García, Vicente, 36–37, 49
García-Martin house (Laredo, Tex.), 179
García Pérez, Benito, 63, 71–72
García Ramírez, Diamantina, 151–152
García Treviño, Anastacio, 99, 140
Garza, Carmen, 132
Garza, Catarino, 76
Garza, Ildefonsa, 60
Garza, Martiniano, 60
Garza, Ofelia, 132
Garza, Pedro, 60
Garza Galán, Andrés, 92–94
Garza Pereda, Gorgonia, 49–50, 55, 62–64, 70
Garza Vásquez, Francisca, 75, 97, 165
General Visita, 36, 49, 179
Gómez, Marte R., 101
González, Darío, 185
González, Elvira and Otila, 140
González, Eulalio, 41
González, Father José Cayetano, 25
González, José María, 20, 22
González, Manuel, 50
González, Pablo, 48, 95
González Benavides, José María, 139, 162
González Garza, Roque, 97
González Pavón, Francisco, 14, 29
González Vela, Lorenzo, 155
Grant, Ulysses S., 184
Grant Street (Laredo, Tex.), 181–182
Great Depression (U.S.), 130, 133, 135, 141
Greene Cananea Copper Company, 78
Greene, William D., 78
Gremio Mercantil (merchants' guild, Guerrero), 163
grito de Dolores, 4
Guadalupe Hidalgo, Treaty of, 20, 22, 39–40, 45, 129, 161, 201
Guardiola, Gustavo, 95–96
Guerra, Matías, 90, 94
Guerra, Vicente, 3, 158, 160
Guerrero, Tamps.: architecture of, 158–176; archives in, 175; bicentennial celebrations in, 156, 172–174; education in, 129, 139–141; and Falcon Dam, 154, 157, 170–171; and Free Trade Zone, 161–165; Indian attacks in, 26–29; and land grants, 39, 44, 49; and Mexican Revolution, 48, 53–54, 64, 71, 92, 94–101, 166; mineral exploration in, 114–115, 118–119; and Republic of the Rio Grande, 13–16, 21, 31–32, 35; social customs of, 138, 141–142, 149–150; and War of Independence, 5; and Zapata bridge, 128
Guerrero, Vicente, 141, 160
Guerrero Viejo (Tamps.), 1, 159, 171, 176
Gutiérrez, Andrea, 55
Gutiérrez, Clemente, 37
Gutiérrez, Cristóbal, 32
Gutiérrez, Eulalio, 97
Gutiérrez, Manuel, 91
Gutiérrez, Sinecio, 94

Gutiérrez de Lara, Angel, 9–10
Gutiérrez de Lara, Father Antonio, 5, 8–10, 26–27, 78, 90
Gutiérrez de Lara, Bernardo: birthplace of, 5; commissioned by Hidalgo, 5; death of, 10–11; as envoy to U.S., 6–7; and execution of Iturbide, 9; exiled to U.S., 8; and Indian problem, 26–27; relations of, with Antonio Zapata, 24, 30; and Republican Army of the North, 7–8; and Republic of the Rio Grande, 13–14; return of, from exile, 9
Gutiérrez de Lara, Januario, 10
Gutiérrez de Lara, Lázaro, 78, 81
Gutiérrez de Lara family, 78, 160
Gutiérrez de Lara papers, 102
Gutiérrez Escamilla, Isidro, 169
Gutiérrez Garza, Francisco, 91
Guzmán, Bishop José de Jesús, 99

Harper, Frank, 116–119
Haynes, J. J., 43
Haynes, John L., 43
Haynes, Leonard, 43
Haynes v. State, 42–43, 45
Heights District (Laredo, Tex.), 181
Hernández, Doroteo, 65–66
Hidalgo, Father Miguel, 4–5, 7, 25, 35, 185
Hidalgo County, Tex., 41, 68–69, 103, 122
Hidalgo Street (Laredo, Tex.), 182, 185, 188
Homestead protection law (Tex.), 135
Hooks, Beatriz, 107
Hooks, Thomas Jefferson, 107
Hotel Flores (Guerrero, Tamps.), 142, 152, 174
Hotel Regis (Mexico City), 115
Houston Street (Laredo, Tex.), 182
Huerta, Victoriano, 49, 52–53, 63, 91–97
huertistas, 94
Humble Oil Company, 118–119

immigration policy of U.S. (toward Mexicans), 128, 133
Improved Order of Red Men, 197
Independence, War of (Mexico). *See* War of Independence
indios bárbaros (hostile Indians), 26–29, 39, 44, 158, 160, 162. *See also* Comanches
International and Great Northern Railway, 118, 164
International Boundary and Water Commission (IBWC), 171–172, 176
International Bridge, Laredo, Tex., 185–187, 198, 201
Iturbide, Agustín de (Agustín I), 8–9, 184
Iturbide Street (Laredo, Tex.), 181–182

jacales (huts), 65, 158, 160, 178
Jarvis, Samuel M., 183–185, 188, 194
Jarvis Plaza (Laredo, Tex.), 188, 200
Jiménez, Mariano, 4–5, 7
Johnson, C. R., 131
Johnson, Pyrle, 131
Jordan, Samuel W., 13, 18–20
Juárez, Benito, 50, 76–77, 158, 173

Karankawas (Indians), 2
Kenedy, Mifflin, 107, 132–33
Keralum, Father Pierre Yves, 179
King, Richard, 132
Kingdom of Zapata (book), 35, 47
King Ranch, 122, 133
Kleberg Town and Improvement Company, 122

La Blanca Land Grant (Tex.), 107
La Bola Tract (Guerrero, Tamps.), 114
La Fraternal (Men's Club, Guerrero, Tamps.), 138
Laguna Espantosa (Nueces River), 17
La Lajilla (*ranchería* in Guerrero, Tamps.), 144

La Loma del Ajo (Guerrero, Tamps.), 118
Lamar, Mirabeau B., 16–18, 22, 34
land grants (Mexican and Spanish), 36–39, 106–107
land scrip (State of Texas), 42
land titles (S. Tex., confirmation), 40–46
language learning (English-Spanish), 190, 192
Laredo, Tex.: architecture in, 17, 181, 189; arrival of Anglo Americans in, 178, 181, 193–194, 197; biculturalism in, 198; and City Hall/Market Hall, 188, 193–195; Civil War in, 56–57, 181, 183; early government of, 183–184, 193–194; founding of, 3, 177–178; and Guadalupe Hidalgo Treaty, 20, 22, 161; languages in, 191, 194, 196–197; and the Mexican Revolution, 92, 95, 186; public library in, 193, 195, 199; and the Republic of the Rio Grande, 2, 11, 16, 18–20; and the Republic of Texas, 161; streets of, 177–178, 183–185, 188–189; town planning in, 177–178
Laredo Junior College, 200–201
Las Brisas (Guerrero, Tamps.), 174
Las Comitas (land grant), 39, 44, 47
Las Escobas Ranch (Zapata County, Tex.): architecture on, 54; cattle and sheep raising on, 58–59; founding of, 55–58; social life on, 60–63
Las Lomas de la Piedra de la Virgen, 95, 158
learning (curriculum; Mexico-Texas contrasted), 191–192
Lerdo de Tejada, Sebastián, 50, 75, 162
Leyes de Reforma (Mexico), 158
Limantour, José Ives, 165
Linares, N.L., 9, 19
Lincoln Street (Laredo, Tex.), 182, 189
Lipan. *See* Apaches, Lipan
Lipantitlán (Tex.), 13, 19
Lizondo, Josepha Gertrudis, 49
Llano, Manuel María de, 15

Llano Grande (land grant), 107
Loma del Degüello (Guerrero), 96
Lopeño, Tex., 170, 172, 175
Lopeño Crossing (on Rio Grande), 54
López, Luis, 18–19
López de Santa Anna, Antonio, 10–12, 20, 22, 24, 198
Los Aldamas, N.L., 31, 164
Louisiana and Louisiana Purchase, 6
Lower Rio Grande Valley (Tex.): business opportunities in, 105; commercial farming in, 123; and Falcon Dam, 154, 157; Great Depression in, 132; land development in, 106–107; railroads in, 107; segregation in, 107–108; town creation in, 107, 122, 132
Lozano, Mikey, 132
Lozano, Paquita P. de, 132

maderistas, 89–90
Madero, Ernesto, 88
Madero, Evaristo, 80
Madero, Francisco I.: assassination, 63, 93; campaign, 79–80, 81–82, 86; election, 74, 87; goals, 52, 80; opposition to, 52, 89, 90–92
Madero, Gustavo, 80, 82, 89
Madero family, 79, 88
Madison, James, 5, 17, 127
Madrigal Barragán, Father José, 154
Magee, Augustus, 7
"Magic Valley," 105–106, 108, 120, 123, 132, 138, 141. *See also* Lower Rio Grande Valley
Marín, N.L., 31
Market Street (Laredo, Tex.), 181
Martínez, Agapito, 162
Martínez, Ignacio, 76
Martínez, Magdalena, 26
Matamoros, Father Mariano, 185
Matamoros, Tamps., 12, 14, 20–21, 30, 92, 95, 145, 183
Matamoros Street (Laredo, Tex.), 182, 185

Maximilian, Emperor of Mexico, 56
Medina, Enrique, 72, 117, 145–146
Medina, Lucio, 145
Mendenhall, Teodora Treviño, 58–59, 142
mercado (N. Laredo), 187
mercedes, 37–38
Mercedes, Tex., 105, 107
mestizaje, 198
mestizos, 4, 26
Mexican Empire, 9
Mexican National Railroad, 164
Mexican Revolution: battles of, 52–53, 64, 66, 82, 84, 91–92, 94–96, 98–99; causes of, 52, 76, 78–80, 85, 88–89, 90–92, 96–97; effects of, 48–49, 53–54, 66, 71–72, 89–90, 101–102, 104, 109–112, 114; and taxation, 48, 98
Mexico City, 64, 97, 115, 153, 157, 160, 173
Mier, Fray Servando Teresa de, 11
Mier, Tamps.: and Falcon Dam, 170; founding of, 3; and the Mexican Revolution, 52–53, 94–95; and the Republic of the Rio Grande, 14, 29, 31; and the Republic of Texas, 161, streets of, 160
Mier y Terán, Manuel, 28
mineral ownership (Mexico), 77, 114
mining laws (Mexico), 77, 114
Mission, Tex., 106–107, 122
Missouri Pacific Railroad (S. Tex.), 131
Moctezuma (Aztec emperor), 184
Molano, Juan Nepomuceno, 15, 19–20
Molano, Refugio, 15
Monroe, James, 6–7
Montemayor, Jesús M., 62, 65–66
Montemayor, Víctor, 62–63, 65, 70
Monterrey, N.L.: business climate of, 88, 110; invasion of, by U.S., 20; and the Mexican Revolution, 80, 83, 96–97; and the Republic of the Rio Grande, 12, 14, 30
Morales, Bartolo, 41
Morelos, Father José María, 7, 26
mulatos, 24–26

municipal autonomy (Guerrero, Tamps.), 170
Muzza, Ana, 71
Muzza, Francisco, 148

Navarro, José Antonio, 16
Neal, Anson, 19
Neutral Ground (U.S. and Spain), 7
Neutrality Act (U.S.), 81, 87
New Orleans, La., 6–7, 76, 81–82, 181
New Spain, 4, 37
noche mexicana, 198
"No Man's Land." *See* Neutral Ground
norteños (Northern Mexicans), 5, 11, 20, 162
Northern Division (División del Norte), 64
novenario (novena), 146
Nueces River (Tex.), 1, 13, 15, 17, 22, 28, 31, 39–41
Nueces Strip (Tex.), 17, 22
Nuestra Señora del Refugio church. *See* Church of Nuestra Señora del Refugio
Nuevo Guerrero (Tamps.), 170, 175, 182
Nuevo Laredo, Tamps.: commerce of, with Laredo, 187; English learning in, 191, 196; and the International Bridge, 186–187; and the Mexican Revolution, 67, 92–96; population growth in, 112, 164
Nuevo León, 1, 5, 12, 15, 22, 24, 31, 79. *See also* Republic of the Rio Grande
Nuevo Santander, 1–3, 5, 9

Oblates of Mary Immaculate (S. Tex.), 61, 179
Obregón, Alvaro, 98, 110, 112, 117, 119, 145
Ochoa, Antonio, 57
Onion Festival, 123
Oreveña Ranch (Zapata County), 31
Original Grantees (Spanish and Mexican grants), 42, 68, 107, 124, 132

Orozco, Pascual, 89
Orozco, Pascual Sr., 92–93
orphans (on S. Tex. ranches), 59–60
Orquesta Flores (Flores Orchestra, Guerrero, Tamps.), 142

Palacio Municipal (Guerrero, Tamps.), 101, 161–162, 173, 175
Palo Alto, Battle of (Tex.), 20
pardos, 25
parián (meat market, Guerrero), 139, 174
parish register (Laredo-Nuevo Laredo), 178
Partido de Guerrero, 89
Partido Liberal Mexicano (PLM), 78, 81
Partido Liberal de Tamaulipas, 90
Partido Socialista Fronterizo (Border Socialist Party), 145
paseo (Sunday promenade, Guerrero, Tamps.), 141–142
Paso Chaveño (on Rio Grande), 54
Paso de Jacinto (on Rio Grande), 3
"Pastry War" (Mexico-France), 12
Pax Porfiriana, 76
Peña, Esther: children of, 84, 96, 100–101, 103–104; death of, 120–122; marriage of, 76; property of, 132, 165
Peña, Francisca, 91, 127, 165
Peña, Juan Martín, 165
Peña Vela, Jesús, 162
peninsulares, 4
Penn, James Saunders, 194
Pereda, Andrés Bautista, 37–38
Pereda, Josefa, 55
Pereda, José Manuel, 37–39, 49, 55
Pérez, Alfredo, 59
Pérez, Antonino, 59
Pérez, Isabel, 145–146
Pérez, María Elena, 59
Pérez, Vidala (Vidalita), 139, 146, 151–152
Pérez, Zoila, 52–55, 59–60, 63, 70–72, 105, 145, 151
Pérez Muzza, Enrique, 71

Pérez Muzza, Gilberto, 147, 153
Pérez Treviño, Gilberto, 71–72, 109–110, 127, 138, 147
Petroleum, Tex., 142
picture postcards (1900s), 51, 68, 80, 100
Pino Suárez, José María, 86–87, 89, 93
Planchet, Father Louis Marie (San Agustín, Laredo), 178
Plan de Ayala, 89
Plan de Guadalupe, 93
Plan de la Soledad, 88
Plan de San Diego, 67–69. *See also* "Bandit War"
Plaza Hotel (Laredo, Tex.), 188–189
plazas (city squares): in Guerrero, Tamps., 141–142, 159, 162; in Laredo, Tex., 177–178, 188
pobladores primitivos (first settlers), 27, 36–37
pocho (dialect), 196
porciones, 36–37, 106–107
porfiriato, 74–75, 85, 89. *See also* Díaz, Porfirio
porfiristas, 52, 89–90
Porter, John Robert, 114–116, 118
Portes Gil, Emilio, 72, 117, 145
Presidio del Río Grande (Coah.), 16, 32
Presidio La Bahía (Tex.), 7
Productos la India (Laredo, Tex.), 182
Prohibition (U.S.), 129–130, 145

railroads (Texas-Mexico border), 107–108, 122, 131, 163–164, 181, 193
Ramireño, Tex., 170, 172
Ramireño de Abajo, 54, 172
Ramírez, Benito, 135
Ramírez, Clemente, 172
Ramírez, Concepción, 51
Ramírez, Cristóbal, 51
Ramírez, José Eugenio, 172
Ramírez, Teresa, 135, 164
Ramírez Martínez, Manuel, 27–28
Ramírez Quintanilla, Jesús, 52

Ramón, José María, 11, 22
Ramos, Basilio, 67
Ramos, Faustino, 82, 84
rancherías (hamlets, in Guerrero jurisdiction), 144, 170
ranchers and ranching (northern Mexico), 48–49, 104–105, 109, 125, 148
Rancho El Tigre de Arriba (Zapata County, Tex.), 135
Rancho Las Tortillas (Guerrero, Tamps.), 29, 76
Rancho Los Moros (Guerrero, Tamps.), 27, 29
Rancho San Juan (Guerrero, Tamps.), 131, 153
Randado, Tex. (Zapata County), 60
Rathmell, Johnnie, 129
Raymond, E. B., 122
Raymond Town and Improvement Company, 122
Raymondville, Tex., 122–123, 126–128, 131, 134–135
"Raymondville Peonage Cases," 123–124
real estate values (Guerrero, Tamps.), 163
Rebelión de la Loba, La, 21
Redmond, Henry, 23–24
Rendón, Candelario, 29
República del Rio Grande, La (newspaper), 21
Republican Army of the North, 7–8, 10, 13
Republican Party: Webb County, Tex., 183; Zapata County, Tex., 47
Republic of Mexico, 1, 39, 43
Republic of Texas, 1, 13, 16, 22, 55, 161
Republic of the Rio Grande, 1–2, 10, 21–22, 24, 31, 39, 55, 161, 178, 203. *See also* Federalist Wars
Resaca de Guerrero, Battle of (Resaca de la Palma), 20
Resguardo Aduanal (customs patrol), 53, 72, 94

Revilla: Act of Possession, 37; architecture in, 158–159; censuses (1757, 1940) in, 32, 158, 169–170; church in, 159; founding of, 3, 158; name of/name change in, 3, 26, 160
Reyes, Bernardo, 76, 79, 83, 86–89, 91–92
Reyes, Isidro, 20, 33
Reyes, Rodolfo, 91, 93
reyista clubs, 79
Reynosa, Tamps., 3, 15, 31, 95
Río Alamo. *See* Alamo River
Río Bravo, 21, 28, 36, 50, 153, 158, 160–161, 175
Rio Grande: colonization of, 2–3; commerce along, 50, 161; crossings of, 54, 66, 71, 128; dividing line of, 6, 22, 129–130, 161; and the floods of 1953 and 1954, 175–176, 187; international dams on, 153–154, 157; land grants (*porciones*) on, 36, 39, 46, 51
Rio Grande City, Tex., 69
Río Salado, 3, 36–37, 125, 154, 159–160, 162, 170, 175. *See also* Guerrero, Tamps.
Río San Juan, 3, 36
Rivera, Fray Buenaventura de, 159
Rocha, Francisco, 26
Rocha, María Antonia, 24, 26
Rodríguez, Juliana, 53
Rodríguez, Lina, 60, 62
Roma, Tex., 23, 57, 61, 69, 128, 170, 179
Rosillo, Josefa, 11
Ross, Col. Reuben, 13–14
Ross, Maj. Reuben, 13
Royal Commission of 1767, 36, 49, 177
rurales (rural police), 52, 94–95

Sabino Seco Land Tract, 131, 153
Salcedo, Manuel, 7
Salinas, Asunción, 32
Saltillo, Coahuila, 12, 19–20
San Agustín Avenue (Laredo, Tex.), 182, 185, 188

San Agustín Church (Laredo, Tex.), 178–179, 185, 189
San Agustín de Laredo, 3, 178
San Agustín Plaza, 2, 11, 17–18, 178, 185, 193–194
San Agustín School (St. Augustine School), 178–181, 190–192, 198–199, 202
San Antonio, Tex., 13, 16–17, 81, 86, 117, 121, 127, 198–199, 202
San Antonio de Béjar, 7–8, 28
San Bernardo Avenue (Laredo, Tex.), 182, 188–189
Sánchez, Amador, 86–87, 92
Sánchez, Darío, 185
Sánchez de la Barrera y Garza, Tomás, 3, 17, 177–178
San Darío Avenue (Laredo, Tex.), 182
San Eduardo Avenue (Laredo, Tex.), 181–182
San Fernando (Zaragoza, Coah.), 16
San Francisco Avenue (Laredo, Tex.), 181
San Francisco de Ampuero Mission, 159
Sanitary Livestock Commission of Texas, 129
San Juan de Carricitos (land grant, Tex.), 132
San Juan River, 3, 36
San Lorenzo Feast Day (Aug. 10), 103, 125, 150
San Miguel, Rafael, 114–115
San Miguel, Rafael Jr., 131, 154
San Patricio, Tex., 13
San Perlita, Tex., 130–132
Santa Gertrudis, Battle of (Tamps.), 21, 162
Santa Rita de Morelos, Coah., 16–17, 33–34
Santa Rosalía, Chih., Battle of, 82, 84
Santa Ursula Avenue (Laredo, Tex.), 182
San Ygnacio, Tex., 23, 54, 57, 66, 172

school holidays (U.S.), 192
segregation (Mexicans in S. Tex.), 107–108, 123–124
Seguín, Juan N., 17–18, 20
seno mexicano, 2
Sewing Academy (Guerrero, Tamps.), 140–141
Shaler, William, 8
sheep raising (Rio Grande plains), 58–59
Sierra, Justo, 89
Sierra Gorda, Count of, 2
Sisters of Divine Providence (Laredo, Tex.), 179
slavery (in Mexico), 25–26
Soberón, Juan, 32
social life in S. Tex. (early twentieth century), 59–62, 124, 133
Sociedad Democrática Estudiantil (Democratic Student Society), 145
Souchon, Father Alphonse Martin, 178
South Texas Chamber of Commerce, 134
Southwest Customs Patrol, 129
Spanglish (dialect), 196
Starr County (Tex.), 23, 40–41, 43, 56, 59, 61, 69
State of Texas, 35, 40, 42–43
St. Louis, Brownsville and Mexico Railway (S. Tex.), 107
Stock Market Crash (1929), 130, 133, 135
sucesión presidencial en 1910, La (book), 78

Tamaulipas [Oil] Company, 118
Tamaulipas (state), 1, 9, 11, 13, 15, 21–22, 39, 43, 45, 161
Teatro Benavides (Guerrero), 75
Teatro Salón Anáhuac (Guerrero), 141
tejanos, 35, 43, 56–57, 61, 69
Teller, Raymond, 123
tequileros, 130
testimonios (land grants), 37

Texas, independence of, from Mexico, 10–11, 16, 24, 160–161
Texas history, teaching of, 198
Texas-Mexican Railway (the Tex-Mex), 164
Texas Rangers, 66, 68, 104, 133
Texas State Library and Archives (Austin), 102
Tex-Mex (dialect), 196
Tienda de Cuervo, José, 32, 49, 158, 160
Tigre de Arriba Ranch (Zapata County, Tex.), 135
town planning (Spanish), 160, 177
Travis County, Tex., 41–42
Treviño, Alejandro, 38, 54–55
Treviño, Ana Josefa, 49
Treviño, Evaristo, 60
Treviño, Felipa, 54, 59
Treviño, Félix, 60, 65
Treviño, Francisca, 59–60
Treviño, Gerónimo, 92–93
Treviño, Gregoria, 62, 65
Treviño, Juana, 60, 70
Treviño, Leonardo, 54–55, 57–58, 60
Treviño, Manuel, 60, 70
Treviño, Teodoro, 54–55, 57–58, 60, 62
Treviño de Cuéllar, Inocente, 60
troneras (gun ports), 54
tuberculosis (early twentieth century), 120–121
Turner, John Kenneth, 78, 81

Union/Unionists (U.S. Civil War), 43, 56, 183–184
Union Fronteriza, La (newspaper), 22
Uribe, Doña Josefa de, 9
Uribeño, Tex., 170, 172
Urrea, José, 12
Ursuline Convent and School for Girls (Laredo, Tex.), 185–186
U.S. War with Mexico (invasion of Mexico), 20, 39, 43, 161, 183

Vallecillo, N.L., 183
Valls, John A., 66–67
Vásquez, Sabás, 75, 161
Vásquez Gómez, Francisco, 86, 89
Vela, Petra, 107
Vela, Santiago, 49
Vela, Ysidro, 56
Vela Ramírez, Manuel, 76
Venegas, Francisco (Viceroy of Mexico), 6
ventiles, 169
Vice Patronato de Tierras y Aguas (land grants), 37
Victoria, Guadalupe, 185
Victoria (Tamps.), 19, 45, 98, 102
Victoria (Tex.), 18
Victoria Street (Laredo, Tex.), 181, 185
Vidaurri y Villaseñor, Francisco, 13, 15
Villa, Francisco (Pancho), 48, 64, 82, 88, 97–98
Villa (land grant), 11, 39, 41, 43
Villa Aldama, N.L., 31, 62, 164, 174
Villa de San Agustín de Laredo, 3, 178
Villar, Lauro, 91
Villarreal, Father Tomás, 62
Villarreal, Otila, 105
Villas del Norte: economy of, 10, 36; and the Federalist Wars, 11, 15–17, 21–22; founding of, 3; and the Indian Wars, 26–29; jurisdiction of, 36; literacy in, 129; and love of land, 35; and town layouts, 31–32; unity of, 3, 22, 161; and the War of Independence, 5
Viva Zapata! (movie), 23
Volpe, Luis, 163
Volpe brothers (Guerrero, Tamps.), 161

War of Independence (Mexico), 4, 8, 16, 25–26, 30, 38, 160
Washington's Birthday celebration (Laredo, Tex.), 92, 186, 197–198
Watchorn, Robert, 116, 118

Watchorn Oil and Gas Company, 116–119
Webb County, Tex., 40–41, 56, 66, 164, 193
Webb County jail (Laredo, Tex.), 86–87, 193
wedding customs (N. Mex., S. Tex.), 60–63, 151–153
Weslaco, Tex., 108, 126
Willacy County, Tex., 122–126
Wilson, Henry Lane, 63, 92–93
Wilson, Woodrow, 63
Winslow, Andrew, 38
Woodmen of the World (life insurance company), 109–110
World War I, effect of, on Mexicans, 104, 106, 128

yndios bárbaros. See *indios bárbaros*

Zacate Creek (Laredo, Tex.), 181, 187
Zapata, Antonio: birth of, 24–26; death of, 34–35; family of, 32; heirs of, 41; house of, 31–32; land grant of, 35, 39, 42–45; reputation of, 24; warrior fame of, 26, 28–29, 33
Zapata, Dolores, 41
Zapata, Emiliano, 23, 64, 89, 97–98
Zapata, Ignacio (the elder), 25
Zapata, Ignacio (the younger), 24–26
Zapata, María Anna, 41
Zapata, María Petra, 41
Zapata, Rafaela, 41
Zapata, Tex., 23, 47, 76, 128, 170, 172, 175
Zapata County, Tex.: and the Civil War, 56–57; and the Cortina War, 56–57; creation of, 24; flooding of, 171–172, 175–176; and land litigation, 42–47; and the Mexican Revolution, 66–67; naming of, 24
Zaragoza, Ignacio, 184
Zaragoza Street (Laredo, Tex.), 17, 179, 185
Zona Libre (Free Trade Zone), 161, 163–165

www.ingramcontent.com/pod-product-compliance
Lightning Source LLC
Chambersburg PA
CBHW022056160426
43198CB00008B/247